WSO2 Developer's Guide

SOA and data services with WSO2 Enterprise Integrator

Fidel Prieto Estrada

Ramón Garrido Lázaro

BIRMINGHAM - MUMBAI

WSO2 Developer's Guide

First published: September 2017

Production reference: 1260917

Published by Packt Publishing Ltd.
Livery Place
35 Livery Street
Birmingham
B3 2PB, UK.
ISBN 978-1-78728-831-7

www.packtpub.com

Credits

Authors
Fidel Prieto Estrada
Ramón Garrido Lázaro

Reviewer
Jack Rider

Commissioning Editor
Smeet Thakkar

Acquisition Editor
Larissa Pinto

Content Development Editor
Roshan Kumar

Technical Editors
Harshal Kadam
Rutuja Vaze

Copy Editors
Safis Editing
Shaila Kusanale

Project Coordinator
Devanshi Doshi

Proofreader
Safis Editing

Indexer
Mariammal Chettiyar

Graphics
Jason Monteiro

Production Coordinator
Shraddha Falebhai

About the Authors

Fidel Prieto Estrada is a fan of new technologieswho has been working with SOA in several integration technologies for 8 years in various industries, which has given him deep integration knowledge and a broad vision for problem solving.

He holds a bachelor of computer science degree from the University of Seville as well as more than 10 certifications, including WSO2 ESB 4 Developer, Oracle SOA Suite 11g, Oracle Unified BPM Suite 11g Essentials, EXIN Secure Programming Foundations, and ISTQB Certified Tester Foundation Level. He also completed the WSO2 ESB for Developers advanced course.

I would like to thank my family for the support they have provided me, especially my late father. I can't thank Marina enough for her support and patience with me throughout the months it took it me to write this book.

Ramón Garrido Lázarois an enthusiast of new technologies and has spent the lasts years understanding and working with WSO2 servers in different projects, companies, and countries. He holds a bachelor's degree in software engineering and two master's degrees focusing on TIC security and software development for computers and smartphones.

He has specialized in SOA environments with multiple certifications, some of them in WSO2 servers. Currently, he works as a WSO2 consultant and teaches WSO2 courses in Chakray Consulting, one of the biggest WSO2-partner specialist companies.

I would like to thank my parents, Mr. Ramón Garrido and Mrs. Pilar Lázaro, for their continuous encouragement and motivation throughout my life. This book is dedicated to them.

About the Reviewer

Jack Rider is both a Spanish and US citizen, but he spends most of his time in the UK and Europe these days. After completing his degree in computer technology in Pittsburgh, Jack began his career in hospitality industry technology before moving to ERP, becoming a SAP consultant and then discovering the open source arena around 21 years ago. Jack has always been a firm believer in open source technology as a principle that led him, almost inevitably, to WSO2 and Chakray Consulting, where he is the CTO. Jack has a keen interest in physics, particularly in quantum theory. He was also the vice chairman of the Spanish Astronomy Association, which is congruous with his philosophy that sleep is overrated.

www.PacktPub.com

For support files and downloads related to your book, please visit www.PacktPub.com.

Did you know that Packt offers eBook versions of every book published, with PDF and ePub files available? You can upgrade to the eBook version at www.PacktPub.comand as a print book customer, you are entitled to a discount on the eBook copy. Get in touch with us at service@packtpub.com for more details.

At www.PacktPub.com, you can also read a collection of free technical articles, sign up for a range of free newsletters and receive exclusive discounts and offers on Packt books and eBooks.

https://www.packtpub.com/mapt

Get the most in-demand software skills with Mapt. Mapt gives you full access to all Packt books and video courses, as well as industry-leading tools to help you plan your personal development and advance your career.

Why subscribe?

- Fully searchable across every book published by Packt
- Copy and paste, print, and bookmark content
- On demand and accessible via a web browser

Customer Feedback

Thanks for purchasing this Packt book. At Packt, quality is at the heart of our editorial process. To help us improve, please leave us an honest review on this book's Amazon page at `https://www.amazon.com/dp/1787288315`.

If you'd like to join our team of regular reviewers, you can email us at `customerreviews@packtpub.com`. We award our regular reviewers with free eBooks and videos in exchange for their valuable feedback. Help us be relentless in improving our products!

Table of Contents

Preface

This book will help you explore the various capabilities of WSO2, from simple and generic to more complex and powerful. It will give you an introduction to a service-oriented architecture in general and is focused on the WSO2 world in order to put into context the principles and the target area where we can apply the knowledge and the techniques outlined in the book. This book will help the reader understand the SOA architecture even without any prior knowledge of it, making the book readable for everyone interested in learning to develop with WSO2 servers, with or without prior experience.

We will also learn how to use mediators to create APIs and proxy services, with which we can perform different actions such as transforming the payload or making a conditional route inside to create smarter web services. We will also learn how to handle the quality of service configuration to apply security, throttling, and caching to the services.

When we develop a service, it is important that it does the actions that its design for, and always gives the same response for the same request. For this reason, it's important that we test our services and debug all that we need. We don't speak about giving more functionality to our services, but about logging and testing them.

The last section will mainly focus on integrating the WSO2 EI with other servers using different protocols. We will learn how to use the VFS protocol to work with files: read, write, move, and so on. Using the JMS protocol, we will learn how to integrate with the WSO2 Message Broker that is inside the WSO2 EI. We will also have a brief introduction to a new programming language called Ballerina, which will be the future of the company.

What this book covers

Chapter 1, *Getting Started with SOA and WSO2,* discusses the issues that gave rise to SOA, describes its main principles, and explains how to make SOA the standard architecture in our organization. In order to achieve this, we have named the WSO2 product we need WSO2 EI. Finally, we will learn how to install it, configure it, and start it up.

Chapter 2, *Developing Integration Projects with WSO2 EI Tooling,* explains the most common tasks a developer performs on a daily basis when working with WSO2 EI, such as creating projects and artifacts. We will also learn how to debug our projects, which is a very important task that's performed on a daily basis. Additionally, we will describe how to use the powerful data mapper.

Chapter 3, *Building Web Services*, explains how to build web services in WSO2 EI and their most commoncomponents, such us endpoints and sequences. We will also explain the different ways of creating services in EIservice when we need to use a Proxy, an API, or an inbound endpoint, and what is the process for adding the logic to that service using sequences and mediators.

Chapter 4, *Building Data Services*, explores how to build the dataservices needed to fetchthe data required in our service orchestration. Additionally, we will learn some tips to save some time when developing and testing our dataservices as well.

Chapter 5, *Transforming the Content of Payload*, explains how to transform the message received in the services. We will also learn how to modify the content of the payload using the `PayloadFactory` mediator or the `enrich` mediator, without needing to have advanced knowledge of transformation languages such as XSLT or XQuery.

Chapter 6, *Conditional Route*, helps us know how to create more intelligent services that can route the flow over different ways, depending on the parameters, the URL, headers, and so on. We will also take a look at the `filter` and `switch` mediators, which we use to check the payload, or a part of it, over a regex expression.

Chapter 7, *Quality of Service*, takes you through the quality of service configuration in depth in order to explain how to configure security in the services, apply throttling policies such as specifying a maximum number of requests that can be done for a user in a period of time, and use the cache to improve the performance of the servers, among other things.

Chapter 8, *Tasks Scheduling,*focuses on the options we have for scheduling tasks inside the EI server. We will also observe the three ways to schedule tasks in the EI server.

Chapter 9, *WSO2 Enterprise Integration Logging,*covers how to log any information about the message received or the properties we set during our service orchestration. We also learn how to log when we are developing a piece of JavaScript code in our service.

Chapter 10, *WSO2 Enterprise Integration Testing*, goes through the process of testing our services using the basic built-in feature, and a more powerful tool--SoapUI. Besides this, we will learn how to build mock services and test suites to create a set of test cases that help us validate that the service is working as we expect.

Chapter 11, *Integrating with VFS*, focuses on the integration of Enterprise Integrator with files, local or remote, handled using the VFS protocol from Apache Commons. We will also cover a variety of file scenarios, such as read, write, and transfer, without processing files over different locations.

Chapter 12, *Integrating with JMS - WSO2 EI Message Brokering*, explains how to send messages to a JMS queue, as well as how to consume them. We will also learn how to build a typical high-performance scenario where a message is stored in a queue to be processed further by another service, which allows the service to handle a high number of messages per second.

Chapter 13, *Introduction to Ballerina*, gives a brief introduction to the new programming language called Ballerina, which will be the future of the company.

What you need for this book

This book will guide you through the installation of all the tools that you require to follow the examples.

Who this book is for

This book is intended for SOA developers with no knowledge of WSO2 Enterprise Integrator, but who are experienced in SOA environment, and are reasonably familiar with XML and JSON message types. Will be useful to have knowledge in XSL, XSD, JMS, VFS, Eclipse IDE and other WSO2 servers.

Conventions

In this book, you will find a number of text styles that distinguish between different kinds of information. Here are some examples of these styles and an explanation of their meaning. Code words in the text, database table names, folder names, filenames, file extensions, pathnames, dummy URLs, user input are shown as follows: "Use `wum check-update wso2ei-6.0.0` to check for updates".

A block of code is set as follows:

```
<messageFormattercontentType="application/json"
class="org.wso2.carbon.integrator.core.json.JsonStreamFormatter"/>

<messageBuildercontentType="application/json"
class="org.wso2.carbon.integrator.core.json.JsonStreamBuilder"/>
```

When we wish to draw your attention to a particular part of a code block, the relevant lines or items are set in bold:

```
wumconfiglocal.product.repo wso2/products
New product repository is \wso2\products
```

New terms and **important words** are shown in bold. Words that you see on the screen, for example, in menus or dialog boxes, appear in the text like this: "In the WSO2EI Tooling top menu, click on**Run|Debug Configurations**."

Warnings or important notes appear in a box like this.

Tips and tricks appear like this.

Reader feedback

Feedback from our readers is always welcome. Let us know what you think about this book-what you liked or disliked. Reader feedback is important for us as it helps us develop titles that you will really get the most out of. To send us general feedback, simply e-mailfeedback@packtpub.com, and mention the book's title in the subject of your message. If there is a topic that you have expertise in and you are interested in either writing or contributing to a book, see our author guide atwww.packtpub.com/authors.

Customer support

Now that you are the proud owner of a Packt book, we have a number of things to help you to get the most from your purchase.

Downloading the example code

You can download the example code files for this book from your account at http://www.packtpub.com. If you purchased this book elsewhere, you can visit http://www.packtpub.com/support and register to have the files e-mailed directly to you. You can download the code files by following these steps:

1. Log in or register to our website using your e-mail address and password.
2. Hover the mouse pointer on the **SUPPORT** tab at the top.
3. Click on **Code Downloads & Errata**.
4. Enter the name of the book in the **Search** box.
5. Select the book for which you're looking to download the code files.

6. Choose from the drop-down menu where you purchased this book from.
7. Click on **Code Download**.

Once the file is downloaded, please make sure that you unzip or extract the folder using the latest version of:

- WinRAR / 7-Zip for Windows
- Zipeg / iZip / UnRarX for Mac
- 7-Zip / PeaZip for Linux

The code bundle for the book is also hosted on GitHub at `https://github.com/PacktPublishing/WSO2-Developer-s-Guide`. We also have other code bundles from our rich catalog of books and videos available at `https://github.com/PacktPublishing/`. Check them out!

Downloading the color images of this book

We also provide you with a PDF file that has color images of the screenshots/diagrams used in this book. The color images will help you better understand the changes in the output. You can download this file from `https://www.packtpub.com/sites/default/files/downloads/B06549_WSO2DevelopersGuide_ColorImages.pdf`.

Errata

Although we have taken every care to ensure the accuracy of our content, mistakes do happen. If you find a mistake in one of our books-maybe a mistake in the text or the code-we would be grateful if you could report this to us. By doing so, you can save other readers from frustration and help us improve subsequent versions of this book. If you find any errata, please report them by visiting `http://www.packtpub.com/submit-errata`, selecting your book, clicking on the **Errata Submission Form** link, and entering the details of your errata. Once your errata are verified, your submission will be accepted and the errata will be uploaded to our website or added to any list of existing errata under the Errata section of that title. To view the previously submitted errata, go to `https://www.packtpub.com/books/content/support` and enter the name of the book in the search field. The required information will appear under the **Errata** section.

Piracy

Piracy of copyrighted material on the Internet is an ongoing problem across all media. At Packt, we take the protection of our copyright and licenses very seriously. If you come across any illegal copies of our works in any form on the Internet, please provide us with the location address or website name immediately so that we can pursue a remedy. Please contact us at copyright@packtpub.com with a link to the suspected pirated material. We appreciate your help in protecting our authors and our ability to bring you valuable content.

Questions

If you have a problem with any aspect of this book, you can contact us at questions@packtpub.com, and we will do our best to address the problem.

Getting Started with SOA and WSO2

1

We will try to introduce this book with a simple, brief, and concise discussion of SOA, talking about its origin and what it means. We will discuss the facts or problems that large companies with a huge IT system had to face, and that finally gave rise to the SOA approach.

Once we know what we are talking about, we will introduce the WSO2 technology and describe the role it plays in SOA, which will be followed by the installation and configuration of the WSO2 products we will use.

So, in this chapter, we will deal with the following topics:

- A basic knowledge of SOA
- Download WSO2 Enterprise Integrator
- WSO2 Update Manager (WUM)
- Update with the official Patches
- Set up WSO2 Enterprise Integrator
- Start Enterprise Integrator

Service-oriented architecture (**SOA**) is a style, an approach to design software in a different way from the standard. SOA is not a technology; it is a paradigm, a design style.

There comes a time when a company grows and grows, which means that its IT system also becomes bigger and bigger, fetching a huge amount of data that it has to share with other companies. This typical data may be, for example, any of the following:

- Sales data
- Employees data
- Customer data
- Business information

In this environment, each information need of the company's applications is satisfied by a direct link to the system that owns the required information. So, when a company becomes a large corporation, with many departments and complex business logic, the IT system becomes a *spaghetti dish*:

Spaghetti dish

The spaghetti dish is a comparison widely used to describe how complex the integration links between applications may become in this large corporation. In this comparison, each spaghetti represents the link between two applications in order to share any kind of information.

Thus, when the number of applications needed for our business rises, the amount of information shared is larger as well. So, if we draw the map that represents all the links between the whole set of applications, the image will be quite similar to a spaghetti dish. Take a look at the following diagram:

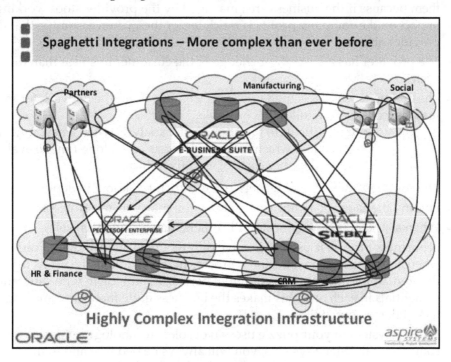

Spaghetti integrations by Oracle (`https://image.slidesharecdn.com/2012-09-20-aspire-oraclesoawebinar-finalversion-160109031240/95/maximizing-oracle-apps-capabilities-using-oracle-soa-7- 638.jpg?cb=1452309418`)

The preceding diagram represents an environment that is closed, monolithic, and inefficient, with the following features:

- The architecture is split into blocks divided by business areas.
- Each area is close to the rest of the areas, so interaction between them is quite difficult.
- These isolated blocks are hard to maintain.
- Each block was managed by just one provider, which knew that business area deeply.
- It is difficult for the company to change the provider that manages each business area due to the risk involved.

- The company cannot protect itself against the abuses of the provider. The provider may commit many abuses, such as raising the provided service fare, violating **service level agreement** (**SLA**), breaching the schedule, and many others we can imagine. In these situations, the company lacks instruments to fight them because if the business area managed by the provider stops working, the impact on the company profits is much larger than when assuming that the provider abuses.
- The provider has a deeper knowledge of the customer business than the customer itself.
- The maintenance cost is high due to the complexity of the network for many reasons; consider the following example:
    - It is difficult to perform impact analysis when a new functionality is needed, which means high costs and a long time to evaluate any fix, and higher costs of each fix in turn.
- The complex interconnection network is difficult to know in depth.
- Finding the cause of a failure or malfunction may become quite a task.
- When a system is down, most of the others may be down as well.
- A business process is used to involve different databases and applications. Thus, when a user has to run a business process in the company, he needs to use different applications, access different networks, and log in with different credentials in each one; this makes the business quite inefficient, making simple tasks take too much time.
- When a system in your puzzle uses an obsolete technology, which is quite common with legacy systems, you will always be tied to it and to the incompatibility issues with brand new technologies, for instance.
- Managing a fine-grained security policy that manages who has access to each piece of data is simply an uthopy.

Something must to be done to face all these problems and SOA is the one to put this in order. SOA is the final approach after the previous attempt to try to tidy up this chaos.

We can take a look at the SOA origin in the white paper, *The 25-year history of SOA*, by *Erik Townsend* (`http://www.eriktownsend.com/white-papers/technology`). It is quite an interesting read, where Erik establishes the origin of the manufacturing industry. I agree to that idea, and it is easy to see how the improvements in the manufacturing industry, or other industries, are applied to the IT world; take these examples:

- The hardware bus in motherboards has been used for decades, and now we can also find the software bus, **Enterprise Service Bus** (**ESB**) in a company. The hardware bus connects hardware devices such as microprocessors, memory, or hard drives; the software bus connects applications.
- A hardware router in a network routes small fragments of data between different nets to lead these packets to the destination net. The message router software, which implements the message router enterprise integration pattern, routes data objects between applications.
- We create software factories to develop software using the same paradigm as a manufacturing industry.
- Lean IT is a trending topic nowadays. It tries, roughly speaking, to optimize the IT processes by removing the *muda* (Japanese word meaning wastefulness, uselessness). It is based on the benefits of the lean manufacturing applied by Toyota in the '70s, after the oil crisis, which led it to the top position in the car manufacturing industry.
- We find an analogy between what object-oriented language means to programming and what SOA represents to system integrations as well.
- We can also find analogies between ITIL V3 and SOA. The way ITIL V3 manages the company services can be applied to managing the SOA services at many points. ITIL V3 deals with the services that a company offers and how to manage them, and SOA deals with the service that a company offers to expose data from one system to the rest of them. Both the conceptions are quite similar if we think of the ITIL V3 company as the IT department and of the company's service as the SOA service.

There is another quite interesting read--*Note on Distributed Computing* from Sun Microsystem Laboratories published in 1994. In this reading, four members of Sun Microsystems discuss the problems that a company faces when it expands, and the system that made up the IT core of the company and its need to share information. You can find this reading at `http://citeseerx.ist.psu.edu/viewdoc/download?doi=10.1.1.48.7969&rep=rep1&type=pdf`.

In the early '90s, when companies were starting to computerize, they needed to share information from one system to another, which was not an easy task at all. There was a discussion on how to handle the local and remote information as well as which technology to use to share that information.

The **Network File System (NFS)**, by IBM was a good attempt to share that information, but there was still a lot of work left to do. After NFS, other approaches came, such as CORBA and Microsoft DCOM, but they still keep the dependencies between the whole set of applications connected. Refer to the following diagram:

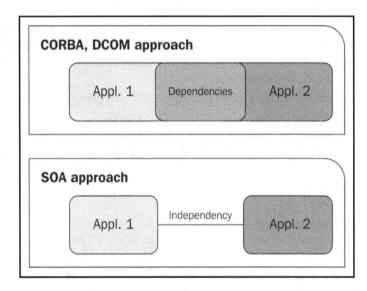

The SOA approach versus CORBA and DCOM

Finally, with the SOA approach, by the end of the '90s, independent applications where able to share their data while avoiding dependencies. This data interchange is done using services. An SOA service is a data interchange need between different systems that accomplishes some rules. These rules are the so-called SOA principles that we will explain as we move on.

SOA principles

The SOA principles are the rules that we always have to keep in mind when taking any kinds of decisions in an SOA organization, such as the following:

- Analyzing proposals for services

- Deciding whether to add a new functionality to a service or to split it into two services
- Solving performance issues
- Designing new services

There is no industry agreement about the SOA principles, and some of them publish their own principles. Now, we will go through the principles that will help us in understanding its importance:

- **Service Standardization**: Services must comply with communication and design agreements defined for the catalog they belong to. These include both high-level specifications and low-level details, such as those mentioned here:
    - Service name
    - Functional details
    - Input data
    - Output data
    - Protocols
    - Security
- **Service loose coupling**: Services in the catalog must be independent of each other. The only thing a service should know about the rest of the services in the catalog is that they exist. The way to achieve this is by defining service contracts so that when a service needs to use another one, it has to just use that service contract.
- **Service abstraction**: The service should be a black box just defined by its contracts. The contract specifies the input and output parameters with no information about how the process is performed at all. This reduces the coupling with other services to a minimum.
- **Service reusability**: This is the most important principle and means that services must be conceived to be reused by the maximum number of consumers. The service must be reused in any context and by any consumer, not only by the application that originated the need for the service. Other applications in the company must be able to consume that service and even other systems outside the company in case the service is published, for example, for the citizenship. To achieve this, obviously, the service must be independent of any technology and must not be coupled to a specific business process. If we have a service working in a context, and it is needed to serve in a wider context, the right choice is to modify the service for it to be able to be consumed in both the contexts.

- **Service autonomy**: A service must have a high degree of control over the runtime environment and over the logic it represents. The more control a service has over the underlying resources, the less dependencies it has and the more predictable and reliable it is. Resources may be hardware resources or software resources, for example, the network is a hardware resource, and a database table is a software resource. It would be ideal to have a service with exclusive ownership over the resources, but with an equilibrated amount of control that allows it to minimize the dependencies on shared resources.

- **Service statelessness**: Services must have no state, that is, a service does not retain information about the data processed. All the data needed comes from the input parameters every time it is consumed. The information needed during the process dies when the process ends. Managing the whole amount of state information will put its availability in serious trouble.

- **Service discovery**: With a goal to maximize the reutilization, services must be able to be discovered. Everyone should know the service list and their detailed information. To achieve that aim, services will have metadata to describe them, which will be stored in a repository or catalog. This metadata information must be accessed easily and automatically (programmatically) using, for example, **Universal Description, Discovery, and Integration** (**UDDI**). Thus, we avoid building or applying for a new service when we already have a service, or several ones, providing that information by composition.

- **Service composability**: Services with more complex requirements must use other existing services to achieve that aim instead of implementing the same logic that is already available in other services.

- **Service granularity**: Services must offer a relevant piece of business. The functionality of the service must not be so simple that the output of the service always needs to be complemented with another service's functionality. Likewise, the functionality of the service must not be so complex that none of the services in the company uses the whole set of information returned by the service.

- **Service normalization**: Like in other areas such as database design, services must be decomposed, avoiding redundant logic. This principle may be omitted in some cases due to, for example, performance issues, where the priority is a quick response for the business.

- **Vendor independent**: As we discussed earlier, services must not be attached to any technology. The service definition must be technology independent, and any vendor-specific feature must not affect the design of the service.

SOA organization

Once we understand what is SOA and its principles, the next question is *How to apply SOA to a standard organization?*

Well, what SOA tries to say to a big organization that has a large number of systems with a high level of integration (remember the spaghetti dish), is, *Stop turning a blind eye! That spaghetti dish is also your business!*

What we mean by this sentence is that companies add new systems on demand as their business grows. In this scenario, the typical way to proceed is to add new systems and configure all the integrations needed with the current systems of the company. This way, little by little, the number of systems grows until they achieve the spaghetti dish.

What is wrong with this scenario is the thinking that interconnections do not play any role in the company business, but only play the simple role of an information socket. At this point, all the interconnections of the company have enough dimension and impact on the business that they should be treated like another part of the business.

SOA tells the company that all that system connections is a business that has to be managed. The company must go deep inside the *spaghetti dish* to understand the business behind it. Then, that business must be digested to turn a large number of wires between applications into *business services*. The beautiful thing about this is that after taking a look at these system connections and discovering the business behind them, the business that we find is the essential business of the company, which defines its identity and what the company is and does.

Once we realize that, let's see how we can bring SOA to our company.

The very first step to do this is service prospection. In service prospection, we look deep inside the connection network to look for the business behind it and turn it into business services. We need to know which systems produce information and which ones consume information. This analysis can be made with the following two strategies:

- **Bottom-up**: This approach starts analyzing the integration from the point-to-point connection (bottom) existing between the systems, building the integration map. These connections are linked together to result in another one in a higher level of abstraction, which will be the very first candidate services. We iterate several times over these connections/services, building high-level services according to the SOA principles until we achieve the business services (up) of the company.

- **Top-down**: This approach is the opposite of the bottom-up approach. It starts designing high-level business services (top) according to the business expert. Starting from that point, we iterate over them, increasing the level of detail in each iteration and splitting them according to the SOA principles. We stop when no new services result from the previous iteration (down).

Take a look at the following diagram:

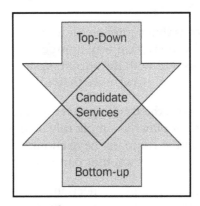

Neither of the strategies are perfect and each one has its pros and cons. The top-down approach is theoretical and lacks the real-world vision, while the bottom-up part is data or real world but does not consider the business theory. Finally, each strategy has its advantages and disadvantages; so, the best practice is to apply both the approaches and stop where they both meet.

For example, we start by defining the high-level business service (top) and identifying the point-to-point connection (bottom); these are the ideally desired business services for the business. We follow this by adding detailed information to top-level services and splitting the services into other services that compose them. On the bottom level, we link or compose the services to generate higher-level ones; these are real-world services that currently form the business. Both the processes continue iterating until they meet each other at a point, where both the processes merge, obtaining the final set of detailed business services. These are the candidate services that have the ideal or desired vision of the business, but use the real-world services that are part of the current business.

These groups of business services will be the SOA catalog. The catalog is a registry where we can find, at the very least, the following information:

- The available services
- The services in progress
- Relationships between services
- Detailed information about each service

Once we have the service catalog of our future SOA organization, the following steps do not differ much from other typical IT projects:

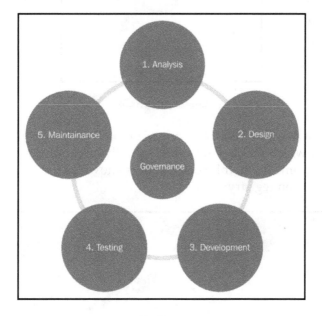

SOA life cycle

We will start with the analysis phase where we determine what to do in each service. In the first iteration, part of this analysis has already been done during the service prospection.

This is followed by the design phase, where we define how to do it in detail. Then, services are implemented according to that detailed design and tested to move them to the production environment of our company. Finally, we are in the maintenance phase, where we control and monitor the business.

There is a new phase that is called SOA Governance, and it is present in all the services. The aim of SOA Governance is to define policies, standards, principles, and processes to uphold the SOA principles; in other words, its role is to ensure that SOA benefits the organization.

Once again, there's nothing new here; governance is a term from politics that is applied to the IT world, but instead of controlling and managing a country, it controls and manages the service catalog of the SOA organization:

Achieving an SOA organization

The last element needed to build our SOA organization is the component that enables the consumer to discover which services are available in the organization, their functionalities, and how they can consume them; this component is known as the Universal Description, Discovery, and Integration registry:

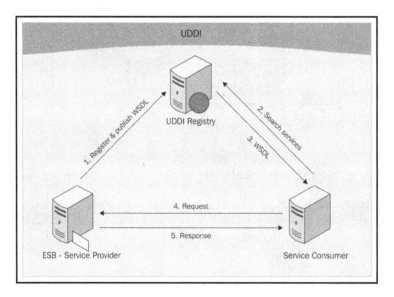

UDDI

So now, we are ready to turn our standard organization into an SOA organization.

Technology for SOA

As we discussed earlier, SOA is an approach and tells us nothing about which technology to use to implement it. Each organization is free to choose the desired technology as long as it ensures the SOA principles.

The most common implementation is based on the following standards:

- **XML**: This is the extensible markup language we all know. It is the typical language used to model the organization's business entities; another option quite popular nowadays is JSON.
- **HTTP(s)**: This is the protocol used to exchange information between systems.
- **SOAP**: **Simple Object Access Protocol** (**SOAP**), is based on XML and defines the structure that will be used to exchange information between systems. A SOAP message contains the following elements:

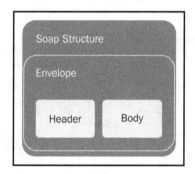

SOAP message

- **Envelope**: The top-level structure that includes everything else
- **Header**: Extra information related to security, how the message must be processed, and the quality of service
- **Body**: The data it sends to the producer, or the response that it sends to the consumer
- **Fault**: Information about the errors produced while processing the message
- **WSDL**: **Web Services Description Language** (**WSDL**), and it is the language for defining the contract of the service. In other words, it defines the input and output of the service black box without any attached vendor technology.

Putting all these standards together, we get the web service technology. Web service is a process that aims to interchange information with other systems. This information exchange is defined by a contact, which is built using the WSDL.

Web service technology will be the instrument that is finally used to build the business services we have been discussing in this chapter. It is important to note that at this point, we can fully define a business service using this technology, without tying it to any specific vendor or technology, such us Java, .Net, or Oracle.

At this time, we can finally introduce the central element of the SOA IT infrastructure ESB. The name is an analogy to the hardware bus we can find in a motherboard, which enables the communication between all components. In this case, as we discussed earlier in the chapter, it communicates software components transporting messages of data instead of communicating hardware components transporting bits of data.

The ESB is a middleware where the SOA services are deployed and published and are ready to be consumed by other systems that may be within the company, in another company, in another country, or even in another continent.

In the following diagrams, we can see an approach of the SOA infrastructure of our company:

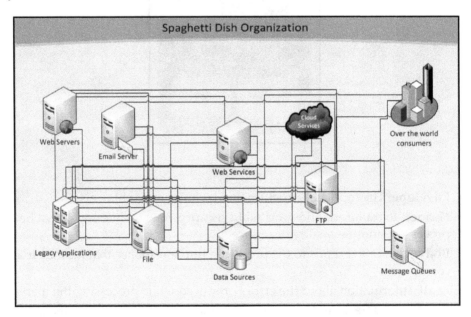

Spaghetti dish organization

In contrast with the spaghetti dish, we can see the following:

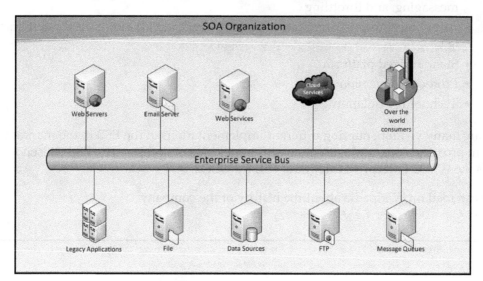

SOA organization

The ESB allows us to accomplish the SOA principles with the following features:

- Deploying, managing, and controlling the SOA services
- Synchronous communication between systems, where the consumer is waiting for the response in the same channel used to send the request
- Asynchronous communication between systems, where the consumers do not wait for the response in the same channel used to send the request
- Fire-and-forget communication, where the consumers do not need a response
- Services orchestration, which wraps business logic that involves several services into a single service
- Complex business services
- Security to ensure authentication and authorization of the consumers

- Quality of the service, such as message signing and encryption, reliable messaging, and throttling
- Applying enterprise integration pattern. You can find out more about it at: `http://www.enterpriseintegrationpatterns.com`.
- Standardized platform
- Protocol conversion
- Technology isolation

There are many vendors offering different implementations of the ESB in the market with different pros and cons, and with many different kinds of licenses. The ESB chosen for this book is the WSO2 **Enterprise Integrator (EI)** by WSO2.

As we can read on Wikipedia about the history of the company (`https://en.wikipedia.org/wiki/WSO2`):

> **WSO2** (sometimes stylized as WSO$_2$) is an open source technology provider that increases the agility of digital businesses and enterprises engaging in digital transformation. It offers an integrated enterprise platform for APIs, applications, and web services—locally and across the internet.
>
> ## History [edit]
>
> WSO2 was founded by Sanjiva Weerawarana and Paul Fremantle in August, 2005, and has been backed by investment from Intel Capital, Toba Capital, Pacific Controls and others. As of 2015, WSO2 has offices in the USA (Mountain View, CA), UK (London), Brazil (São Paulo), and Sri Lanka (Colombo), with the bulk of its research and operations being conducted from its main office in Colombo. The company rose to prominence after eBay revealed that a key element of their transaction processing software used the open source WSO2 ESB.[2]

Based on the experience of working with WSO2 products for more than five years, we have to follow how the company has grown and expanded due to its innovative culture. Along with this experience, we have witnessed the evolution of the WSO2 components since the successful early version of the ESB and DSS to the current ones, and the brand new WSO2 EI.

In the following chart from the WSO2 site, we can see the WSO2 vision of the SOA infrastructure:

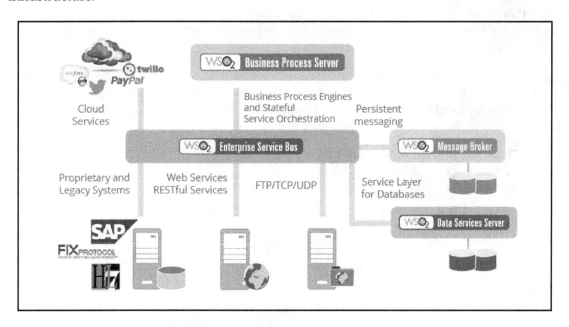

WSO2 ESB (http://b.content.wso2.com/sites/all/technology-microsites/integration/
images/integration-micro-complete-enterprise-ready-integration.png)

Here, we can see how WSO2 ESB is the heart of the infrastructure and relies on the other components:

- **WSO2 Data Services Server**: This is a very successful component that lets you expose data from a very diverse source, such as web services or REST resources, in a couple of minutes without any code.
- **WSO2 Message Broker**: This is a message broker, as its name says, that supports the Publish/Subscribe model, Java Message Service (JMS), and Advanced Message Queuing Protocol among other features, which allows us to build complex business services.
- **WSO2 Business Process Server**: This a business process engine. Business processes are a higher level of abstraction called Business Process Management (BPM). BPM is based in business services that compose business processes, and supports BPMN 2.0, WS-BPEL 2.0 , WS-Human Task 1.1, and BPEL4People 1.1 standards.

The SOA component missed in the preceding chart is the UDDI registry. WSO2 offers this UDDI registry with its component called **WSO2 Governance Registry**; this component is more than a simple UDDI registry. It also provides a service catalog as well as a repository for the whole set of governance elements, such us policies, documents, schemas, and web services descriptors, for the SOA Governance.

As we said earlier, the WSO2 is a very dynamic company that tries to be cutting edge. The last component for SOA from WSO2 is the **WSO2 EI 6**. In this component, they put the most important SOA functionalities in just one component. Those functionalities were previously encapsulated in the following components:

- WSO2 Enterprise Service Bus
- WSO2 Data services Server
- WSO2 Message Broker
- WSO2 Business Process Server
- WSO2 Application Server

So, this brand new component offers a new vision of the SOA infrastructure:

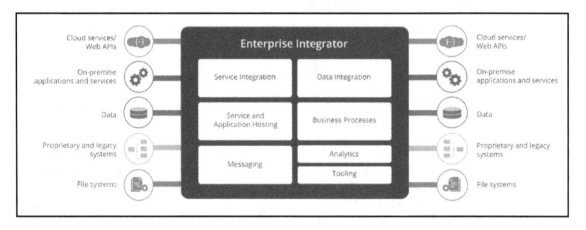

WSO2 Enterprise Integrator (http://wso2.com/integration)

We have already discussed all these components in the preceding figure about the WSO2 SOA infrastructure, except **WSO2 Application Server**. WSO2 Application Server, as the name says, is a Java application container for web applications, web services, and RESTful services. This container is called the **Carbon platform**. According to the level of this book, we will focus on the following WSO2 EI functionalities:

- Service Integration

- Data Integration
- Messaging
- Analytics
- Tooling

In the subsequent chapters, we will learn how to install WSO2 EI, create web services and data services, and how to test and manage them. We will also learn how to build services that use message queues, data services, and connectors to integrate with third-party applications.

Downloading WSO2 Enterprise Integrator

WSO2 EI can be downloaded from the WSO2 page for this component at `http://wso2.com/integration`. We just need to click on the download button, and we will be redirected to a download page:

WSO2 EI download page

- On this page, the email field is mandatory to download the server, so after writing our email, we will be able to download WSO2 EI by clicking on the **Download Server** button.
- If you already have a WSO2 portal account, you can just log into the site and browse to the product. Here, you can download the server without being asked for the email.

- In case you do not have an account, you can sign up for one for free at `https://wso2.com/user/register`. This will be useful to be up to date with the WSO2 world, and it will be necessary to use the WSO2 Update Service.
- Our recommendation is to obtain a WSO2 user account as we will need it later in the chapter to use the WSO2 Update Manager.
- Once our download is complete, we will have a ZIP file ready for installation.
- If an update is available for the component when downloading, we will have to use the WSO2 Update Service to apply it.

WSO2 Update Manager

WSO2 Update Manager will allow us to download many of the WSO2 products with the latest improvements and fixed bugs applied. They can be downloaded from `http://wso2.com/update/wum/download`, where we have to just choose the right version for our operating system and follow the instructions provided to install it.

Once installed, we can access WSO2 Update Manager by opening a terminal and typing:

```
>wum
```

And if everything is okay, we will see this in the console:

```
WUM keeps WSO2 products up-to-date.
* Find more information at http://wso2.com/update
Usage:
wum [command]
Available Commands:
init         Initialize WUM with your WSO2 credentials
search       Search products containing specific keyword(s)
add          Add or download a product
check-update Check for new updates for products
update       Update products in your local repository
list         List products in your local repository
describe     Show details of products in your local repository
delete       Delete products in your local repository
config       Change WUM configuration
version      Display wum version information
Flags:
  -h, --help     help for wum
  -v, --verbose  enable verbose mode

Use wum [command] --help for more information about a command.
```

This tool allows us to download and update our products so that we will always be up to date with fixed bug and improvements. It is important to note that, as we can see on the product page, WUM is not Apache 2.0 like the rest of the components, and it can only be freely used in non-production environments. For production environments, it is necessary to pay a subscription.

We will go through the most useful command needed to download and update our server.

The mandatory first step we always have to perform is to initialize the tool using a WSO2 user account. When we do this, we type this:

```
>wum init
```

Then, we will be asked for a WSO2 username and password. In case we have already launched the init command, only the password will be requested in the console:

You need a WSO2 account to start using wum. Don't have one yet? Sign up at https://wso2.com/user/register:

```
Please enter your WSO2 credentials to continue
    Username: my@email.com
    Password for 'my@email.com':
    Authenticating...
    Done!
    -- Welcome to WUM 1.0-beta --
    * Find more information at http://wso2.com/update
    * Please contact us for further information at http://wso2.com/contact
What's next? Have a look at the following list of wum commands. Add WSO2
products to your product repository:
    wum search          Search WSO2 products
    wum add             Add or download WSO2 products

Update WSO2 products available in your product repository:
    wum check-update    Check for new updates
    wum update          Update your WSO2 products

Manage WSO2 products available in your product repository:
    wum list            List WSO2 products
    wum describe        Show details of WSO2 products
    wum delete          Delete WSO2 products

Use wum [command] --help for more information about a command.
```

Now we are ready to download or check for updates for our products. By default, the tool places the repository in the operating system user's home directory; to avoid this, we will change the location of the repository to our working folder.

We will place our repository in the `wso2/products/` path; so, we type as follows:

```
>wumconfiglocal.product.repo wso2/products
New product repository is \wso2\products
```

In this repository, WUM places all the distributions in the download, and the new distributions are generated when there is a new update.

At this point, the most common tasks will be as follows:

1. Adding an existing downloaded product to the repository.
2. Downloading a new product.
3. Checking for updates of the server added to the repository.
4. Deleting a product from the repository.

Add an existing product to WUM repository

In cases where we have downloaded the product from the product page of wso2.com, we can add this download to the repository so that we can check for updates.

If we have previously downloaded, for example, WSO2 ESB 5.0.0, the previous version of WSO2 EI, and we want to add it to the repository to check whether any update is available for it, we type the following:

```
C:>wum add --file wso2esb-5.0.0.zip
Connecting to WSO2 Update...
Adding product wso2esb-5.0.0...
Successfully added to following location:
C:\wso2\products\wso2esb\5.0.0\wso2esb-5.0.0.zip
What's next?
use wum check-update wso2esb-5.0.0 to check for updates
use wum update wso2esb-5.0.0 to install latest updates
```

Remember that in Mac, you need to put the full path when typing the name of the file; in this case, we need to type the full path for the file, `wso2esb-5.0.0.zip`.

Now, we have WSO2 ESB 5.0.0 in the local repository. The ZIP containing the original server will remain in the source location, and an updated/patched copy will be placed under `[product.repo]/wso2esb/5.0.0/` in the repository location.

Next step, as we can read in the message displayed in the console, is to check for updates.

Download a product using WSO2 Update Manager

We can download a product using the WUM tool. This is our recommendation as it is the best way to keep your server up to date. In case you need to install an update in a server that is manually downloaded, you will have to install WUM and add that server to the repository anyway, so it is better to use it from the beginning.

To download WSO2 EI using WUM and add it to the repository, we just need to type the following in the console:

```
>wum add wso2ei
    Connecting to WSO2 Update...
    The following product(s) will be downloaded.
    wso2ei-6.0.0.zip
    After this operation, 600.8MB of additional disk space will be   used.
    Do you want to continue? [Y/n] y
    Successfully added to following location:6MB/600.8MB]
    What's next?
    product wso2ei-6.0.0... [566.7MB/600.8MB]
    use wum check-update wso2esb-5.0.0 to check for updates
    use wum update wso2esb-5.0.0 to install latest updates
```

When the download is complete, we will have WSO2 EI 6.0.0 in our repository. We can list the products existing in the repository by typing as follows:

```
C:\wso2\products>wum list
Product                 Updated         Filename
wso2ei-6.0.0            -               wso2ei-6.0.0.zip
wso2esb-5.0.0           -               wso2esb-5.0.0.zip
```

What's next? Use `wum describe [<product-pattern>]` to get more details of products. Also, if we ask for details, we get this:

```
C:\>wum describe wso2ei-6.0.0
Filename:               wso2ei-6.0.0.zip
Product Name:           wso2ei
Product Version:        6.0.0
Kernel Version:         4.4.14
Last Updated Time:      -
Product File Path:      C:\wso2\products\wso2ei\6.0.0\wso2ei-6.0.0.zip
```

We can get the absolute path in the filesystem where the product is located using this command. We can verify that the ZIP file containing the server is available in the path where we located the WUM repository in the filesystem.

Check for product updates using WSO2 Update Manager

Now that we have all of our products in the repository, as we can check with the `wum Gstlist` command, we are ready to check for updates. To achieve that, we type the following:

```
C:\ >wum check-update wso2ei-6.0.0
Connecting to WSO2 Update...
Checking for latest updates for wso2ei-6.0.0...
Product is up to date.
```

In this case, WSO2 EI is up to date, so no action is required. However, if we check for updates for the other product, WSO2 ESB 5.0.0, in our repository, we have this:

```
>wum check-update wso2esb-5.0.0
Connecting to WSO2 Update...
Checking for latest updates for wso2esb-5.0.0...
37 updates are available
[WARNING] 17 critical security updates. WSO2 strongly recommends that
you install these updates now.
```

What's next? Use `wum update` to install the latest updates.

In that case, due to WSO2 ESB 5.0.0 being released in 2016, there are updates available. In spite of the fact that it is not the product we are focused on in this book, we will show the update procedure using this product since the procedure is the same for all the products managed by WSO2 Update Manager.

So, to install the latest updates in all the products in the repository, we type this:

```
C:\>wum update
Connecting to WSO2 Update...
Validating your subscription status for product wso2ei...
[WARNING] Your credentials are not associated with an active WSO2
Updating wso2ei-6.0.0...
Product is up to date.
Validating your subscription status for product wso2esb...
[WARNING] Your credentials are not associated with an active WSO2
subscription.
```

Please remember that updates are not licensed for use in production without a valid WSO2 subscription. See `http://wso2.com/update` for more details:

```
Updating wso2esb-5.0.0...
37 updates are available
Downloading updates... [36/37]
Installing updates...
Preparing update summary...
Building updated product...
Update summary:
  Installed updates: 37
  * [WARNING] WSO2 strongly recommends to use this updated product for
  production as soon as possible.
  Security updates: 17
  Updated Product: C:\wso2\products\wso2esb\5.0.0\wso2esb-
  5.0.0.1488178152499.zip
  * More information about updates are available inside the above
  product archive
  Update summary(pdf): (product-archive)/updates\summary-2017-02-
  28T19-31-14\update-summary-1488178152499.pdf
```

What's next? Use `wum list [<product-pattern>]` to list products in your local repository. Use `wum describe [<product-pattern>]` to get more details of products.

The result is a new ZIP generated with all the updates ready to be installed.

Deleting a product from the WSO2 Update Manager repository

We can remove a product from the repository in a very simple way; we just have to type as follows:

```
C:\>wum delete wso2esb-5.0.0
The following product file(s) will be deleted.
wso2esb-5.0.0.1488178152499.zip
wso2esb-5.0.0.zip
Do you want to continue? [y/N] y
```

This command removes the ZIP file containing the product as well as all the releases generated as a result of new updates to the product.

Installing WSO2 Enterprise Integrator

Once we have obtained the up-to-date product ZIP, we are ready to install it. According to the level of the book, we will assume a target reader who will use WSO2 EI for development or testing purposes. We will also assume that the reader has a basic knowledge of WSO2 EI or this is their first contact with WSO2 EI. Advanced users may need to refer to the official product documentation at

`https://docs.wso2.com/display/EI600/WSO2+Enterprise+Integrator+Documentation`.

We will describe the installation under the following assumptions that *are not recommended for a production environment*:

- WSO2 EI runs using the default H2 embedded database
- WSO2 EI H2 embedded registry
- Standalone configuration

The prerequisites are quite simple, and for most cases, for a development or testing environment, these are enough:

- Memory of 2 GB minimum and 1 GB heap size.
- Space disk of 1 GB for installation. This is space just for the component; additional space is needed for logs and databases.
- JDK 1.8.
- JavaScript enabled browser.

If we meet these requirements, we will be able to run WSO2 EI. The installation for both the Linux and Windows operating systems are quite simple as well; we just need the `JAVA_HOME` environment variable properly configured, pointing to the JDK installation. Of course, there are several ways to create environment variables, but we will focus on a standard one, that is valid for most scenarios:

- Linux:
    1. Edit the BASHRC file in your home directory to add the `JAVA_HOME` variable definition at the top. The `JAVA_HOME` variable must point to the JDK installation folder. In this example, we are supposing that it is installed in the following:

    ```
    /usr/java/jdk1.8.0_121:
    export JAVA_HOME=/usr/java/jdk1.8.0_121
    export PATH=${JAVA_HOME}/bin:${PATH}
    ```

2. Verify that the `JAVA_HOME` variable is properly set in the console using the echo `$JAVA_HOME` command. The result must be the JDK installation path we set earlier.

- Windows:

    1. Go to **System properties** | **Advanced** | **Environmental variables**.

    2. In the **System Variable** section, add new.

    3. Set the name as `JAVA_HOME`

    4. Set the value as the JDK installation path, for example, `C:\Program Files\Java\jdk1.8.0_121`.

    5. Verify that `JAVA_HOME` is properly set, executing the `set JAVA_HOME` command in the console. The result must be the JDK installation path.

Now we are ready to launch WOS2 EI. As we discussed in the previous sections, WSO2 EI encapsulates six products that were previously independent of the following:

- WSO2 ESB.
- WSO2 Data Services Server (WSO2 DSS).
- WSO2 Application Server (WSO2 AS). In EI 6.1.1 and so on, it is not a feature anymore.
- WSO2 Analytics.
- WSO2 Business Process.
- WSO2 Message Broker.

The first three products have been merged into just one component called WSO2 EI, so WSO2 EI is made up of the following:

- WSO2 EI
- WSO2 EI Analytics
- WSO2 EI Business Process
- WSO2 EI Broker

So, when we talk about starting the WSO2 EI, we have several options:

- Start the four components manually in a specific order
- Start the four components automatically using the script provided
- Start the component on demand. According to the level of the book, WSO2 EI Business Process and WSO2 EI Broker require a deeper knowledge of WSO2, so we miss them in this book

Starting components manually

We can start the component one by one on demand. For example, we cannot create business processes in this book, so we do not need to start WSO2 Business Process. In such cases where we do not need a message queue, we do not need to start the WSO2 EI Broker. WSO2 EI Analytics will be useful to check message traces when invoking a service and to get the services statistics, so we will use this component.

We need to start the components in a specific order, as follows:

1. WSO2 EI.
2. WSO2 EI Analytics.
3. WSO2 EI Business Process.
4. WSO2 EI Broker.

In the following sections, we will see that all of them start and stop the same way.

Starting/stopping WSO2 Enterprise Integrator

To start WSO2 EI, we have to follow these steps:

1. Open a console and go to the `<WSO2EI_HOME>\bin` directory.
2. Type the following command:
   - **On Linux or macOS**: `sh integrator.sh`
   - **On Windows**: `integrator.bat --run`

3. You will see a log that the boot up is generating. The server will start up when you see a message log as shown:

   `WSO2 Carbon started in X sec`

4. We will also see the URL to access the WSO2 EI console in a message as follows:

```
Mgt Console URL   : https://<EI HOST>:<PORT>/carbon/
Where <PORT> is:
              8243 for WSO2 EI version 6.0.0
              9443 for WSO2 EI version 6.1.0 o higher
```

This port number will not change depending on the version for the rest of the components provided with WSO2 EI.

We will see, similar to the following screenshot, that the server is up:

```
INFO - StartupFinalizerServiceComponent Server          :  WSO2 Enterprise Integrator-6.0.0
INFO - StartupFinalizerServiceComponent WSO2 Carbon started in 88 sec
INFO - CarbonUIServiceComponent Mgt Console URL  : https://192.168.0.163:8243/carbon/
```

WSO2 EI boot up finished

In this screenshot, we can see the Management Console URL. We can see that the URL is shown using the host IP. When we access the console from the host that WOS2 EI is running on, we use localhost instead of the host IP. We will use the host IP to access the console from other hosts in the LAN or from internet:

- WSO2 EI 6.0.0:
  - `https://[your_IP]:8243/carbon/`
  - `https://localhost:8243/carbon/`
- WSO2 EI 6.1.0 or greater:
  - `https://[your_IP]:9443/carbon/`
  - `https://localhost:9443/carbon/`

You may have noted that the Management Console uses the HTTPS protocol. This is a secure protocol that encrypts the traffic between the browser and the server for security reasons; to do this, a certification is needed. All WSO2 products are provided with a default certificate that is not signed by a well-known certification authority but is okay for testing purposes. For this reason, when we access the Management Console, the browser will show an untrusted connection warning. We have to accept that certificate to access the Management Console. For a production environment, we will need a certificate generated by a well-known certification authority and then, there will not be any warning when accessing the Management Console.

All these considerations are valid for all the components, so we have to proceed in the same way when starting the other components.

Now we are able to browse to the Management Console:

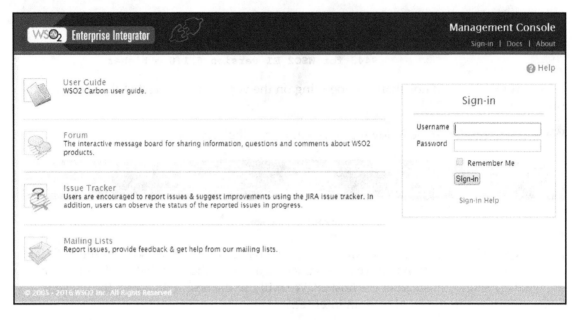

WSO2 EI Management Console

Now we just have to type the default username and password to sign in:

- **Username:** admin
- **Password:** admin

Then, the browser will show the WSO2 EI home page:

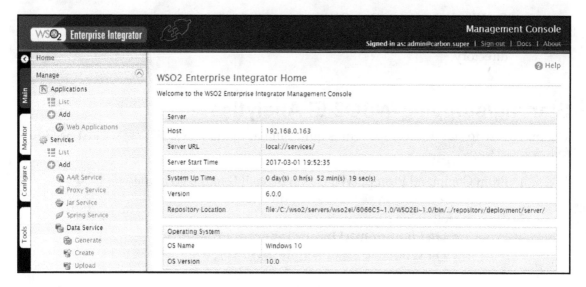

WSO2 EI home page

WSO2 EI can be shut down/restarted using the console. We can find this option in the **Main** tab by clicking on the **Shutdown/Restart** option:

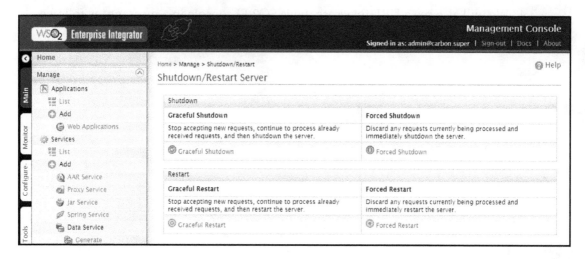

Shutdown and restart from Management Console

We also can shut down the product this way:

- **On Windows**: Using *Ctrl+C* in the command window
- **On Linux/macOS**: Using `sh integrator.sh` stop from the `<EI_HOME>/bin/` directory

Starting/stopping WSO2 EI Analytics

The procedure to start this component is quite similar to the WSO2 IE one; we just need to follow these steps:

1. From Command Prompt (Windows) or shell (Linux), go to the `<EI_HOME>/wso2/analytics/bin` directory.
2. Type the following command:
   - **On Linux or macOS**: `sh integrator.sh`
   - **On Windows**: `integrator.bat --run`

3. You will see a log that the boot up is generating. The server will start up when you see a message log as illustrated:

   `WSO2 Carbon started in X sec`

4. We will also see a URL to access the WSO2 EI console in a message, as follows:

   `Mgt Console URL  : https://<EI HOST>:port/carbon/`

The same considerations for accessing WOS2 EI Management Console are valid here. The port, in this case, is offset by 1, so we will browse to `https://localhost:9444/carbon`. Take a look at the following screenshot:

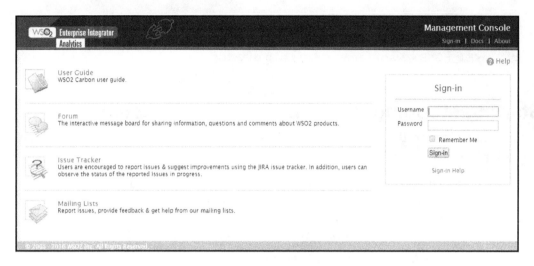

WSO2 EI Analytics Management Console

We sign in with the **Username** as `admin` and **Password** as `admin` to get the WSO2 EI Analytics Home:

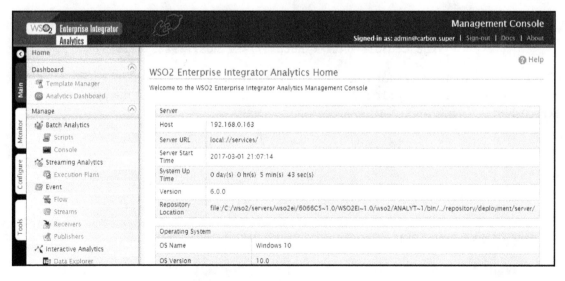

WSO2 EI Analytics Home

WSO2 EI Analytics can be shut down/restarted using the console. We find these options in the **Main** tab by clicking on the Shutdown/Restart option. We also can shut down the product this way:

- **On Windows**: Using *CTRL+C* in the command window
- **On Linux/macOS**: Using `shwso2server.sh` stop from the `<EI_HOME>/wso2/analytics/bin` directory

Starting/stopping WSO2 EI Business Process

The procedure to start this component is quite similar to the WSO2 IE one; we just need to follow these steps:

1. From Command Prompt (Windows) or shell (Linux), go to the `<EI_HOME>/wso2/ business-process/bin` directory.
2. Type the following command:
    - **On Linux or macOS**: `sh.ws02server.sh`
    - **On Windows**: `ws02server.bat`
3. You will see a log that the boot up is generating. The server will be started when you see a message log as follows:

    `WSO2 Carbon started in X sec`

4. We will also see a URL to access the WSO2 EI console in a message, as illustrated:

    `Mgt Console URL  : https://<EI HOST>:9445/carbon/`

The same considerations as for accessing WOS2 EI Management Console are valid here, so we will browse to `https://localhost:9445/carbon`. Take a look at the following screenshot:

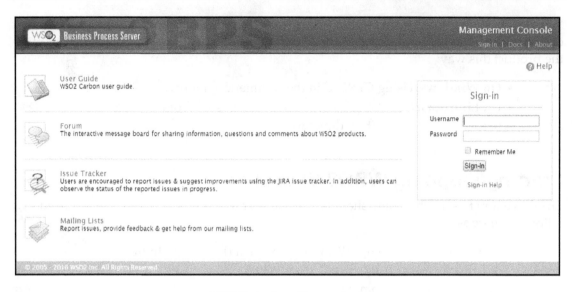

WSO2 EI Business Process Management Console

We sign in with the **Username** as `admin` and **Password** as `admin` to get the WSO2 EI Business Process Home:

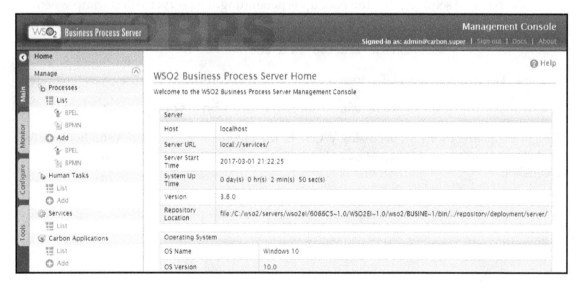

WSO2 EI Business Process Home

WSO2 EI Business Process can be shut down/restarted using the console. We can find this option in the **Main** tab by clicking on the Shutdown/Restart option. We can also shut down the product this way:

- **On Windows**: Using *CTRL+C* in the command window
- **On Linux/macOS**: Using `sh wso2server.sh` stop from the `<EI_HOME>/wso2/business-process/bin` directory

Starting/stopping WSO2 EI Broker

The procedure to start this component is quite similar to the WSO2 IE one; we just need to follow these steps:

1. From Command Prompt (Windows) or shell (Linux), go to the `<EI_HOME>/wso2/ broker/bin` directory.
2. Type the following command:
   - **On Linux or macOS**: `sh.wso2server.sh`
   - **On Windows**: `wso2server.bat`

3. You will see a log that the boot up is generating. The server will start up when you see a message log as shown:

   WSO2 Carbon started in X sec

4. We will also see a URL to access the WSO2 EI console in a message, as illustrated:

   Mgt Console URL   : https://<EI HOST>:9446/carbon/

The same considerations for accessing WOS2 EI Management Console are valid here, so we will browse to `https://localhost:9446/carbon`. Take a look at the following screenshot:

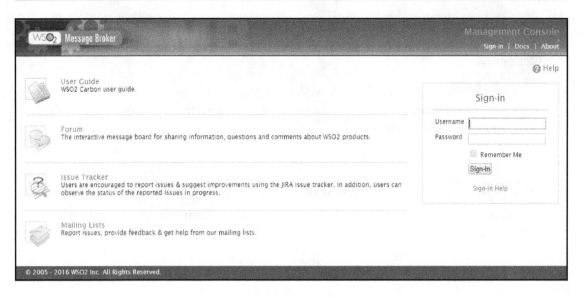

WSO2 EI Broker Management Console

We sign in with the **Username** as admin and **Password** as admin to get the WSO2 EI Broker Home:

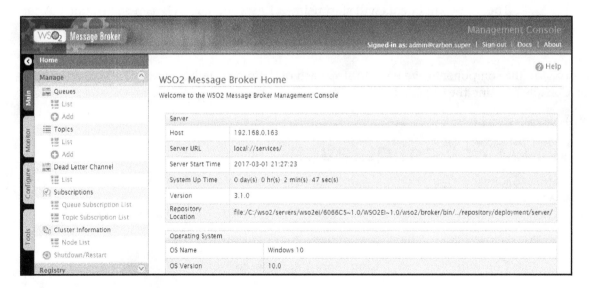

WSO2 EI Broker Home

WSO2 EI Broker can be shut down/restarted using the console. We can find this option in the **Main** tab by clicking on the Shutdown/Restart option. We also can shut down the product this way:

- **On Windows**: Using *CTRL+C* in the command window
- **On Linux/macOS**: Using `sh wso2server.sh` stop from the `<EI_HOME>/wso2/broker/bin` directory

Starting all the products

In cases where we need to start all the components, we can do it using just one command; we just need to follow these steps:

1. From Command Prompt (Windows) or shell (Linux), go to the `<EI_HOME>/bin` directory.
2. Type the following command:
    - **On Linux or macOS**: `shstart-all.sh`
    - **On Windows**: `start-all.bat`

3. The four components will start using a 10-second gap between each launch. After a few seconds, all the components will be up and each Management Console will be available.

To stop the components, we have to stop each of them manually, using each Management Console or using the console instructions.

WSO2 EI Configuration

There are some configuration tasks that must usually be done when developing real-world services:

- Configuring JDBC drivers
- Configuring transports
- Configuring message formatters and message builders

Configuring JDBC drivers

This is a mandatory configuration task when using data services. JDBC drivers allow WSO2 EI to connect to databases. By default, there are many JDBC drivers installed, so we have to configure the drivers' need for connecting the data sources that will provide us with the data in the orchestration.

We can do that with these simple steps:

1. Locating the correct JDBC drivers for the databases that will play in our orchestration.
2. Copying them to the `<EI_HOME>/lib/` folder.
3. Restarting the server.

Once the server is restarted, we will be able to connect to the databases.

Configuring transports

WSO2 EI supports several transports that we can use when building our services, such as the following:

- **JMS transport**: This enables sending and receiving messages to queues and topics that implement the JMS specification
- **Mailto transport**: This enables sending emails
- **VFS transport**: **Virtual File System** (**VFS**) transport allows us to process files in a directory of the filesystem

We can enable this transport and many others in the `<EI_HOME>/conf/axis2/axis2.xml` file. All the transports available can be found in that file with a default configuration. We have to configure these transports for input and output connections. The input transports are configured using the `transportReceiver` XML tag, while the output transports are configured with the `transportSender` tag:

```
<transportSender name="jms"
class="org.apache.axis2.transport.jms.JMSSender"/>

<transportReceiver name="jms"
class="org.apache.axis2.transport.jms.JMSListener">
<parameter name="myTopicConnectionFactory" locked="false">
<parameter name="java.naming.factory.initial"
locked="false">org.wso2.andes.jndi.PropertiesFileInitialContextFactory</par
ameter>
```

```
<parameter name="java.naming.provider.url"
locked="false">conf/jndi.properties</parameter>
<parameter name="transport.jms.ConnectionFactoryJNDIName"
locked="false">TopicConnectionFactory</parameter>
<parameter name="transport.jms.ConnectionFactoryType"
locked="false">topic</parameter>
</parameter>

<parameter name="myQueueConnectionFactory" locked="false">
<parameter name="java.naming.factory.initial"
locked="false">org.wso2.andes.jndi.PropertiesFileInitialContextFactory</par
ameter>
<parameter name="java.naming.provider.url"
locked="false">conf/jndi.properties</parameter>
<parameter name="transport.jms.ConnectionFactoryJNDIName"
locked="false">QueueConnectionFactory</parameter>
<parameter name="transport.jms.ConnectionFactoryType"
locked="false">queue</parameter>
</parameter>

<parameter name="default" locked="false">
<parameter name="java.naming.factory.initial"
locked="false">org.wso2.andes.jndi.PropertiesFileInitialContextFactory</par
ameter>
<parameter name="java.naming.provider.url"
locked="false">conf/jndi.properties</parameter>
<parameter name="transport.jms.ConnectionFactoryJNDIName"
locked="false">QueueConnectionFactory</parameter>
<parameter name="transport.jms.ConnectionFactoryType"
locked="false">queue</parameter>
</parameter>
</transportReceiver>
```

Configuring message formatters and message builders

Message formatters and **Message builders** are the components that allow us to send and receive different types of messages according to the content type specified in the request. It is important to enable the content type used in the messages exchanged because if the content type received is not configured in the system, the message will not be understood.

Message builders are used to process incoming messages, and Message formatters are used to build the outgoing messages.

We can enable the Message formatters and builders in the file located in `<EI_HOME>/conf/axis2/axis2.xml`. Message formatters are under the same name in XML tag, and so are Message builders. Most values that messages content type can be received are already configured, but they are commented. We just have to find the one we need and uncomment it for Message formatters and/or message builders, depending on the case.

For example, to enable us to send and receive JSON messages, we have to enable that content type for input and output messages in `axis2.xml`:

```
<messageFormattercontentType="application/json"
class="org.wso2.carbon.integrator.core.json.JsonStreamFormatter"/>

<messageBuildercontentType="application/json"
class="org.wso2.carbon.integrator.core.json.JsonStreamBuilder"/>
```

Summary

In this chapter, we discussed the issues that gave rise to SOA, described its main principles, and explained how to make our standard organization in an SOA organization. In order to achieve this aim, we named the WSO2 product we need as WSO2 EI. Finally, we learned how to install, configure, and start it up.

In the next chapter, we will learn how to create the artifacts that will be deployed in WSO2 EI. These artifacts are packaged in so-called carbon files, which are generated by the WSO2 EI IDE, named WSO2 Tooling.

2
Developing Integration Projects with WSO2EI Tooling

In the last chapter, we kept up-to-date with **Service-Oriented Architecture (SOA)**, the original problem that gave birth to SOA, and the benefits of SOA. Additionally, we learned how to build our SOA infrastructure using WSO2 products, and, more concretely, using WSO2 EI 6.0.0.

In this chapter, we will introduce WSO2 Enterprise Integrator Tooling. This is an Eclipse-based IDE and we will use it to develop our services, as well as to build the deployable artifacts. The topics we will cover are as follows:

- Installing and running WSO2EI Tooling
- Creating carbon projects
- Debugging applications
- Data mappings

WSO2EI Tooling is a single tool used to develop our entire application, including artifacts from any of the components that comprise WSO2EI.

WSO2EI Tooling is based on Eclipse IDE for Java developers, also called Mars 2.

We can do either of the following:

- Download the Eclipse plugin and install it to our Eclipse, where the Eclipse version must be Mars 2 compatible
- Download the full distribution

We will choose the second option, since it is suitable for most cases, is the simplest one, and avoids any configuration issues.

Installing and running WSO2EI Tooling

In order to install and run the WSO2ESB Tooling, let's look at the following steps:

1. The first step is to download the tooling from the WSO2 product site at: `http://wso2.com/integration`:

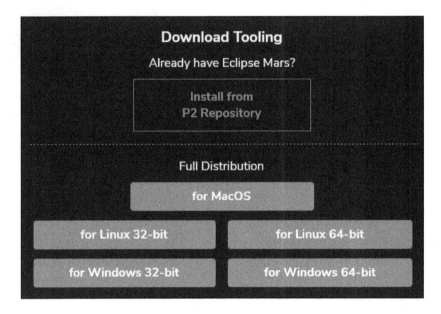

2. We just have to choose the full distribution that matches our operating system and it will start to download.

3. Once the download is complete, we will have a ZIP file containing the prepackaged WSO2EI Tooling in Eclipse Mars 2. We just have to unzip this file in the desired folder (`$WSO2EITOOL`) and then we will have Eclipse WSO2EI Tooling ready to be launched as a regular one. For Mac users, you can download a `.dmg` file. For specific installation instructions and known issues, refer to the official documentation at `http://wso2.com/integration`.

 We are working with version 4.1.0, which is the most recent version at the time of writing this book.

4. The only requirement for starting Eclipse is Java 7 or 8 JRE/JDK. Assuming that it is installed, we can launch Eclipse by typing in this command line:

```
Linux/Mac: ./$EITOOL/eclipse
Windows: $EITOOL\eclipse.exe
```

5. Once Eclipse is up, we can find the WSO2EI Tooling features in the **Developer Studio** option on the menu:

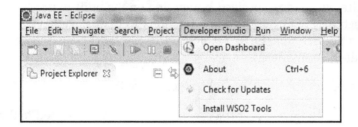

6. Click on **Developer Studio | Open Dashboard**, and a new tab will open, where we can find everything we need to develop our WSO2EI applications:

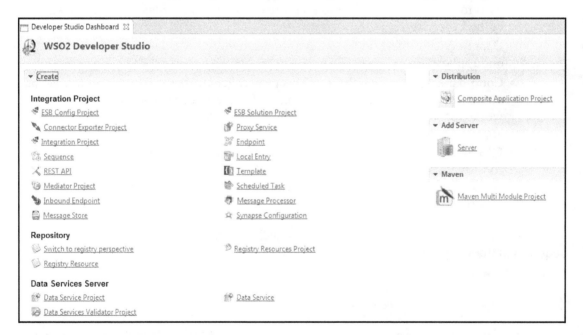

Creating carbon projects

When we develop a WSO2 Enterprise Integrator application, we can create different types of projects depending on the functionality required. These projects are called carbon projects, and there are several kinds of projects depending on the functionality needed.

As you may remember from Chapter 1, *Getting Started with SOA and WSO2*, WSO2 Enterprise Integrator is a bundle made up of previous individual products. Hence, we will have to create different kinds of projects depending on the built-in product in which we are implementing each part of our application functionality. Thus, we have different projects for the **Enterprise Service Bus (ESB)**, **Data Services Server (DSS)**, or **Business Process Server (BPS)** built-in components.

Focusing on the scope of the book, we will make use of the following:

- **ESBConfig Project**: This project contains all artifacts related to the functionality developed in the ESB.
- **Registry Resource Project**: This project will be used to add resources such as XSL transformations, WSLD files, and XSD files to the EI registry. Some of the artifacts used to develop our application require complementary files that must be stored in the EI registry.
- **Data Service Project**: In this kind of project, we add the data services required in our application.
- **Composite Application Project**: This project generates the deployable artifact of our application. It detects the existing artifacts in the projects within the workspace and allows us to select which ones will be packaged in a composite application that will be deployed in WSO2EI.
- **ESB Solution Project**: This project is not a real project; rather, it can be considered as a wizard, as it can make a developer's life easier. It allows us to create the most common projects needed in a service development using just one wizard.

All these projects use Maven technology, so we will find the mandatory pom.xml file required in these types of projects in all of them.

ESBConfig projects

This type of project is focused on web services and REST artifacts. We will create all the artifacts needed to develop the web services or REST services of our application inside this project.

To create a new project of this kind, we go to Developer Studio dashboard and click on **ESB Config Project**.

Then, we follow these steps:

1. Select **New ESB Config Project** and click on **Next**.
2. Type the name for the project and click on **Next**. We can keep the default values for the other options:

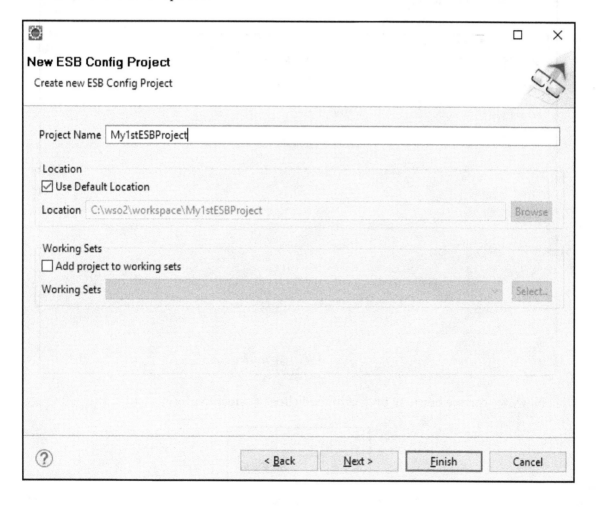

3. Finally, we introduce some Maven-required information for the pom.xml file that will be generated, that is, **Group Id**, **Artifact Id**, and **Version**. If needed, we can **Specify Parent Project from the Workspace** as well, and then click on **Finish**:

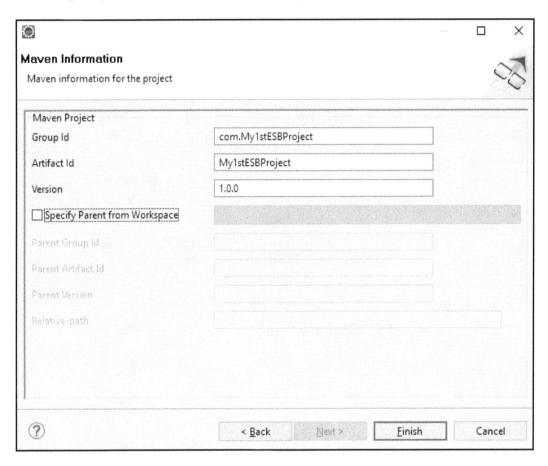

Now, we can see our new project in the Eclipse **Project Explorer**:

Now we are ready to add the artifacts that comprise our composite application to the project. The most common artifacts available are listed here:

- **Proxy services**: We use this artifact to create any kind of service different from REST services, for instance, **Simple Object Access Protocol** (**SOAP**) web services, VFS services, **Java Message Service** (**JMS**) services, and so on.
- **REST API**: With this artifact, we build REST services.
- **Sequences**: These artifacts allow us to structure service flow in little pieces so that the code will be more understandable, reusable, easy to read, and so on.
- **Endpoints**: These artifacts will be used to define communication endpoints the messages may be sent to, in other words, the destination we can send messages to.

However, how do all these artifacts work together to comprise our service?

Well, just take a look at the following diagram to clarify that:

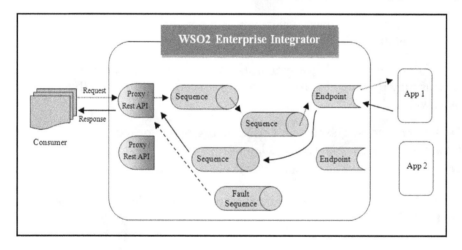

4. The dotted arrow specifies the path followed by the incoming message, until it is sent to the final backend, in this case App1, and the black arrow indicates the response patch.
5. The **Consumer** sends a message to the service that can be implemented using a Proxy (SOAP Service) or a Rest API. In this element, we specify the interface configuring parameters such as **Web Services Description Language** (**WSDL**) or protocol.

6. From **Proxy/Rest API**, the message is sent to a sequence where we implement the service functionality. We can abstract our logic in several sequences that we can chain as desired. The incoming flow finishes sending the message through an endpoint to the backend, **App1** in this case. We can set a specific sequence that processes the endpoint response; otherwise, a default sequence will be used.

7. The backend receives the message, processes it, and sends the response back to the out **Sequence** if using send mediator, or to the next mediator in the sequence if using call mediator. The endpoint will send the message to a sequence where the response can be processed or just sent back to the proxy.

8. Then, the outcoming flow finishes with the proxy replying to the consumer with the response.

Additionally, we need to define a sequence that will be executed when any error occurs during the process; this sequence is called **Fault Sequence**. The most common behavior of this sequence is to build an error message and respond to the consumer. This flow is reflected in the diagram with a striped arrow.

This is the best practice; however, you can omit creating a custom fault sequence, which means that the default fault sequence will be called in case of an error.

The flow described here matches a synchronous scenario where the consumer awaits the response. This may probably be the most common scenario; however, there are other scenarios as well:

- Asynchronous: The consumer does not remain blocked waiting for the response; the response may be received later
- Fire and forget: The consumer does not need a response

Once we know which artifacts we will need to build our service, we will learn how to create them with the IDE.

Creating a proxy

When we need to create a service based on a SOAP web service, we will open the Developer Studio dashboard and follow these steps:

1. Click on **Proxy Service**.
2. Choose **Create a New Proxy Service** and click **Next**.

3. In this window, we will enter the following information:

- **Proxy Service Name**: The name of the service.
- **Proxy Service Type**: These are common and simple scenarios where only a little information is needed to build the service, so we will be asked for that information here. Thus, the proxy will be created with all the needed artifacts and further customizations will not be necessary. In other words, we will create our server at once in this wizard. Depending on which service type we choose, the advanced configuration option will change, showing the required information in each case. The available types are as follows:
    - **Pass Through Proxy**: In this scenario, the service just sends the information to the endpoint without any content processing. The WSDL exposed in this case is a generic one, and, of course, different from the backend web service.
    - **Custom Proxy**: This is the scenario we must choose when we are building a complex service that suits none of the other scenarios.

- **Transformer Proxy**: In this scenario, the service modifies the message content, performing an **Extensible Stylesheet Language** (**XSL**) transformation. This transformation can be executed in the incoming flow, prior to sending it to the backend, and/or in the outcoming flow, transforming the response received from the backend before responding to the consumer.
- **Log Forward Proxy**: This scenario is similar to the **Pass Through Proxy**. The message is sent as is, but it allows you to log the message sent to the backend as well as the received one.
- **WSDL Based Proxy**: This scenario is the same as for the **Pass Through Proxy** and allows you to set the WSDL for the proxy. This may be the same as the backend or a custom one.
- **Secure Proxy**: Again, this scenario is a pass-through scenario but, additionally, it allows you to secure the web service, attaching a secure policy to the proxy.

- **Save the proxy service in**: As it says, here we choose the **ESBConfig Project** where we add the service.
- **Advanced configuration**: Here, we add the additional information required by the **Proxy Service Type** established earlier.

4. Click on **Finish**, and we will see our service in the **ESBConfig Project** chosen:

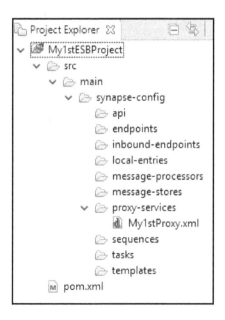

5. We can start editing our proxy by double-clicking on the `My1stProxy.xml` file that you can see in the preceding image. The edition screen will be shown, as follows:

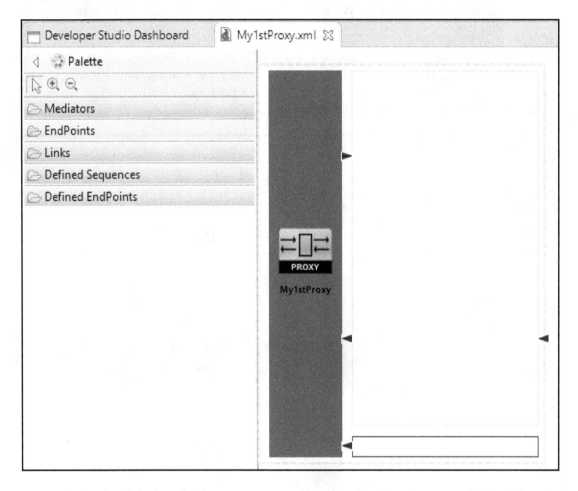

6. On the right-hand side, we can see a diagram showing the proxy design. The proxy design can be structured in these parts:
    - **In flow**: Here, we place the logic that processes the incoming messages sent to the proxy.
    - **Out flow**: Here, we place the logic for the outcoming messages; these are the responses received from an endpoint.
    - **Fault flow**: Here, we implement the behavior that must be triggered when an error occurs during the flow.

7. On the left-hand side, we can see the palette where we have all the artifacts available to build our services.

8. To use these components, we just have to drag them from the palette and drop them in the correct area. We will discuss these components further in the next chapter.

As a best practice based on our experience, it is better for the incoming sequence, outcoming sequence, and the fault sequence to define sequences where we implement the logic. In other words, in proxy, we just link to sequences instead of implementing the logic in the proxy itself as you see in the following image:

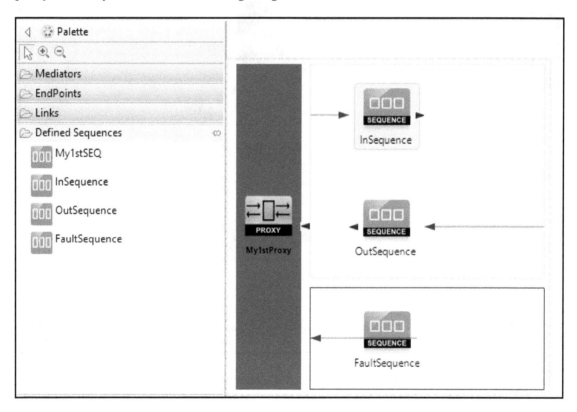

We shall discuss more about sequences in the next section.

The truth behind the scene can be seen if we click on the **Source** tab, which we can find in the left-bottom corner of the proxy editor:

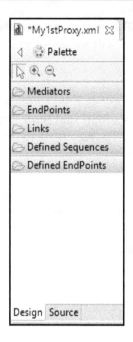

In this tab, we can see the proxy XML code:

```xml
<?xml version="1.0" encoding="UTF-8"?>
<proxy name="My1stProxy" startOnLoad="true" tra
    <target>
        <inSequence>
            <sequence key="InSequence"/>
        </inSequence>
        <outSequence>
            <sequence key="OutSequence"/>
        </outSequence>
        <faultSequence>
            <sequence key="FaultSequence"/>
        </faultSequence>
    </target>
</proxy>
```

As we acquire knowledge on WSO2EI, sometimes it will be useful to edit this XML code rather than using the visual editor in Eclipse.

Creating a REST API

Here, we will learn to create a **Representational State Transfer** (**REST**) API, that is, how RESTful services are created in WSO2EI. We create them from the Developer Studio dashboard by following these steps:

1. Click on REST API:

2. Choose **Create A New API Artifact** and click on **Next**.
3. Add the following information:
    - **Name**: Name of the API; here, we will set it to `my1stapi`
    - **Context**: This is the root context our services will have, for example, `my1stapi`. Thus, when calling the API, the URL will look like `http://localhost:8280/my1stapi`. It must start with `/`.
    - **Host name**: We can leave it blank. It is used to filter the host that can invoke this API; if it is blank, everyone can call it.
    - **Port**: This is used if we need to bind the API to a specific port; here, we leave it blank.
    - **Save location**: Choose an ESB project to save it. Here, we choose **My1stESBProject**.

4. Click on **Finish**, and the API structure will be added to the project. It will be placed in the **My1stESBProject** project in the project explorer in the path:

5. If we double-click on the `my1stapi.xml` file, the API editor will open and will look like this:

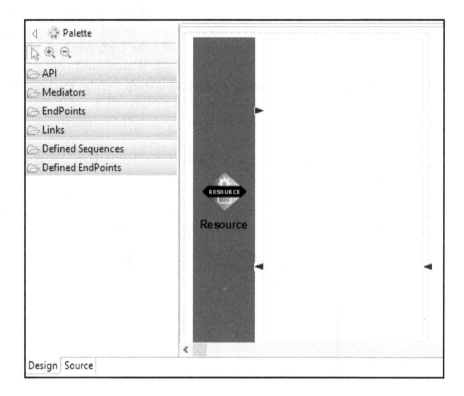

6. Now we are ready to implement our API functionality. API works the same way as proxy services. They both use in sequence, out sequence, and fault sequence, where logic is implemented.

We will go over RESTful services again later in the book.

Creating a sequence

In this section, we will create the sequences that implement the logic for our service. Sequences are the building blocks of our service. We can create them from the Developer Studio dashboard by following these steps:

1. Click on **Sequence**.
2. Select **Create New Sequence** and click on **Next**.

3. In this window, we enter this data:
   - **Sequence Name**: The name of the sequence
   - **Save Sequence in**: Project where we create the sequence

There are some advanced configurations that are not mandatory:

- **On Error Sequence**: Here, we can specify which sequence will be triggered when an error occurs during the sequence flow. This behavior is similar to that described for fault sequences in proxies. If no sequence is specified, the fault sequence of the proxy that executes this sequence is thrown.
- **Available Endpoints**: Here, we can select a default endpoint to send the message.
- **Make the sequence as Dynamic Sequence**: This option means that the sequence will be stored in the WSO2EI registry, which allows you to share the sequence and can be stored in the two kinds of locations: **Configuration** and **Governance**. We are not using this feature due to the scope of this book, but to give a brief idea of its application, we can say that the configuration registry artifacts are shared by all the WSO2EI nodes in a cluster, while the governance registry artifacts are shared by all the WSO2 products of our environment.

4. Click on **Finish** and the sequence will finally be created:

5. We can begin implementing our sequence logic by double-clicking on the file My1stSEQ.xml in the project explorer, which will open the sequence editor:

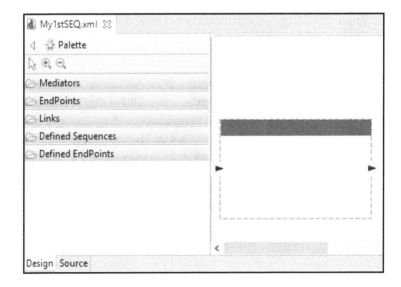

As you may note, this editor is quite similar to the proxy editor. On the left-hand side, we have the **Palette**, where we can find the artifact we use to compose our logic. We just need to drag and drop components from the palette to the design section.

In most of the common scenarios, logic is implemented using **mediators** that allow us to modify the content of the message. We will discuss more on mediators in the subsequent chapters.

As is the case with proxies, we also have a source tab where we can see the XML code behind the design display. Consider this design:

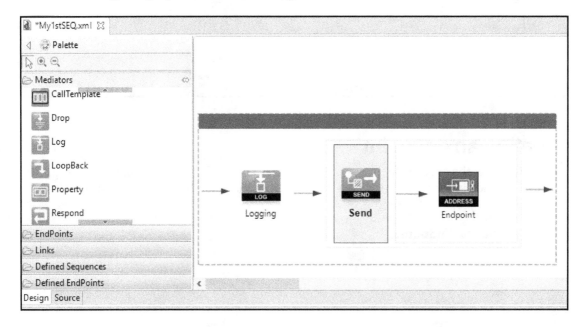

We have the following source code for the preceding design:

```xml
My1stSEQ.xml
1  <?xml version="1.0" encoding="UTF-8"?>
2  <sequence name="My1stSEQ" trace="disable" xmlns="http://ws.apache.org/ns/synapse">
3      <log description="Logging"/>
4      <send>
5          <endpoint>
6              <address uri="http://www.example.org/service"/>
7              <description>Endpoint</description>
8          </endpoint>
9      </send>
10 </sequence>
11
```

Design | Source

Creating an endpoint

The endpoint is the only artifact left for us to learn to create in the ESB project. The endpoint specifies the destination the message is sent to. From the Developer Studio dashboard, we follow these steps:

1. Click on **Endpoint**.

2. Select **Create a New Endpoint** and click on **Next**:

3. In the preceding screen, we fill in the following information:
    - **Endpoint Name**: The name of the endpoint.
    - **Endpoint Type**: There are many ways to specify the endpoint. Adapting to the scope of this book, we will use the **Address Endpoint**, where we just need to specify the URL of the endpoint. These are also the types of endpoint used for most cases.
    - **Address**: The endpoint of the backend.
    - Choose between **Static Endpoint** and **Dynamic Endpoint**. Like sequences, endpoints can also be dynamic, which means that they will be stored in the WSO2EI registry. In this book, we use static endpoints.
    - **Save endpoint in**: The project where we add the endpoint.

4. Finally, clicking on **Finish** will add the endpoint to the project:

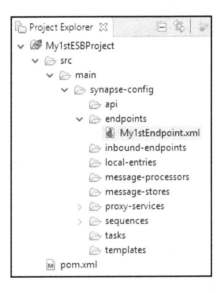

In this case, we usually do not need to edit this artifact again as all information is provided in the wizard. However, if we need to edit, we can double-click on the file and the editor will be shown:

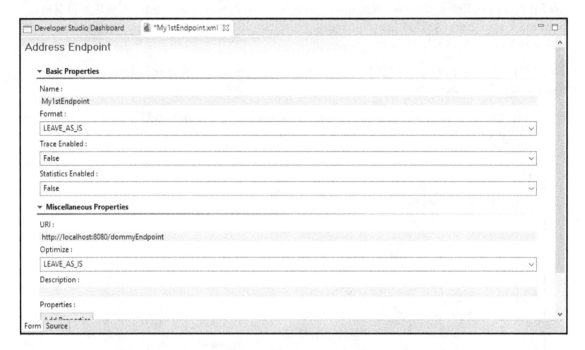

We can also see the XML source code in the **Source** tab:

```
1  <?xml version="1.0" encoding="UTF-8"?>
2  <endpoint name="My1stEndpoint" xmlns="http://ws.apache.org/ns/synapse">
3      <address uri="http://localhost:8080/dommyEndpoint"/>
4  </endpoint>
5
```

Form Source

Registry Resource Project

This kind of project will be needed to create resources for same mediators that provide useful functionalities, such as message validation or XSL transformation. WSDL and **XML Schema Definition (XSD)** files required to establish the proxy WSDL also need to be uploaded to the WSO2EI registry.

To add a resource to the WSO2EI, we start from the WSO2 Developer Studio dashboard as usual and follow these steps:

1. Click on **Registry Resources** project and enter the name and location of the project:

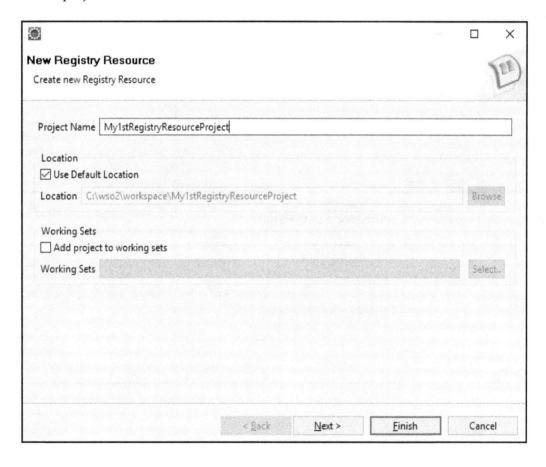

2. Click on **Next** and introduce the Maven information for the project, that is, **Group Id**, **Artifact Id**, and **Version**. If needed, we can specify the parent project as well; then, click on **Finish**:

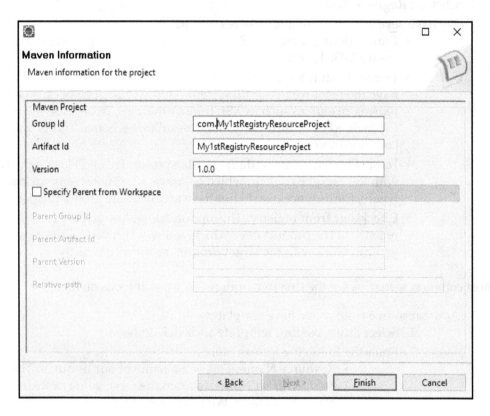

Now, we can see the new project in the Eclipse **Project Explorer**:

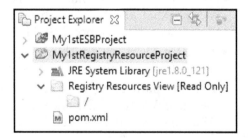

Now we are ready to add resources to this project from the WSO2 Developer Studio dashboard. We just have to follow these steps:

1. Click on **Registry Resource**.
2. We have several options to add new resources:
    *   **From existing template**: This helps us create the resource, starting from a WSDL or XSD template.
    *   **Import from the system**: Many times, it so happens that we already have the resource in our filesystem. This may happen because we are reusing resources such as XSL transformations, or because the resource is provided by a third party, such as an XSD schema. This is quite a common option.
    *   **Import registry dump file from file system**: This will load a package with the registry content, which we must work with, only for cases where, for instance, we do not have access to the product registry.
    *   **Check-out from registry**: This option allows you to connect to the registry of the product over which you will run your service so that you can work with the target product repository directly.

The most common scenarios are the first two options, so we will focus on them:

1. Add a resource from an existing template:
    1. Select **From existing template** and click on **Next**.
    2. Enter the following information:
        *   **Resource Name**: This is the name of our resource. The next field, **Artifact Name**, is set to the same value as **Resource Name** by default. We recommend for you to leave the default value.
        *   **Template**: There are many types of templates, such as WSDL, XSD, and XSL, which are the most common ones. We can choose, for instance, **XSL File**.
        *   **Registry**: Here, we can choose **gov** or **conf**. Due to the scope of this book, we always choose the **conf** registry.
        *   **Registry path**: Here, we type the path where we locate the resource. We type **XSL** since we are adding an XSL file. Thus, the file will be stored in the registry in the `$ConfRegistry/XSL/My1stRegistryResource.xsl` path.
        *   **Save resource in**: Here, we choose a **Registry Resource Project** to save the resource.

3. Click on **Finish** and the resource will be added:

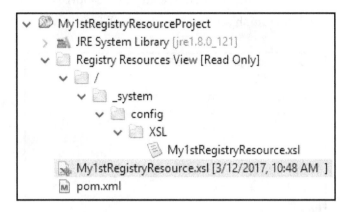

Here, we can see the resource we have just added. You can also note the path where the resource is located under the **Registry Resources View [Read Only]** tree, that is, the conf registry (**_system** | **config**), plus the (**_system** | **config** | **XSL**) path.

2. Import from file system:
    1. We choose Import from file system and click on **Next**.
    2. Now, we provide the following information:
        - **From file**: Here, we can browse to a file or folder. In this case, we will add another XSL transformation from the `XSLTransformation.xsl` file.
        - **Artifact Name**: A name for the artifact. This is populated by default when choosing the file in the from file field. We recommend keeping this name.
        - **Registry**: Here, we choose the configuration registry (**conf**).
        - **Registry path to deploy**: The folder where the resource will be located. We set the folder to XSL since we are adding an XSL transformation as well.

- **Save resource in**: Here, we choose the **Registry Resource Project** where we add the resource.

2. Click on **Finish** and the resource will be added:

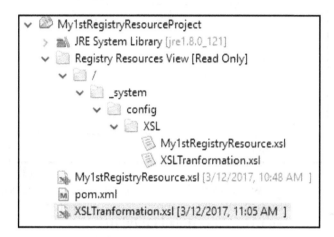

Now, we already have our resources in the project. Whether it is an existing resource or a new one from a template, we edit them by double-clicking on them. This will open the Eclipse plain text editor, which we can start editing in.

Data Service Project

Data Service Project will be used to add data services that allow us to access multiple data sources and expose their data in a very simple way. To create this kind of project, we will start from the Developer Studio dashboard, as usual, and follow these steps:

1. Click on **Data Service Project** and add the name and location of the project.
2. Click on **Next** and enter the Maven information for the project, that is, **Group Id**, **Artifact Id**, and **Version**. If needed, we can specify the parent project as well, and then click on **Finish**:

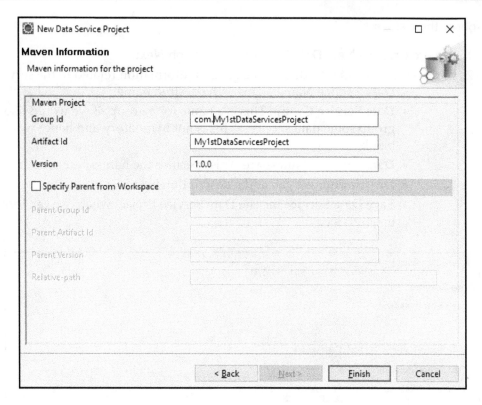

3. Now, we have added the new data service project to the workspace:

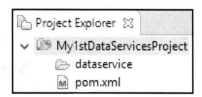

Now, we can create the data services needed for our application.

To add a new data service, go to the Developer Studio dashboard and click on **Data Service**.

Then, follow these steps:

1. Choose **Create a New Data Service** and click on **Next**.
2. In this step, we will introduce some general information related to the service:
    *   **Data Service Name***: This is the desired name.
    *   **Data Service Group**: This is a name for a group, if we would like to group some data services. This is not mandatory and hence we leave it blank.
    *   **Data Service Namespace**: This specifies the namespace for our service.
    *   **Description**: We can add a description here.
    *   **Save Data Service in:** The Data Service Project where we can locate the data service.

3. Click on **Next**. Now, we will add the data source information for our data service. There are many ways to create data sources, but according to our experience, the best practice is to create the data sources in the WSO2EI and create references from data services. This way, we can have just one point of data source configuration that provides many advantages. Thus, we will add the following information:

- **Data Source Id**: This is a name for the datasource.
- **Data Source Type**: As we discussed earlier, we choose **Carbon Data Source** here, which means that we reference a data source already created in the system.
- **Data Source Name**: This is the name of the data source we are referencing.

4. Click on **Finish** and the data service will be added:

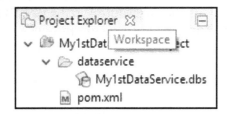

We can start building our data service by double-clicking on the file. We are now done with the data service edition, and we will go deeper into it in the later chapters.

Composite Application Project

Composite Application Project will be used to generate the deployable artifacts. This project is aware of the existing artifacts in the rest of the project within the workspace and allows us to choose which one we want to add to the deployable **Carbon Application aRchive (CAR)** file.

Once again, we go to the Developer Studio dashboard, click on the **Composite Application Project** and follow these steps:

1. We enter the name and location of the project as we did earlier, in the other projects:

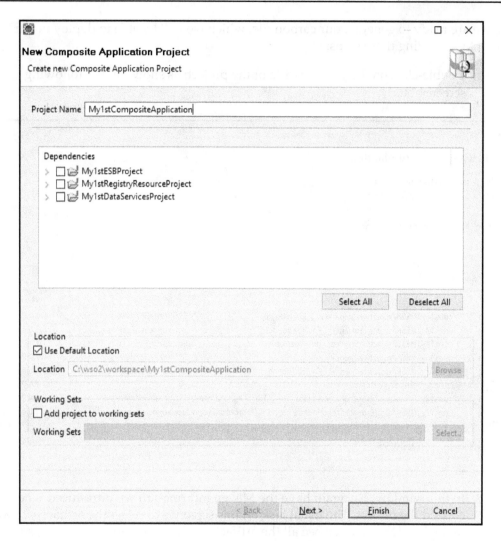

2. Click on **Next** and add the Maven information: **Group Id**, **Version**, and **Artifact Id**.

3. Click on **Finish**, and the project will be added to the **Project Explorer**:

Then, we are ready to generate our carbon file, which we will be able to deploy in our WSO2EI by following these steps:

1. Double-click on the `pom.xml` file of the project; as shown in the following screenshot:

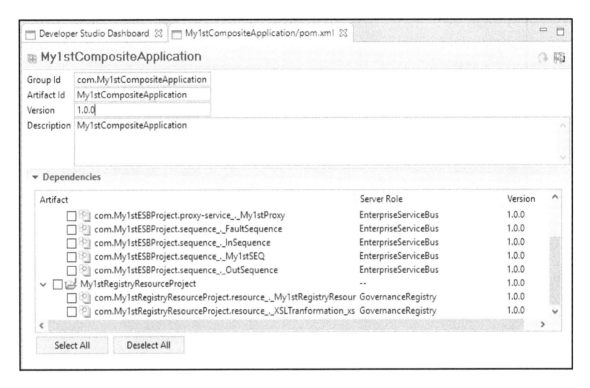

2. In this window, we again have the Maven information we introduced when we created the project. The usual task on this screen is to select the artifacts we want to deploy. Here, we can see all the artifacts we have previously created, such as proxy, sequences, and endpoint.

3. In this case, we select all of them but `My1stDataServiceProject`. As we said earlier, we need to go further into data services; the data service sample created to illustrate how to create Data Service Projects is not completed and will generate errors if we try to deploy it.

For the registry resources project, we need to change the server role. By default, as we can see in the preceding image, the registry resource artifacts have the server role **Governance Registry**. Since we are not working with the product WSO2 governance registry in this book, we have to choose the WSO2EI built-in registry. In other words, we have to set the **EnterpriseServiceBus** role for the artifacts of the Registry Resource Projects:

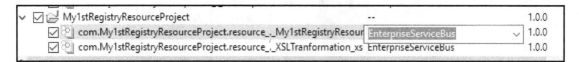

4. We generate the deployable artifact by clicking on the icon in the top-right corner:

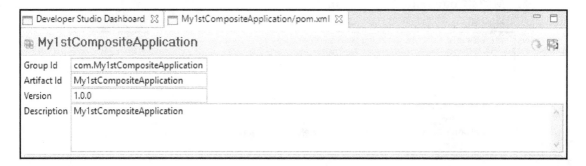

5. We choose the location to save the file, for instance, in the `carbonApp` folder. We can check whether the `*.car` file has been created in the folder:

Once we have generated the car file, the next step is to deploy to the server. To do this, we follow these steps:

1. Sign in to the WSO2EI management console.
2. Go to **Main** | **Carbon Applications** | **Add**:

3. Select the *.car file generated; in this case, **My1stCompositeApplication_1.0.0.car**:

4. Clicking on Upload will show an upload confirmation message. We will need to go to the WSO2EI console to check whether the deployment was successfully completed or not:

```
INFO - ApplicationManager Successfully Deployed Carbon Application : My1stCompositeApplication_1.0.0 {super-tenant}
```

5. Additionally, if the carbon application is deployed successfully, we will see this application in the WSO2EI management console in the **Main** | **Carbon Applications** | **List** path:

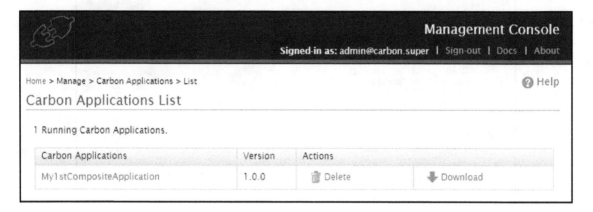

6. To undeploy the carbon application, we just click on the **Delete** action and it will be removed from the WSO2EI.

ESB Solution Project

This kind of project is not really a new kind of project. As you might have noted, most of the time, we will need to create at least three kinds of projects when implementing our project. This is a quite repetitive task that can be automated using this kind of project.

When we choose to create an **ESB Solution Project** from the Developer Studio dashboard, we can choose to create one or several of the following projects at once:

- ESBConfig Project (mandatory)
- Registry Resource Project (optional)
- Composite Application Project (optional)

Note that you can also **Create Connector Exporter Project**, which is optional. We uncheck this option, since we are not working with this kind of project in this book:

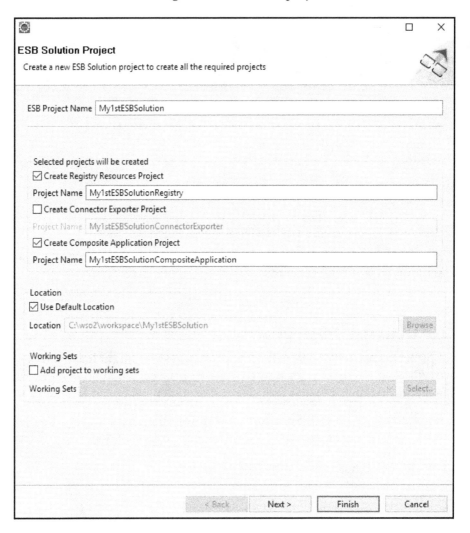

We can omit the Maven information step, leaving that information as the default, use the **Default Location**, and click on **Finish**. Then, the following projects will be generated:

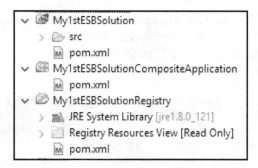

Now, we can work with this project as we mentioned in the previous sections.

Debugging mediation

With debugging mediation, we will be able to debug our service code as we usually do with our Java applications, for instance. In this case, this feature allows us to check how the message is being changed after every step that happens inside our service. Thus, we can see how an operation performed by a mediator modifies the message.

To enable debugging mediation, you have to follow these steps:

1. In the WSO2EI Tooling top menu, click on **Run | Debug Configurations**.
2. Double-click on **ESB Mediation Debugger**, and a new configuration window will show.
3. We keep the default values, except for the following:
    - **Name**: A name for the configuration; for instance, WSO2EIDebugging
    - **Serverhost**: The host in which we will perform the debugging; in this case, **localhost**

Note that *we do not click on* **Debug** *yet*, we remain in this screen. We have to wait for a special event during WOS2EI start up to press the debug button.

4. Now we will start the WSO2EI in debug mode. For this purpose, we will start the server as usual, adding in the -Desb.debug=true command line:
    - On Linux or Mac OS: shintegrator.sh -Desb.debug=true
    - On Windows: integrator.bat --run -Desb.debug=true

5. We can verify that the ESB has started up in debug mode, and the following messages are shown in the startup log. We have to keep an eye on the startup log, since we should return to the WSO2EI Tooling to click on the debug button when the marked message is shown:

```
INFO - ServiceBusInitializer Starting ESB...
INFO - ServiceBusInitializer Initializing Apache Synapse...
INFO - ServiceBusInitializer ESB Started in Debug mode for super tenant
INFO - SynapseDebugInterface Listen on ports : Command 9005 - Event 9006
```

We only have a minute to return to the WSO2EI Tooling to click on the debug button. Otherwise, the WSO2EI will start up without the debugging ability.

6. When the message is shown, we should return to the WOS2EI Tooling. The debug configuration screen may still be there, waiting for us to finish it. Now, we will click on the debug button, and a new **Message Envelope** tab should appear in Eclipse:

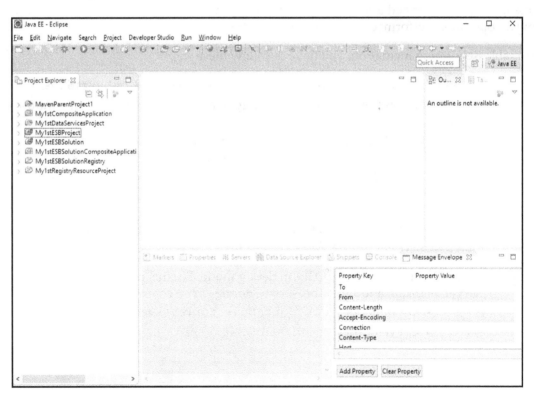

Now, we are ready to debug our services. In order to illustrate how debugging works, we will work with a simple service that will just set a variable, change the message, and respond. We have still not gone far enough into how to implement our service logic. This will be explained in detail in later chapters.

However, you don't need to understand how the logic is implemented to learn how to debug a service. This is our sample sequence where the logic is implemented:

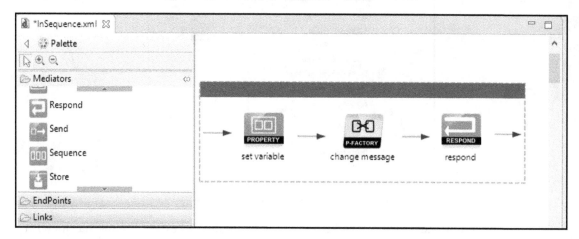

This sequence is attached as in sequence to a proxy, so that when invoking the proxy this sequence will be launched.

We have generated a new version of the carbon application we built in the previous section that includes the needed artifacts. This carbon application can be found in the book resources, and its name is `My1stCompositeApplication_1.0.1.car`. We just need to undeploy the previous version; the current version is 1.0.0, which must be replaced with version 1.0.1.

We will follow these steps to debug the service:

1. The first thing we need prior to debugging our service is to set the breakpoints. We can do that by right-clicking over the mediator in which we want to set the breakpoint. In this case, we set a break point in each mediator:

2. Check whether there is a red circle in the top-left corner over the mediators with a breakpoint.

3. Now, we will invoke our **My1stProxy** service. We can do that by browsing to `https://localhost:8243/services/My1stProxy?tryit`, which looks like this:

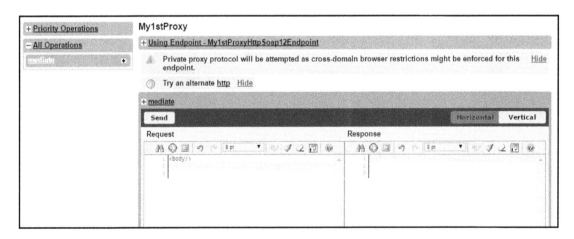

This is a simple testing page that WSO2EI enables for each service deployed. It is called **Tryit** and we will go further into it later in the book.

4. We will send a greeting message to the service, so we will replace the default request build by the tryit page with the following one:

```
<body>
    &lt;message>How are you?</message>
</body>
```

Hence, the tryit request should look as follows:

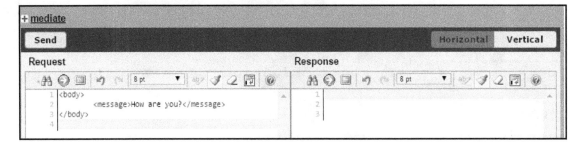

5. Now, we will click on **Send** to send the message to our service; this will trigger the debug mode in WSO2EI Tooling.
6. We will go to WSO2EI Tooling, and the debugging mode should have been triggered. The first time it is triggered, we should see a message like this:

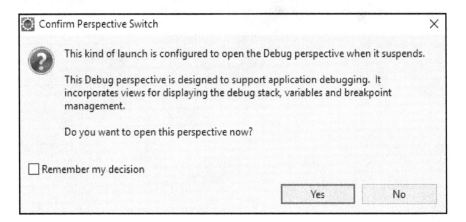

7. When we click on **Yes**, the debug perspective will open:

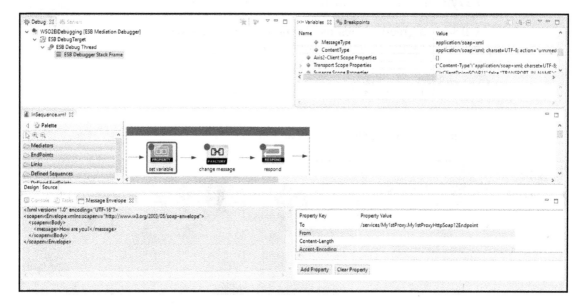

8. Congratulations, now you are debugging your first service. We will describe the most useful section on the screen. We can recognize the artifact where debug stops because it has a red square.

9. You can see the current content of the message in the **Message Envelope** tab or just by placing the mouse over the current mediator:

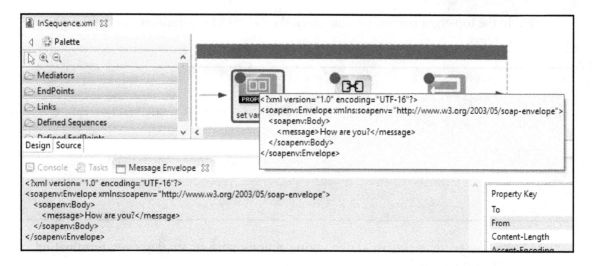

10. In the **Message Envelope** tab, we can see the raw envelope on the left-hand side, as we said before, and on the right-hand side, we can see other low-level properties sent in the post request, such as **Content-Length**, **host**, and **SOAP Action**:

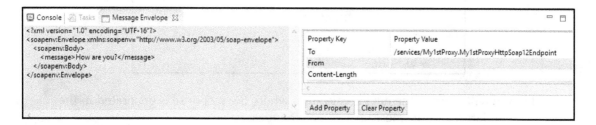

11. In the top-right corner, we can check the values of the variables in the flow context:

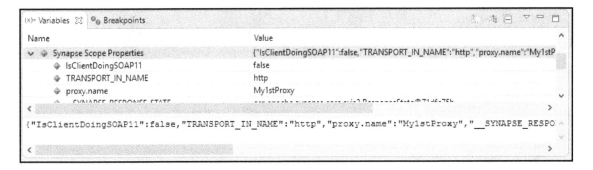

12. We can perform the usual debugging actions, such us steping over, terminating, or resuming the flow.

13. We will step over to the next breakpoint and watch how the variable called **MyProperty** is populated with the value of the XML tag called &<message> in the request:

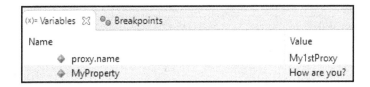

14. We will jump to the next breakpoint, where the response is generated in the mediator, and the message content changes:

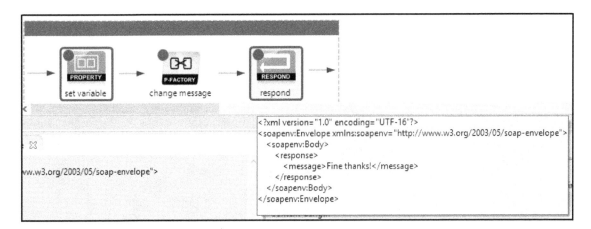

15. Finally, we will finish the execution and check how that message is received in the testing page of the service:

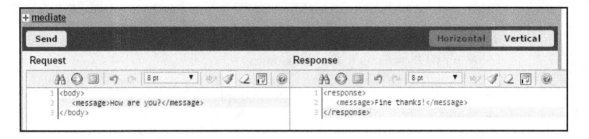

Data mapping

Data mapping is a very common task when developing services. This task is performed with many integration patterns, some of them quite common, such as the following:

- **Message Translator**:
  http://www.enterpriseintegrationpatterns.com/patterns/messaging/Messag eTranslator.html

- **Normalizer**: http://www.enterpriseintegrationpatterns.com/patterns/ messaging/Normalizer.html

- **Canonical Data Model**:
  http://www.enterpriseintegrationpatterns.com/patterns/messaging/Canoni calDataModel.html

This task entails translating, transforming, or converting data from one data format to another, such as XML to JSON. For instance, we may receive a message in our service in the XML format, and we have to send the information within this XML payload to a JSON endpoint and to an XML endpoint in which the XML format is different from the XML format specified in our service contract.

In such situations, we will have to transform the message, or create a new one from the original. To achieve this task, WSO2EI has a mediator called Data Mapper Mediator. Our life can be even easier with the graphical tool that WSO2 Developer Studio gives us.

We need these three things to perform a data mapping:

- **Input schema file**: This will allow the mediator and the diagram editor to know which information is there in the input file. This can be an XML schema file (`*.xsd`), for instance, or a JSON schema. When using JSON schema, we can create it using the WOS2 Developing tool by adding the JSON element needed to define our JSON schema to the blank output schema.
- **Output schema file**: This allows the mediator and the diagram editor how the target information is stored. The procedure explained for the input schema files can be applied here for the output schema files as well.
- **Mapping configuration file**: This is the file that has the information about how the translation takes place. This is a JavaScript file; therefore, the data mapping is performed using a JavaScript engine.

The schema files supporter for both input and output schema files are as follows:

- **XML**: An XML file whose content has the structure we need. When using XML files, it is important to note that every single tag must be qualified with its namespace, so tags such as `<book>This book</book>` are not allowed in this tool. We should use `&<ns:book>This book</ns:book>`, assuming that `ns` is the namespace of this tag in the XML file.
- **JSON**: A JSON file containing the structure needed.
- **CSV**: A CSV file with column definition in the first record.
- **XSD**: A proper schema file (`*.xsd`).
- **JSONSCHEMA**: AWSO2 data mapper JSON schema.
- **CONNECTOR**: A connector to use the JSON schemas defined for their operations.

This tool, called WSO2 data mapper, is an independent component that is not tied to any WSO2 product. So, to create our first data mapping, we just need to add the data mapper mediator to a sequence. You may remember the sequence we used to show how to debug our service. In this case, we will use a similar sequence that transforms the incoming message before it responds to us.

Assuming that we are editing a sequence, we call it `InMappingSequence`. The steps to use the data mapper are as listed:

1. Drag and drop the **Data Mapper** to the sequence:

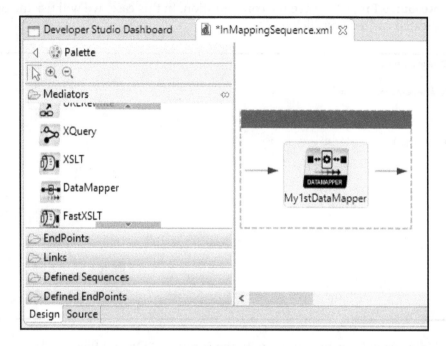

2. Double-click on the mediator in our sequence. We set the name for it as **My1stDataMapper**.

3. The input and output files we mentioned earlier must be stored in the WSO2EI registry, so when we double-click on the mediator, we are asked whether to create a new data mapper configuration or use an existing one. We choose **Create new Configuration** and set a name for it. We also need to choose a **Registry Resource Project** to save the configuration. In this case, we will use the one we created earlier, and click on **OK**:

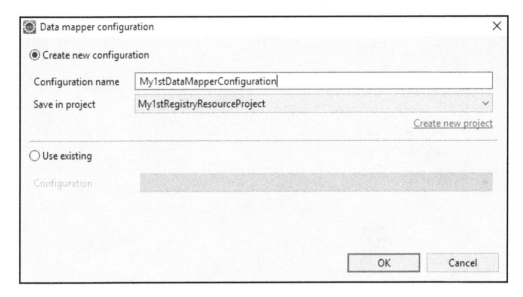

4. Now, we will see the canvas with the **Input** and **Output** files:

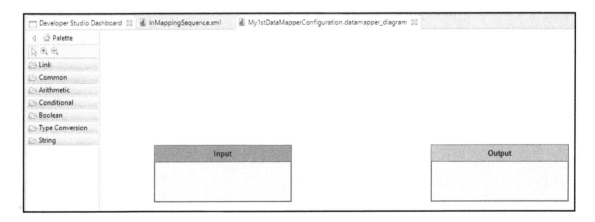

In this canvas, we have three sections:

- **Palette**: Here, we find the operators we use to build the logic of our data mapping. We have several categories of operators.
- **Input**: Here, we load the input file that defines the input message.
- **Output**: Here, we load the output file that defines the output message.

In our example, we will build a service that receives a greetings message and responds to our greetings. We will achieve this with a data mapper that will use these operators, which are quite common and useful:

- Constant
- Compare
- IfElse

We will use XML messages for input and output messages. For the input message, we will use an XML Schema Definition (*.xsd file) you can find in the book resources, and for the output, we will build the response from the editor.

To build this data mapper, we need to follow these steps:

1. Load the input schema by right-clicking on input and clicking on **Load Input**:

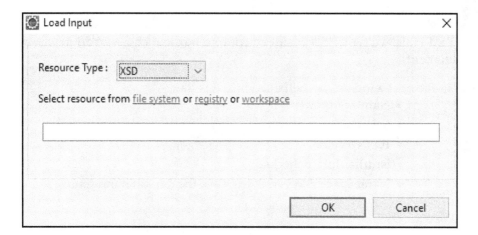

2. Choose XML value for the **Resource Type** and select the resource from the file system. We will select the `greetings.xsd` file you can find in this book's resources and click on **OK**:

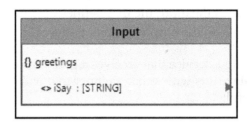

The input box will show the XML defined by the schema we have loaded. This is a simple XML that looks like this:

```
. If we do not send a message in the differen<greetings>
    <iSay>Hi!</iSay>
</greetings>
```

3. Now, we will create the response that will look like this:

```
<response>
    <youSay>Hi!</youSay>
    <iSay>What's up</iSay>
</response>
```

To do this, we right-click inside the output box and choose **Add new root element**.

4. In the next window, we will introduce this data:
    - **Name: response**
    - **SchemaType: object**
    - **ID**: No value
    - **isnullable**: Unchecked
    - **Namespace**: No value; we leave the default namespace

We click on **OK**.

5. Now, we have the root element called **response**:

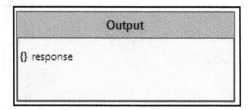

6. We need two more elements, both children of **response**. To add them, click on **response** and right-click on the **response** label. Then, click on **addField**.

7. We add the following information for the **youSay** XML tag:

   - **Name**: youSay
   - **SchemaType**: **string**
   - **isNullable**: Unchecked
   - **Namespaces**: Blank

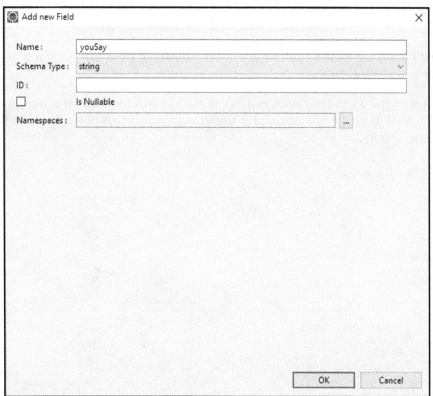

8. Click on **OK**:

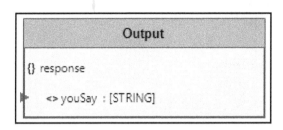

9. Repeat steps 8 and 9 to add the **iSay** XML tag. Now, we have finished building the response:

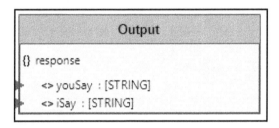

Now, we will build the logic to build the response message from the incoming message. Our service will work as follows:

1. If we send a message such as Howareyou?, it will respond with our greetings in an XML tag called youSay, plus the Fine, thanks! response in an XML tag called iSay.

This is the request:

```
<greetings>
    <iSay>Hi!</iSay>
</greetings>
```

This is the response:

```
<greetings>
    <youSay>Hi!</youSay>
    <iSay>What's up!</iSay>
</greetings>
```

2. If we do not send a message in the different form How are you?, the response
   will always be What's up!.

   This is the request:

   ```
   <greetings>
       <iSay>Hi!</iSay>
   </greetings>
   ```

   This is the response:

   ```
   <greetings>
       <youSay>Hi!</youSay>
       <iSay>What's up!</iSay>
   </greetings>
   ```

So, to implement this functionality, the use case will be as shown:

- Copy the <iSay> value from the request to the <youSay> value in the output
  message
- Consider that <iSay>from the input message is How are you?:
    - Set the <iSay> value to Fine,thanks! in the output message
- Otherwise, do this:
    - Set the <iSay> value to What's up! in the output message

Now, we will implement this logic:

1. We have the input and output messages already defined from the previous steps,
   and they look like this:

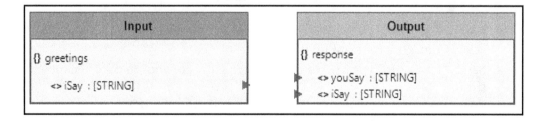

We begin assigning the `<iSay>` value from the input to the `<youSay>` value in the output. We just drag the `iSay` field and drop it over the `youSay` field. Then, a link between both the fields will appear:

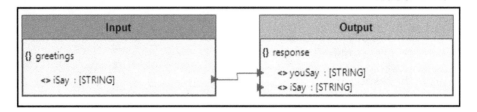

2. Now, we will add the comparison between the `iSay` field and the `How are you?` string:

In the **Palette**, we open the **Common** tab, and drag the **Constant** operator and drop it in the canvas:

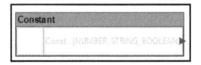

3. Right-click over the square in the left-hand side of the **Constant** window, and select **Configure constant operator**.
4. Set the **Constant Type** to **String** and assign **How are you?** to the constant value. Click on **OK**.
5. Then, the **Constant** operator will look like this:

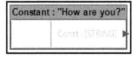

6. The next step is to create the comparison:

We can do that by dropping the **Compare** operator in the canvas from the palette:

7. We need to set the two strings we are comparing in this operator. This is quite easy, since we just need to drag and drop the values over the left boxes in the comparison window. Note that you can read **In** in these boxes. So, we set the **iSay** field from the input message over the first **In** box and our canvas will now be like this:

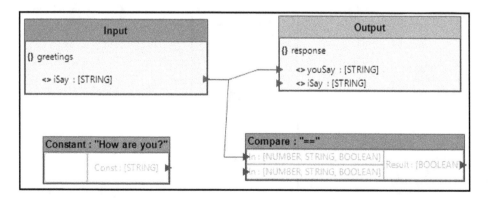

We drag the right arrow in the **Constant** window over the second **In** box in the **Compare** window:

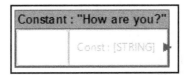

Thus, we have set the two values of the comparison. Our canvas should look as follows:

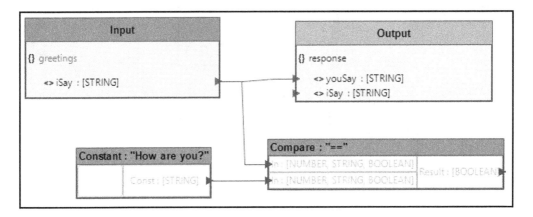

8. We have the initial comparison (step 1 in the use case). The next step is to build the if-then structure. We add it in the canvas by dropping the **IfElse** operator from the **Palette** on the canvas. This operator can be found in the **Conditional** tab:

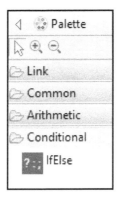

This operator has three inputs: condition, then, and else. You can read the name of the input in the box; these values will be the following:

- **Condition**: This input will be the output of the comparison operator we created earlier
- **Then**: This input will be a constant with the value `Fine, thanks!`
- **Else**: This input will be a constant with the value `What's up!`

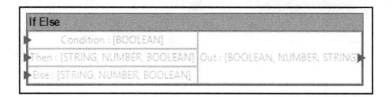

9. We set the condition by dragging the right arrow in the compare operator over the condition input:

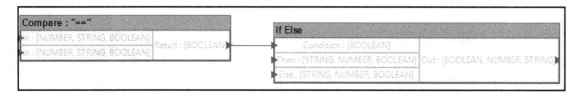

10. Now, we will create a new constant operator with the value `Fine, thanks!` and assign it to the `Then` input. The result will be as follows:

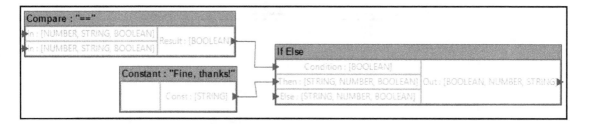

11. We create the left constant operator we need for the `Else` input and assign it to the `Else` input. In this case, we use the `What's up!` value (note that we need to escape the quote). Finally, the **If Else** operator will look as shown:

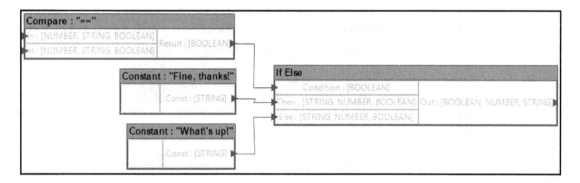

12. The last step is to assign the **If Else** output to the **iSay** field in the output message. We just need to drag the right arrow in the **If Else** operator and drop it on the **iSay** field:

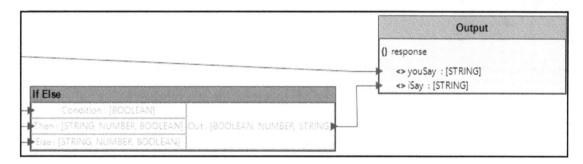

The whole picture will look like this:

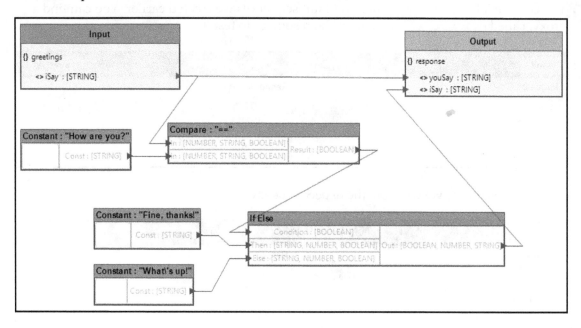

Now, we save the file and return to the sequence where we add the **datamapper** mediator. We add the **Respond** mediator, and save and close the sequence. It will look as illustrated:

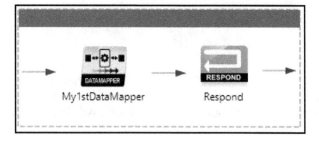

You can easily test this by creating a proxy and setting this sequence as the input sequence. You can use it for the out sequence and fault sequences we created earlier. You can find a proxy, called `My1stProxyMapping`, in the resources to test it:

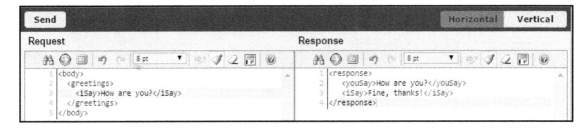

If we call this proxy, we will note the expected behavior:

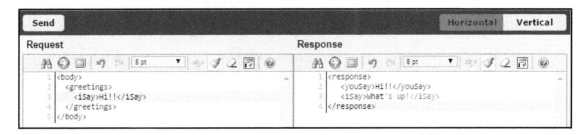

You can find more about the data mapper mediator in the official documentation.

Summary

In this chapter, we learned the most common tasks a developer performs in his daily working with WSO2EI, such as creating projects and artifacts. We also learned to debug our projects, which is a very important task on a daily basis. Additionally, we described how to use the powerful data mapper.

In the next chapter, we will learn how to build web services in WSO2EI and their most commons components, such us endpoints and sequences. Additionally, we will go over the most important set of mediators used for implementing our service orchestration.

3

Building Web Services

In this chapter, we will look at the main concepts of WSO2 Enterprise Integrator. What is the nomenclature and the parts that have a role inside different types of services that offer us the EI server:

- How to build SOAP Proxies and REST APIs
- Creation of inbound endpoints for dynamic services
- Different mediators such as send, log, script, and property
- Transport configuration
- Creation and configuration of sequences
- Scheduling tasks

WSO2 EI has multiple entry types to start a service:

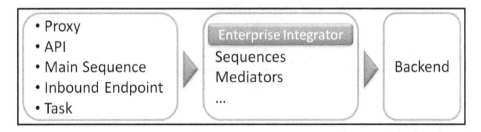

- **Proxy**: Acts as a virtual service: receives messages and mediates them before sending them to the endpoint
- **Main Sequence**: Default sequence for all messages not sent to a proxy service
- **API**: Accepts REST messages that allow clients to provide additional information on how to manage the message
- **Inbound Endpoint**: A message source that can be configured dynamically

- **Task**: Scheduled jobs to execute proxy service or a named sequence

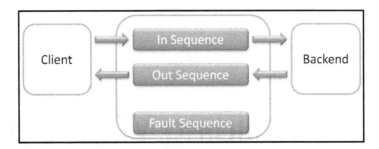

When we create a service, it's necessary to configure the following:

- **Transport**: Carry the payload in a specific format
- **Mediators**: Simplest message processing units that are placed inside sequences
- **Sequences**: List of mediators executed sequentially
- **Endpoints**: Define destination for the current payload

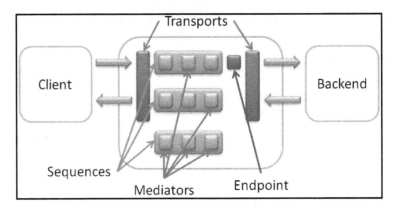

Mediators

In WSO2, a mediator is a piece of code that has a logical behavior and a final purpose for using it, having an XML structure. By default, we have a list of mediators that we can use *Out of the Box*, but we can also develop a custom mediator to extend the default functionality.

When we have a set of mediators that perform an action together, it's called sequences: We can use it in Proxies and APIs.

The property mediator

A property is a variable that stores some information during a time that depends on the *scope* it has configured.

Here's the syntax:

```
<property name="string" [action=set|remove] [type="string"]
(value="literal" | expression="xpath")
[scope=default|transport|axis2|axis2-client] [pattern="regex"
[group="integer"]]>
    <xml-element/>?
</property>
```

We have three different types of properties:

1. **Static**: Get a static value in the creation:

   ```
   <property name="color" value="red" />
   ```

2. **Dynamic**: Get a dynamic value:
   - From an xpath expression:

     ```
     <property name="dynamic1" expression="//xpath"/>
     ```

   - From any other property:

     ```
     <property name="dynamic2"
                         expression="get-
     property('dynamic1')"/>
     ```

3. **Action**: Do an action with an existing property:

   ```
   <property name="To" action="remove"/>
   ```

The properties can have seven different types of scope:

- **Axis2**: It's the shortest scope and is only used to send parameters to Axis2 engine
- **Axis2-client**: The same duration as synapse, but the property can be read through custom mediators
- **Synapse**: The property will live in the same sequence; it's the default scope
- **Operation**: It's the largest scope; the property will live until the end of the service through the different sequences

- **Registry**: It is used to get properties from the registry
- **System**: To get Java system properties
- **Transport**: The property will be sent as a transport header

Depending on the content, the properties can be of eight different types:

- BOOLEAN
- DOUBLE
- FLOAT
- INTEGER
- LONG
- OM
- SHORT
- STRING

The log mediator

The log mediator allows us to show and save some information in the console and server log, which is useful to audit the services.

Now, let's look at the syntax:

```
<log [level="string"] [separator="string"]>
    <property name="string" (value="literal" | expression="[XPath|json-
    eval(JSON Path)]")/>*
</log>
```

We have six different categories, sorted by informational purpose to error logs:

- TRACE
- DEBUG
- INFO
- WARN
- ERROR
- FATAL

We also have four levels of log:

- **Custom**: Show the properties configured inside
- **Full**: The `Show To`, `From`, `WSAction`, `SOAPAction`, `ReplyTo`, and `MessageID` headers and the current payload
- **Headers**: Log all the SOAP headers
- **Simple**: Log `To`, `From`, `WSAction`, `SOAPAction`, `ReplyTo`, and `MessageID` headers

For example, to log the full content of the payload, we can use the following syntax:

```
<log level="full"/>
```

Alternatively, to only log a custom property, use this:

```
<log category="INFO" separator=",">
    <property name="dynamicProperty"
    expression="//xpathExpression" />
</log>
```

By default, the log is placed at:
`<WSO2_HOME>/repository/log/wso2carbon.log`.

The send mediator

The send mediator is used to make a non-blocking request to a backend with the current payload. The backend is configured with the endpoints that can have implicit, inline, named, or store in the registry. When the send mediator is used in the out sequence, it will perform a response to the client.

This is the implicit send syntax:

```
<send/>
```

The following is the endpoint send syntax:

```
<send [receive="string"]>
    (endpointref | endpoint)+
</send>
```

Here, keep the following things in mind: `endpointref` is a named or registry `endpoint`. `endpoint` is an anonymous endpoint defined inline, `receive` is the sequence that processes the backend response.

For example, consider `send` with inline definition (`endpoint` type):

```
<send>
   <endpoint>
      <address uri="http://localhost:8280/services"/>
   </endpoint>
</send>
```

Now, consider `send` with a named endpoint (`endpointref` type):

```
<send receive="OutSequence">
   <endpoint key="CreditEpr"/>
</send>
```

The respond mediator

Stop processing the current message and send the payload back to the client that made the request to the service.

This is the syntax:

```
<respond/>
```

The loopback mediator

The loopback mediator moves the current message to the out sequence.

Here's the syntax:

```
<loopback/>
```

The drop mediator

The drop mediator stops processing the current message. Only if it's configured in the in sequence, send an HTTP 202 accepted response to the client.

The following is the syntax:

```
<drop/>
```

The sequence mediator

The sequence mediator throws the processing of a named sequence or registry sequence.

This is the named sequence syntax:

```
<sequence key="namedSequence"/>
```

The registry sequence syntax is as follows:

```
<sequence key="conf:/path/to/registrySequence"/>
```

The script mediator

We can use different scripting languages to process the payload and get some information or make a transformation, such as JavaScript, Groovy, and Ruby.

Inline script syntax is as follows:

```
<script language="js">
  <![CDATA[
       //script code
  ]]>
<script/>
```

This is the registry script syntax:

```
<script key="path/to/script" language="(js | groovy | rb)"
[function="nameOfTheFunction"]>
     [<include key="string"/>]
</script>
```

The following is a list of the available methods:

- `getPayloadXML()`: Returns the current XML payload.
- `setPayloadXML(payload)`: Set the body with the content of the payload parameter.
- `addHeader(mustUnderstand, content)`: Add a new SOAP header.
- `getEnvelopeXML()`: Return the full payload.
- `setTo(reference)`: Set the value of the `To` header (receiver).
- `setFaultTo(reference)`: Set the value to the `FaultTo` header.
- `setFrom(reference)`: Set the value to the `From` header (sender).
- `setReplyTo(reference)`: Set the value to the `ReplyTo` header.

- `getPayloadJSON()`: Return the current JSON payload.
- `setPayloadJSON(payload)`: Set the body with the content of the payload parameter.
- `getProperty(name)`: Get the value of a property.
- `setProperty(key, value)`: Create or update the content of the property from the first param with the value of the second param.

For example, this is the script to print the current value of a property and set the new value:

```
<script language="js">
  <![CDATA[
    var property = mc.getProperty("static");
    print("property: " + property);
    mc.setProperty("static", "newValue");
  ]]>
</script>
```

Sequences

A sequence is a list of mediators processed one by one in order. By default, the Enterprise Integrator has two sequences--main and fault--but we can create the sequences we need in our requirements, containing a combination of mediators.

Main sequence

This sequence is triggered when a call to the EI server doesn't have a correct instance for an axis2 service; for example, when we make a request to the URL: `http://localhost:8280/services/NonExistingService`, the sequence returns a 202-accepted HTTP code and logs the incoming message to the console, unless there are one of the sample services:

```
<?xml version="1.0" encoding="UTF-8"?>
<sequence name="main" xmlns="http://ws.apache.org/ns/synapse">
    <in>
        <!-- Log all messages passing through -->
        <log level="full"/>
        <!-- ensure that the default configuration only sends
                                        if it is one of samples -->
        <!-- Otherwise Synapse would be an open proxy by default (BAD!) -->
        <filter regex="http://localhost:9000.*"
```

```
                                      source="get- property('To')">
        <then>
            <!-- Send the messages where they have been sent
                                (i.e. implicit "To" EPR) -->
            <send/>
        </then>
        <else/>
    </filter>
</in>
<out>
    <send/>
</out>
<description>The main sequence for the message mediation</description>
</sequence>
```

The fault sequence

The fault sequence is used for exception handling when we haven't configured a custom fault sequence. This sequence logs the error code and the current payload, and then the message is dropped:

```
<?xml version="1.0" encoding="UTF-8"?>
<sequence name="fault" xmlns="http://ws.apache.org/ns/synapse">
    <!-- Log the message at the full log level with
                            the ERROR_MESSAGE and the ERROR_CODE-->
    <log level="full">
        <property name="MESSAGE"
                        value="Executing default 'fault' sequence"/>
        <property name="ERROR_CODE"
                        expression="get-property('ERROR_CODE')"/>
        <property name="ERROR_MESSAGE"
                        expression="get-property('ERROR_MESSAGE')"/>
    </log>
    <!-- Drops the messages by default if there is a fault -->
    <drop/>
</sequence>
```

A custom sequence

The two previous sequences are defined by default in the Enterprise Integrator, but we can create the custom sequences that we need. The principal idea of a sequence is that it needs to be as generic as possible, because every sequence can be used by different services, no matter whether they are SOAP or REST, Proxy, or API.

Here's the syntax:

```
<sequence name="string" [onError="string"] [key="string"] [trace="enable"]
[statistics="enable"]>
    mediator*
</sequence>
```

- The `onError` attribute sets the sequence that will be triggered when there's a problem during the processing of the sequence, instead of using the default fault sequence
- `statistics` enable or disable the statistics collection to track the number of messages processed and the processing times
- `trace` enables or disables the trace collection in which the messages will write tracing information through each mediation step

Proxies

In this section, we will see the different ways that the Enterprise Integrator server offers us to create SOAP proxy services. We have a wizard for the most common types of proxy that lets us create a proxy quickly; also, we can create a custom proxy for more complex scenarios.

We can configure a different setup for a proxy service, such as transport, security, caching, throttling, and so on.

The transformer proxy

The transformer proxy receives the request and then applies a transformation using the XSLT language before sending it to the backend service. Also, it can be used to transform the backend service response before sending it back to the client.

Extensible Stylesheet Language Transformations (XSLT) is a language for transforming XML payload:

Secure proxy

The proxy that we create using this wizard will be secured using WS-Security standard, and can be used to secure a backend service that has no security restriction.

Consider that we have a legacy backend service with no security, and it does not support any type of authentication. We can create a secure proxy, configure to use a WS-Security policy, and then consume the insecure backend; this proxy will be the public service available to the final consumer instead of the legacy one:

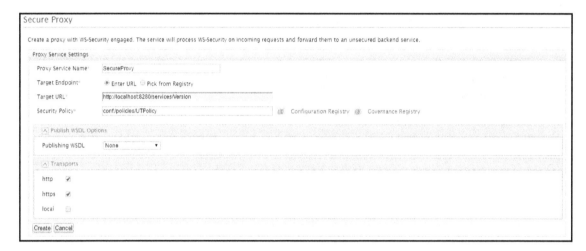

WSDL based proxy

We need to use this wizard when we currently have a service that already has a WSDL definition, so the server will create the proxy with the information of this file.

WSDL is a standard for web service definition, based on the XML language:

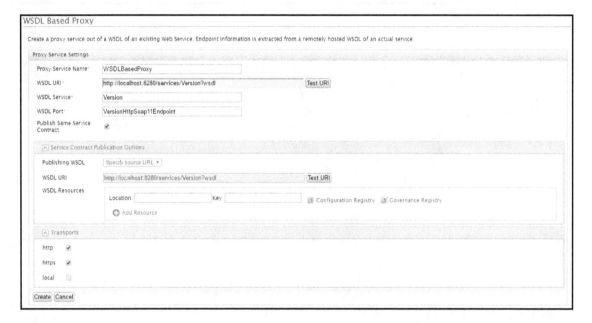

Logging proxy

This proxy is similar to the pass through proxy with the difference that this will log all the incoming requests before forwarding them to the final endpoint. Also, we can log the response of the backend service before sending back to the client:

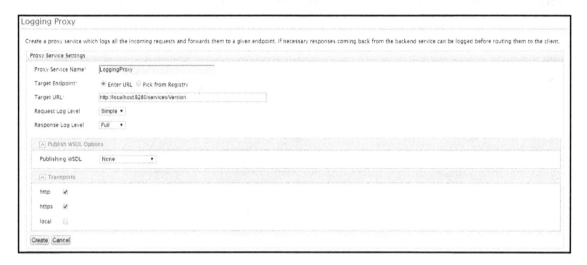

Pass through proxy

This type of proxy is the simplest; it only gets the message and forwards it to the backend without any type of processing:

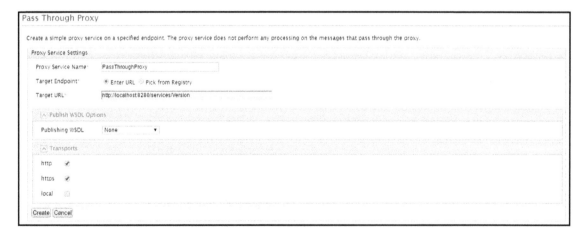

Custom proxy

When we want to create a proxy that is not possible with the previous templates because it's more complex, we need to use this wizard in which we can configure the in, out, and fault sequences, endpoints, transport, and so on:

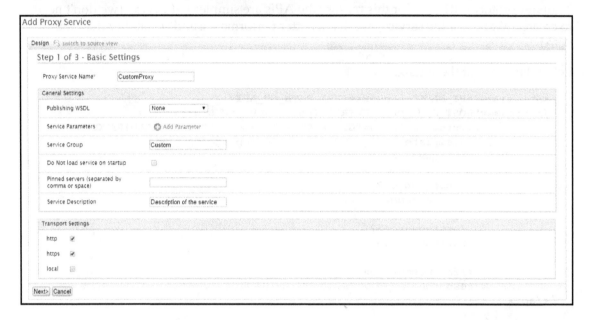

APIs

In this section, we will go deep into the process for creating APIs with Enterprise Integrator. The main difference between the APIs and the Proxies is that Proxies use the **Simple Object Access Protocol** protocol (**SOAP**), meanwhile the APIs use the **Representational State Transfer** protocol (**REST**). For this reason, the APIs are simpler to develop (we don't need to create a WSDL for the service) and have better performance and scalability than the SOAP services.

Let's take a look at the syntax:

```
<api name="API_NAME" context="URI_PATH_OF_API"
[hostname="HOST_NAME_OF_SERVER"] [port="PORT_NUMBER"]>
        <resource [methods="GET|POST|PUT|DELETE|OPTIONS|HEAD|PATCH"]
        [uri-template="URI_TEMPLATE"|url-mapping="URL_MAPPING"]>
            <inSequence>
              . . .
            </inSequence>?
            <outSequence>
              . . .
            </outSequence>?
            <faultSequence>
              . . .
            </faultSequence>?
        </resource>
</api>
```

Where `name` is the name of the API and must be unique, `context` is the endpoint of the API and must be unique, `hostname` and `port` is the host and port to consume the service methods specify the HTTP verb to consume the service.

When we design a resource inside an API, we can choose between the URL mapping or the URI template approach. Now, we will look at the differences and how to use both of them.

URL mapping

If we use the URL mapping, we need to specify a pattern for the resource, and only the requests that satisfy this pattern will go through the API service.

We can use three different types of patterns:

1. **Path mappings**: All the requests that start with the resource and/or path will be listened to; for example, `/resource/*`.
2. **Extension mappings**: Only the requests that have the same extension will be listened to; for example, `*.jag`.
3. **Exact mappings**: Only the requests that match the exact pattern will be listened to; for example, `/resource`.

To read the incoming parameter for all the previous types, we can use the following expressions depending on the HTTP methods:

- POST: `json-eval($.nameParameter)`
- GET: `$ctx:query.param.nameParameter`

For example, we can create the following URL mapping API for type 3, exact mappings, which will only be triggered when a call that matches the resource context is received:

```
<api xmlns="http://ws.apache.org/ns/synapse" name="UrlMappingAPI"
context="/urlmappingapi">
    <resource methods="GET" url-mapping="/getParam">
        <inSequence>
            <log>
                <property name="Value of GET param"
                                    expression="$ctx:query.param.param"/>
            </log>
            <respond/>
        </inSequence>
    </resource>
    <resource methods=" POST" url-mapping="/postParam">
        <inSequence>
            <log>
                <property name="Value of POST param"
                                    expression="json-eval($.param)"/>
            </log>
            <respond/>
        </inSequence>
    </resource>
</api>
```

This API gets the value of the incoming parameter and shows in the server log. We can invoke these resources with the following curl commands:

- **getParam** resource:

```
Request:
    curl http://localhost:8280/urlmappingapi/getParam?param=GetParam
LogMediator:
    To: /urlmappingapi/getParam?param=GetParam,
    MessageID: urn:uuid:cde7830c-0c95-460d-9e05-ec0c7956d6cd,
    Direction: request,
    ***Value of GET param = GetParam
```

- **postParam** resource:

```
Request:
    curl -H "Content-Type: application/json" -X POST
        -d {"param":"postParam"}
        http://localhost:8280/urlmappingapi/postParam
Log Mediator:
    To: /urlmappingapi/postParam,
    MessageID: urn:uuid:54538723-3b3c-4c5b-81be-ce0c44c733d5,
    Direction: request,
    ***Value of POST param = postParam
```

URI template

When we use this type of API, we need to define patterns and variables in order for the resources that will be processed, so only the requests that match this template will trigger the resource.

The way to define input parameter or variables is with curly braces, as shown:

```
/resource/{param1}/{param2}
```

For reading the parameters defined in the template, we can use the following expression:

```
get-property('uri.var.nameParameter')
```

In the next example, we have one resource that can be consumed by the GET or POST methods, and will be listened to two incoming parameters:

```
<api name="UriTemplateAPI" context="/uritemplateapi">
    <resource methods="POST GET"
                        uri-template ="/resource/{param1}/{param2}">
        <inSequence>
```

```
        <log>
                <property name="Value of param1"
                                expression="get-
property('uri.var.param1')"/>
                <property name="Value of param2"
                                expression="get-
property('uri.var.param2')"/>
                </log>
                <respond/>
        </inSequence>
    </resource>
</api>
```

We can use the following curl commands:

- GET method:

  curl http://localhost:8280/uritemplateapi/resource/P1/param2

- POST method:

  **curl -X POST
  http://localhost:8280/uritemplateapi/resource/P1/param2**

The following line will be shown in the log file:

```
LogMediator:
To: /uritemplateapi/resource/P1/param2,
MessageID: urn:uuid:fc7e5bda-8a78-4991-937c-eaf705911df0,
Direction: request,
Value of param1 = P1,
Value of param2 = param2
```

Inbound endpoints

Until now, we have studied two different ways of creating services in the Enterprise Integrator server: Proxies and APIs. Both of them are using the axis2 layer, and although we can configure the incoming ports, these are static and are applied globally for all the services deployed in the server. Also, after every change in the setup, we need to reboot the server in order to apply the changes.

However, this is different with the inbound endpoints; it's a message entry point that does not use the axis2 layer, but directly gets the message from the transport layer and sends it to the mediation layer. The Enterprise Integrator has four different inbound endpoint types:

- **Listening**
- **Polling**
- **Event-Based**
- **Custom**

We can see that in the following diagram:

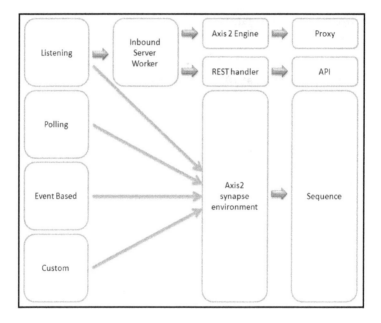

Inbound Endpoints

Listening

In the listening inbounds endpoints, we configure the specific port in which the server will be waiting for the incoming request. By default, we can use different protocols such as HTTP, HTTPS, HL7, CXF, WebSocket, and Secure WebSocket.

For a basic configuration of the inbound endpoint, we need to configure the following:

- **Endpoint Name**: Unique identity of the inbound endpoint
- **Type**: Protocol for listen
- **Sequence**: Sequence that will be processed on an incoming request
- **inbound.http.port***: Port that will be open dynamically for the listen request

For example, we can define an HTTP inbound endpoint named **HttpInboundEndpoint**, which listens to the port 8765 and triggers the main sequence, as follows:

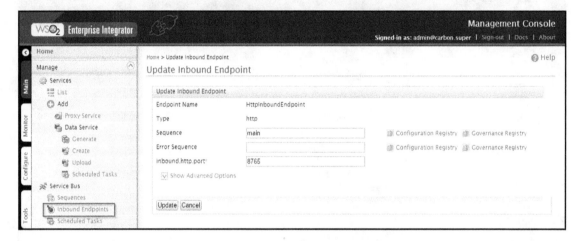

Dynamically, the Enterprise Integrator server will open that port and keep listening to a request to launch the main sequence. For testing, we only need to make a request to that port with the browser or using a curl command:

```
curl http://localhost:8765
```

Polling

This type of inbound endpoints is polling continuously for data at every interval time configured in the parameter. When data is available, it will be able to trigger a specific sequence with the original data as a payload.

By default, the Enterprise Integrator has three different polling types:

- **File**: For FTP, SFTP, and FILE connections
- **JMS**: For Java Message Service protocol
- **Kafka**: For Apache Kafka protocol

For example, to configure a polling inbound endpoint that is polling a local directory for a specific file to process a sequence, we can set up as follows:

For testing this inbound endpoint, we only need to create a pollingInboundEndpoint.txt file in the C:\Temp path and wait until the following interval polling, in which the enterprise integrator will get the file and inject it to the configured sequence.

Event based

The event based inbound endpoint will establish the connection with the configure server when it's created, and then stay waiting for a specific configured event.

Out of the box, we have the **Message Queue Telemetry Transport (MQTT)** and RabbitMQ protocols:

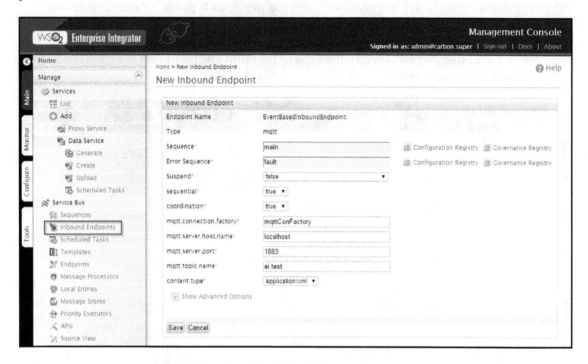

In the preceding example, we set up an MQTT event based inbound endpoint that will trigger the main sequence when receiving an event for the server `localhost:1883` in the topic called `ei.test`.

Custom

When our requirement can't be processed with the previous types of inbound endpoints, we can create our ad hoc inbound endpoint that covers the necessities of our scenario. For that, we need to define a Java class implementation with the logic we need for our requirement, and then we can specify the type of inbound endpoint that we have created in the Enterprise Integrator server:

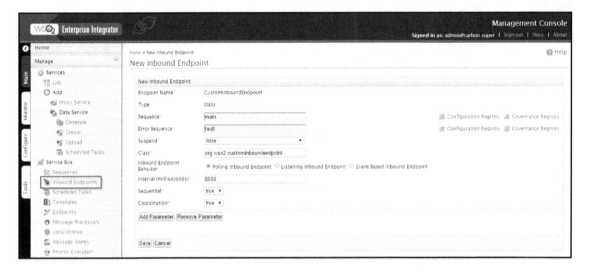

Tasks

With tasks scheduled, we can set up the execution of a service to be processed on a specific date and time, periodically for a specified number of times.

Consider that we have a service that automatically updates the information of a database, and it works with a lot of information. So, we can schedule a task for that service in order to be triggered at night when the server is more idle, without the request of the final users making request to all the services deployed in that server.

Depending on the type of service we want to schedule, we can use the wizards that we'll discuss in the subsequent headings.

Scheduling data services

This wizard allows us to create and configure tasks specifically for data services, where we can specify what operation will be processed. This wizard is located in the Enterprise Integrator in the following path:

Main | Manage | Services | Add | Data Service | Scheduled Tasks:

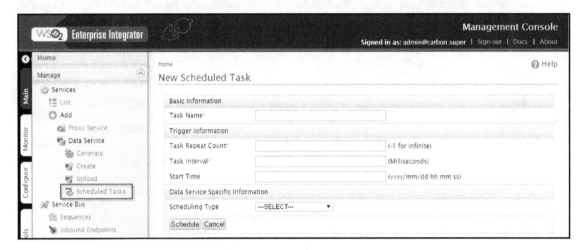

Scheduled Data Services Tasks

Here, keep the following in mind:

- **Task Name**: Identifier of the scheduled task.
- **Tasks Repeat Count**: Number of times that the service will be executed without regard for the first invoking.
- **Task Interval**: Time between the different executions.
- **Start Time**: Time to launch the first execution. When we don't specify, this parameter will be processed just after creating the task.
- **Scheduling Type**:
    - **Data Service Operation**: For invoking an existing data service operation.
    - **Data Service Task Class**: For invoking a custom task class.

Scheduling other services

On the other hand, when we need to schedule other types of services, we need to use another wizard that is located in **Main** | **Manage** | **Service Bus** | **Scheduled Tasks**:

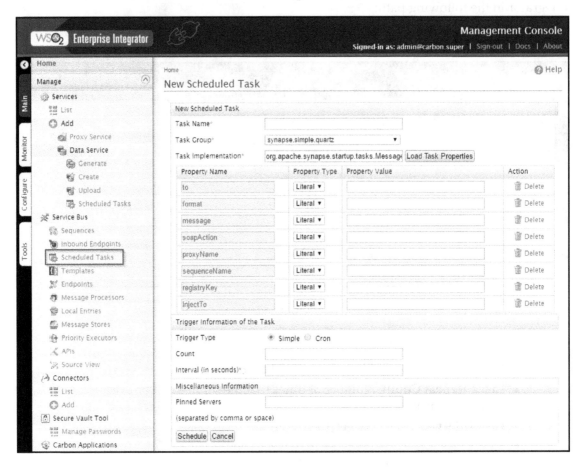

This wizard is more powerful than the previous one, and allows us to create tasks for launch proxy, sequences, endpoints, and so on. We can schedule tasks in three different ways:

1. Specifying the number of times and the interval to launch the process.
2. Setting up a cron expression.
3. Design a task that will be executed only once the server starts.

We have the following parameters to configure when we want to create an inbound endpoint:

- **Task Name**: Identifier of the scheduled task
- **Task Group**: Name of the group for grouping tasks
- **Task Implementation**: Java class implementation to execute the task; the default is `org.apache.synapse.startup.tasks.MessageInjector`
- **to**: Endpoint address
- **format**: Format of the message that the task will send
- **message**: Payload of the message in literal or XML style
- **soap Action**: Set the SOAP Action header for the endpoint
- **proxy Name**: Name of the proxy to launch
- **sequence Name**: Name of the sequence to launch
- **registry Key**: Path in the registry to execute the task
- **inject To**: Specify whether the task invokes a proxy ('proxy') or sequence ('sequence')
- **Trigger Type**:
  - **Simple**: We need to specify the count and interval properties
  - **Cron**: We need to specify the cron expression
- **Pinned Servers**: List of servers to launch the task

Summary

In this chapter, we learned the different ways of creating services in the Enterprise Integrator service, when we need to use a Proxy, an API or inbound endpoint based on our requirement, and what is the process for adding the logical to that service using sequences and mediators.

At the end of the chapter, we also learned how we can schedule tasks in the server to start a service automatically, based on periods of time.

In the next chapter, we will focus on how to create services specifically defined to work with different types of data sources, and what is the configuration needed in the service to operate with any source of data: **Relation Database Management System (RDBMS)**, CSV, Excel, ODS, Cassandra, Google Spreadsheets, RDF, and any web page. Regarding databases, it supports MSSQL, DB2, Oracle, OpenEdge, TerraData, MySQL, PostgreSQL/EnterpriseDB, H2, Derby, or any database with a JDBC driver.

4
Building Data Services

WSO2 Enterprise Integrator allows us to build web services that easily manage tables in our data sources. These services are called data services, as their aim is to manage the service interaction with our data sources. These services support our service orchestration and offer a facade that isolates each data source particularly under a web service technology.

In this chapter, we will cover the following topics:

- Configuring data sources
- Using the wizard to manage a table with a single data service
- Using the wizard to manage multiple tables with a single data service and with several data services
- Using several data sources in the same data service
- Defining custom requests and responses for our data service
- Creating multiple operations
- Exposing the data service as a REST API

WSO2 EI data services support any source of data, such as **relational database management systems (RDBMS),** CSV, Excel, ODS, Cassandra, Google Spreadsheets, RDF, and any web page. Regarding databases, it supports MSSQL, DB2, Oracle, OpenEdge, TeraData, MySQL, PostgreSQL/EnterpriseDB, H2, Derby, and any database with a JDBC driver. So, with this in mind, nearly all scenarios are covered.

A data service definition is made up of the following steps and definitions:

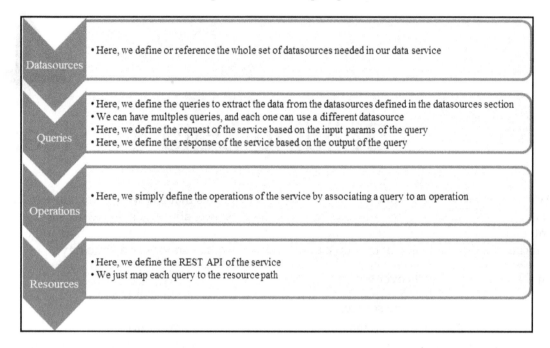

The main task when building a data service is to focus on the queries' definitions, which is where we define what the input and output parameters will be.

We can create our data services in the following different ways:

- **Using the WSO2 EI management console**: This may be the fastest way and may help developers start from a base data service, but it is not recommended for a production environment. In the console, there are two wizards available to design a data service:
    - **Generate Wizard**: This wizard automatically creates a data service with the CRUD operations required to manage one or several tables.
    - **Create Wizard**: This wizard creates a data service, allowing you to customize every step's configuration.

- **Using the WSO2 EI Tooling**: This is the recommended option; the forms and steps you have to follow are quite similar to the management console's Create Wizard. Additionally, this allows you to generate carbon files for the deliveries, as well as manage your code in an SVN or a GitHub repository.

Both options are compatible; actually, they complement each other on a daily basis. The management console enables you to quickly perform modifications over your data service deployed with your carbon application, as well as test them. In addition, the console wizards will also allow you to build a base data service to start with.

Configuring data sources

Instead of having to define each data source in each data service's definition, the best practice is to define the data source in the WSO2 EI console and refer it to your data service definition. This allows you to easily control and manage your data source configurations within a single point for all data services.

WSO2 EI allows you to create the following data sources, and its data services support any source of data, such as--RDBMS, CSV, Excel, ODS, Cassandra, Google Spreadsheets, RDF, and any web page. When used with RDBMS, it supports any database with a JDBC driver.

RDBMS data sources are the most commonly used in most scenarios, so we will use this kind of data source to illustrate the process; in particular, we are using a MySQL database version 5.7.

We are using MySQL Community Server edition, as its vendor affirm; the edition is also known as *...the world's most popular open source database*. You can download and install it from `https://dev.mysql.com/downloads/`.

We need to create a simple schema in this database called **wso2ei**. Over this schema, we will execute the script file provided in this chapter's resources:

The file name is WSO2EI_Chapter4_Scripts.sql; it will create a table called the city in the schema and populate it with some data:

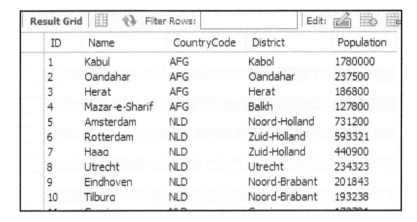

ID	Name	CountryCode	District	Population
1	Kabul	AFG	Kabol	1780000
2	Oandahar	AFG	Oandahar	237500
3	Herat	AFG	Herat	186800
4	Mazar-e-Sharif	AFG	Balkh	127800
5	Amsterdam	NLD	Noord-Holland	731200
6	Rotterdam	NLD	Zuid-Holland	593321
7	Haaa	NLD	Zuid-Holland	440900
8	Utrecht	NLD	Utrecht	234323
9	Eindhoven	NLD	Noord-Brabant	201843
10	Tilbura	NLD	Noord-Brabant	193238

Now that we have the data source over which we will work, we can start creating a data service to manage one, several, or all of them. In order to illustrate how a data service works, we will build a data service with the following functionalities:

- An operation for listing the cities in a SOAP service using the XML format
- An operation for listing the cities in a REST service using the JSON format
- An operation for listing the cities, filtered by country
- An operation for adding a city to the city table
- An operation for updating the population of a city
- An operation for deleting a city from the city table

We follow these steps to create our data source:

1. Download the proper JDBC driver for the database version used and the JDK version that WSO2 EI is using. We can download MySQL from the MySQL JDBC driver (`https://dev.mysql.com/downloads/connector/j/`).

2. Copy the downloaded JAR to `$EI_HOME/lib`.

3. Start or restart WSO2 EI and sign into the management console.

4. Go to **Configure** | **Datasources**:

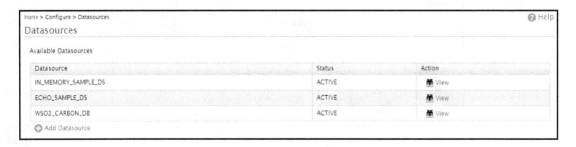

5. Click on **Add Datasource**:

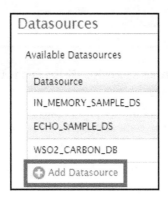

6. Then, type the following information:

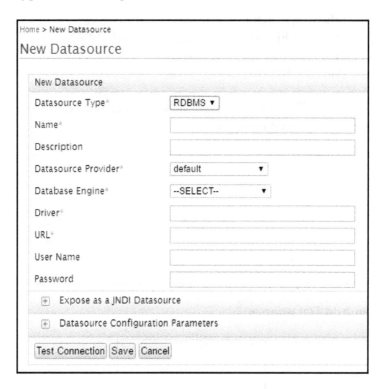

- **Datasource Type**: **RDBMS**; this is the type for the database data source.
- **Name**: This is a name for the datasource. This name will be used later in the data service to refer to the data source; here, we will type MySQLWorld.

- **Description**: This is the description for this data source; here, we can type `Data source for MySQL World schema`.
- **Datasource Provider**: This should be set as default, as we are using a regular JDBC connector.
- **Database Engine**: Set this to **MySQL**. When choosing this option, a template value for the connection will be set in the **Driver** and **URL** fields.
- **Driver**: The default value populated when choosing the MySQL database engine is correct in most cases, so we leave the `com.mysql.jdbc.Driver` value.
- **URL**: This is the JDBC URL to connect the database. We type `jdbc:mysql://localhost:3306/wso2ei` here.

- **User Name**: This is the user that will connect to the database.
- **Password**: This is the password of the user.

7. We can leave the rest of the values as they are entered by default. Before saving the datasource, we should test whether everything is okay by clicking on the **Test Connection** button. We should see the following window saying that all database parameters are **OK**:

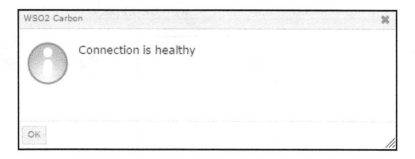

8. Finally, we click on **Save**, and we will see our **MySQLWorld** datasource in the **Datasources** list:

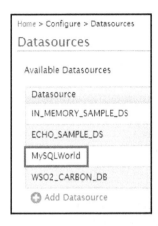

This may be the typical way to create data sources, but you can create these data sources in the filesystem. You can define custom data sources using XML and place them in `$EI_HOME/conf/datasources`. You can see a sample of XML in the `$EI_HOME/conf/datasources /custom-datasources.xml` file.

Data sources added in the filesystem can be viewed in the management console. For example, the following data sources are shipped with the EI package by default:

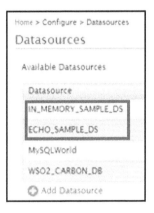

Their definition can also be checked in the `$EI_HOME/conf/datasources /custom-datasources.xml` file.

Now that we have created the data sources, we can use them from both the management console data services wizard and from the WSO2 EI Tooling.

Create wizard

The Create wizard can be found in the WSO2 EI Management Console in **Main | Data Service | Create**. We will use this wizard in the Management Console because for a reader new to WSO2 EI, it is easier to understand data services when they are created by the Create wizard rather than the WSO2 EI Tooling. The best practice is to use the WSO2 EI Tooling, though.

When creating a data service using the Management Console, we have to follow these steps:

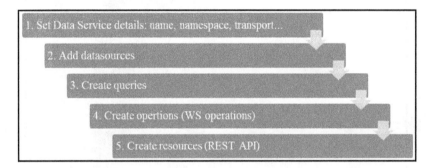

Data service details

This is the first step, where we set the data service details:

As we mentioned earlier, you can get here by navigating to **Main** | **Data Service** | **Create** in the Management Console:

According to this book's aims, the most useful information we have to provide here is the following:

- **Data Service Name**: This is the name of the data service; here, we type `My1stDataService`.
- **Data Service Namespace**: This is the namespace of the service; here, we type `http://www.my1stdataservice.com`.

- **Description**: Here, we can add a description for the service; for instance, `This is my first data service to connect to MySQL`. This field is not mandatory.
- **Advanced Configuration**: We leave these options as they are by default.
- **Transport Settings**: Here, we enable the transport over which we want to publish our service. The default available transports are as follows:
    - **http**: If checked, the data service can be invoked via HTTP.
    - **https**: If checked, the data service can be invoked via HTTPS.
    - **local**: If checked, the data service can be invoked using a fast call between services in the same virtual machine. In other words, when calling other services inside the same virtual machine, the message does not leave the machine and will return to it during the invocation; it is a kind of function or internal method call.
    - **jms**: If checked, the data service will consume the messages received in the message queue set in the **Java Message Service (JMS)** protocol configured in the WSO2 EI:

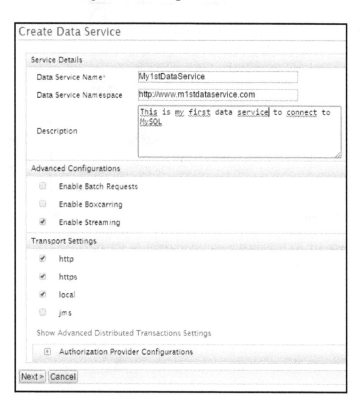

Now, click **Next** and go to the next step.

Adding datasources

This is the second step for building our data service, where we add the data sources needed for the service:

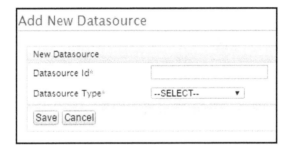

We click on **Add New Datasource** and proceed to the following window:

Here, we add the following information:

- **Datasource Id**: This is just a name to refer to the data source later in the process. Here, we type MySQL.

- **Datasource Type**: Here, we will choose the datasource we created in the first step. We will set this value to **Carbon Datasource**, and then the list of datasources for the Management Console will show up for us to select the one we need:

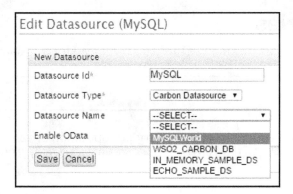

- **Datasource Name:** Here, we choose the **MySQLWorld** datasource, which, as you may remember, is the one we created in the first step.
- **Enable OData**: This enables open data, which automatically creates CRUD operations. In this case, we keep this unchecked.

Finally, we click on **Save** and return to the list of datasources added to the data service:

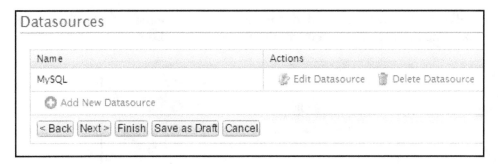

Here, we can edit or delete the added datasources. We can add as many datasources as we want by repeating the steps mentioned earlier. We can use a datasource in as many queries as needed.

This works in the same way when, for instance, an operation of your data service uses a PostgreSQL data source and another one uses the MySQL data source. In this case, you will add both data sources to the list before going to the next section, where we will define the queries that will use them.

In this case, we just need one datasource, so all the work has to been done here. We click on **Next** to go the next step.

Adding queries

In the third step, we will add as many **Queries** as we need for our data service:

The most common practice is to have one query per operation or resource. These queries will be consumed via the SOAP service (in the Operation step) or REST service (in the Resources step).

Assuming the common use case of one query per operation/resource and a database-type data source, the aim of the query definition is to extract data from the data source. In order to do that, we need to design the following:

- The query and data source over which it will be launched
- Input parameters based on query parameters
- Output parameters based on query column results

We can add as many queries as needed, and each one can use the same or different datasources. The the steps for each query definition are as follows:

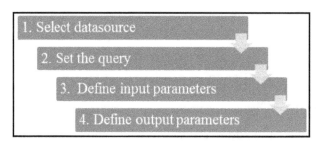

We will add the following queries:

- A query for listing the cities using XML.
- A query for listing the cities using JSON.
- A query for listing the cities filtered by the country and population.
- A query for adding a city to the `city` table.

- A query for updating the population of a city.
- A query for deleting a city from the `city` table.

Now that we know what to do in this step, we are ready to go to work. After adding the **Datasources**, we should see the following window:

Adding new queries using XML responses

In this case, we are focusing on generating the response using XML for the output type of the service; this is the default value for the output.

We click on **Add New Query** to start with the first query, and the following window will open:

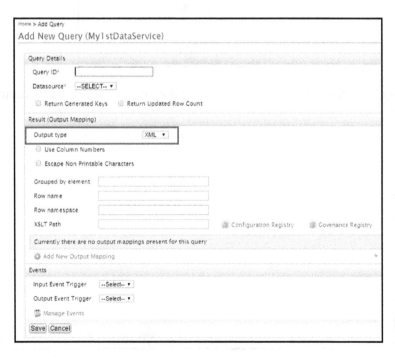

This form has three main sections, as follows:

- **Query Details**: In this section, we set the **Query ID** (the name of the query), the **Datasource**: and the SQL that will be executed on it, and the input parameter mappings
- **Result (Output Mapping)**: Here, we see how the result of the query will be exposed; in this case, we chose the XML format
- **Events**: This is an advanced feature that we will not be using according to the scope of this book

So, now we focus on the **Query Details** section and add the following information:

- **Query ID**: This is the identification for the query; we will call this one `citiesXML`
- **Datasource**: Here, we have the list of datasources that were added in the first step; as we just added one, we will select **MySQL**:

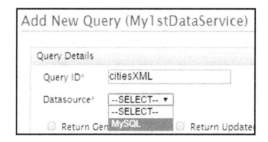

After selecting the datasource, the box for typing the query and other functionalities will appear, as follows:

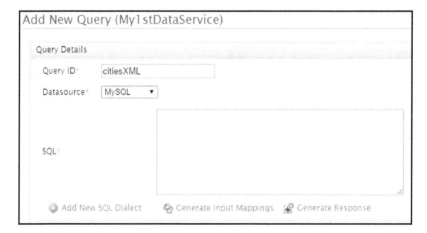

Now we type the **Data Manipulation Language** (**DML**) sentence in the **SQL** box. For the first operation needed in our service--listing the cities and countries--we will type the following SQL:

```
SELECT ID, Name, CountryCode, District, Population FROM city
```

The output of the query will usually be mapped using XML and the following structure:

- Each column will be an XML tag containing the value of the column:

```
<column>columnValue</column>
```

- Each row returned by the query, which is made up of an XML tag per column, will be grouped in an XML tag:

```
<row>
<column1>column1Value</column1>
<column2>column2Value</column2>
<columnN>columnNValue</columnN>
</row>
```

- All the returned rows will be grouped again in another global XML tag, as follows:

```
<queryResult>
<row>
<column1>column1Value</column1>
<column2>column2Value</column2>
<columnN>columnNValue</columnN>
</row>
<row>
<column1>column1Value</column1>
<column2>column2Value</column2>
<columnN>columnNValue</columnN>
</row>
</queryResult>
```

Once we have the SQL set, we will be able to automatically generate the input and output mapping. To take advantage of this feature, it is mandatory to set all column names while avoiding the wildcard *, as, in this case, WSO2 EI cannot infer which column returns the query. Thus, our recommendation is always to define the SQL column, because the autogeneration feature will save you a lot of time. Unfortunately, this option is only available when choosing XML as the language for the response. If we choose a JSON or RDF format for the output, we will have to manually design the response.

You may think that the autogenerated mappings will not match your needs, and this can be true. After generation, you will have to customize the generated mappings, but the time saved makes it worthwhile.

Now that we have discussed the mapping auto-generation, we will show you how it works. To start autogenerating the input mapping, click on **Generate Input Mappings**:

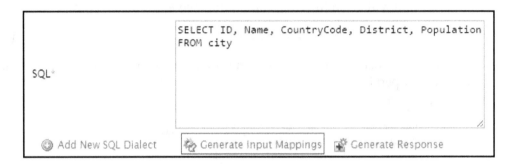

The result will be as illustrated in the following screenshot since there are no input parameters:

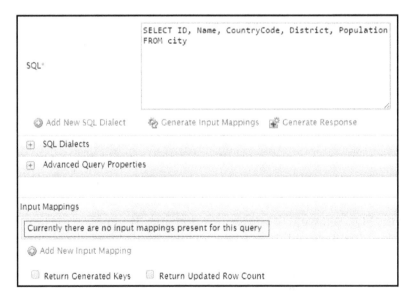

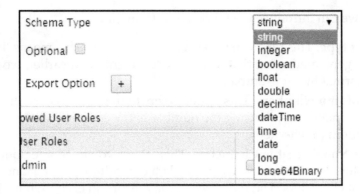

Now we click on **Generate Response**:

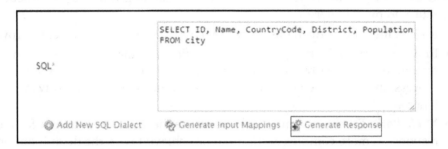

This will show the generated output mappings, as follows:

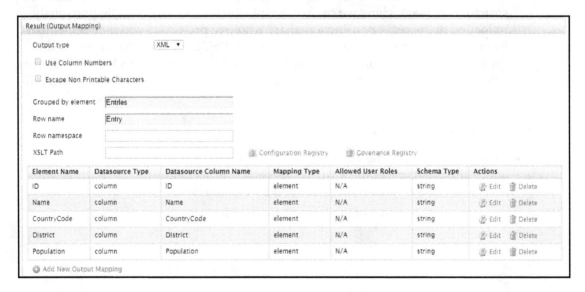

Element Name	Datasource Type	Datasource Column Name	Mapping Type	Allowed User Roles	Schema Type	Actions	
ID	column	ID	element	N/A	string	Edit	Delete
Name	column	Name	element	N/A	string	Edit	Delete
CountryCode	column	CountryCode	element	N/A	string	Edit	Delete
District	column	District	element	N/A	string	Edit	Delete
Population	column	Population	element	N/A	string	Edit	Delete

In this window, we can introduce the following information:

- **Output type**: This field can be **XML**, **JSON**, or **RDF**. This means that the response will be generated using that format. As we mentioned earlier, we are using the XML format in our example.
- **Use Column Numbers**: This option refers to the reference for the query columns in the response design using the number of the column (checked) or the name of the column (unchecked).
- **Escape Non Printable Characters**: This allows you to escape nonprintable characters in the response when the data of a column, for instance, contains these kinds of characters. These characters may throw an exception in WSO2 EI if you do not check this option.
- **Grouped by element**: Here, we set the XML tag to group the whole set of rows returned by the query.
- **Row name**: This is the name of the XML tag that will group an entire row.
- **Row namespace**: Here, we can set a specific namespace for the rows. As you may remember, we already set a namespace for the service at the beginning of this process. In case we need to have a different namespace for the row tag, we can set it here.
- **XSLT Path**: There are some scenarios where the structure required for the response is more complex and cannot be achieved with the default options the wizard gives us. We can solve this situation by defining a simple structure and building an XSLT transformation for that response, which results in the final structure we need. Here, we can set the transformation that must be previously uploaded to the registry using a registry resource project, as you may remember from Chapter 1, *Getting Started with SOA and WSO2*. For instance, if we need to group the result by country, we can do an XSL to transform the plain XML list of cities into a list of cities grouped by country. That XSL will be set here, and it will be launched after building the XML according to the output mapping.

Now, we will customize this mapping by performing the following modification:

- Change the name of the XML element that groups the whole response of the query and the name of the XML tag for each row, as follows:
  1. Set the value of the **Grouped by element** to Cities.
  2. Set the value of the **Row name** field to City.

Following these fields, we now have the list of the autogenerated XML tags for each row mapping, which we can change as desired by adding new mappings, modifying the existing ones, or deleting any of them:

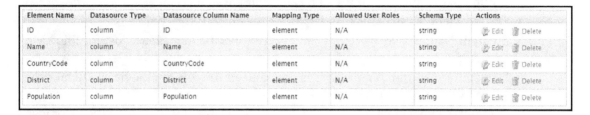

Element Name	Datasource Type	Datasource Column Name	Mapping Type	Allowed User Roles	Schema Type	Actions
ID	column	ID	element	N/A	string	Edit Delete
Name	column	Name	element	N/A	string	Edit Delete
CountryCode	column	CountryCode	element	N/A	string	Edit Delete
District	column	District	element	N/A	string	Edit Delete
Population	column	Population	element	N/A	string	Edit Delete

For each column mapping, we have the following information that can be found when editing any row. The same form can be found by clicking on **Add New Output Mapping**:

- **Mapping Type**: This is the type of XML object used for the mapping; the most common one is an XML element.
- **Datasource Type**: Here, we set whether the value of the field will come from a column of the query, or if it will be an input parameter.
- **Output Field Name**: This is the name of the output XML object.
- **Element Namespace**: Here, we can define a specific namespace just for this XML element.
- **Datasource Column Name**: This is the name of the column the field will take the value from.
- **Parameter Type**: Here, we define whether the element will be an ARRAY or just a simple value (**SCALAR**).
- **Schema Type**: Here, we define the type of data that the XML element will contain. This allows WSO2 EI to set the proper type of XML element in the WSLD. The values allowed are the following XSD types:

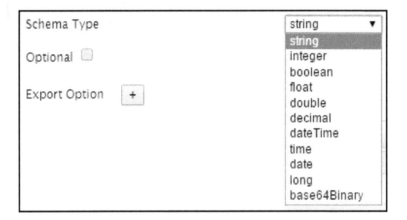

- **Optional**: This specifies whether the field will be optional. If checked, it will be optional in the WSDL of the service.
- **Allowed User Roles**: Here, you can define which roles are allowed to be seen in this field, so this information will be shown just to the roles you check. The most common case is to allow everyone to see the entirety of the service's information, so we can keep the default value. All roles are unchecked.

Now that we have learned how to add or modify the output mappings, we will perform using this modification:

1. Change the name of some fields in order to clarify the response. Here, we will work with the following elements of the mappings list:
2. Change the element with the name `Name` for `CityName`. Click on **Edit** in the row with the **Element Name** as `Name` that corresponds to the name of the city entered in the query. In the edit form, change the **Output Field name** to `CityName` and save.
3. Change the element with the name `ID` ti `CityID`. Click on **Edit** in the row with **Element Name** as `ID` that corresponds to the ID of the city entered in the query. In the edit form, change the **Output Field name** to `CityID` and save.

We can check the result in the output mapping list, as follows:

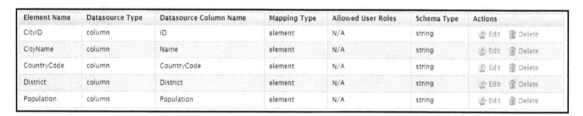

Element Name	Datasource Type	Datasource Column Name	Mapping Type	Allowed User Roles	Schema Type	Actions	
CityID	column	ID	element	N/A	string	Edit	Delete
CityName	column	Name	element	N/A	string	Edit	Delete
CountryCode	column	CountryCode	element	N/A	string	Edit	Delete
District	column	District	element	N/A	string	Edit	Delete
Population	column	Population	element	N/A	string	Edit	Delete

We are done with the query definition, so we can now just click on **Save** and the query will be added to our data service:

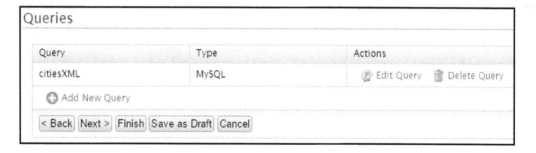

Query	Type	Actions	
citiesXML	MySQL	Edit Query	Delete Query

Queries

➕ Add New Query

< Back | Next > | Finish | Save as Draft | Cancel

Adding new queries using JSON responses

We can now add a new query similar to the one we added earlier. Actually, it will be identical, except for the **Output type**. This time, we will choose JSON for the output type, so we will have to manually define the response using JSON. We will choose this query for the REST version of the service.

Before using the JSON output, we have to ensure that the following configuration is correct:

- `$WSO2_EI/conf/axis/axis2.xml` and `$WSO2_EI/conf/axis/axis_client.xml` must have the following parameter set to `true` and uncommented. Restarting is required after modifying these files:

```
<parameter name="httpContentNegotiation">true</parameter>
```

So, now we proceed in the same way as described in the previous section, by creating a new query using the following information:

- **Query ID**: `citiesJSON`
- **Datasource**: **MySQL**
- **Query**: `SELECTID, Name, CountryCode, District, and PopulationFROMcity`
- **Output type**: JSON

The generated response feature does not work for the JSON output type, so you can omit that step. After setting the previous information, the form has only the result JSON left to be completed. Take a look at the following screenshot:

We check the **Use Column Numbers** to easily reference the columns in the JSON template with the $ character and use the number of columns instead of their names. We will set the following JSON template to achieve the JSON version of the previous XML query:

```
{
 "Cities": {
 "City": [
 {
 "CityID": "$1",
 "CityName": "$2",
 "CountryCode": "$3",
```

```
  "District": "$4",
  "Population": "$5"
}
   ]
      }
}
```

The form will look like this:

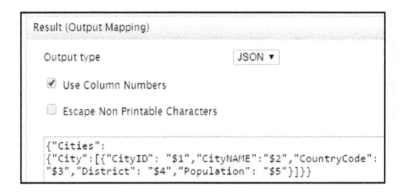

Finally, saving will add the new query.

Adding new queries using a filter

In this case, we are adding a query where we will have input parameters. These parameters will be used in the `where` clause to filter the cities from the country received in the input parameter. To build this query, we will operate as we did in the *Adding new queries using XML responses* section, with the only difference we have an input parameter, a country, and a population that we want to filter by in this case. Thus, we can create a query with the following information:

- **Query ID**: `citiesFromCountryXML`
- **Datasource: MySQL**
- **Query**: `SELECT ID, Name, CountryCode, District, Population FROM city WHERE CountryCode = :countryCode AND population < :population`
- **Output type: XML**

We can set the parameters of our query as follows:

- Using the '?' character
- Using : followed by a name--: countryCode

In this case, we will proceed in the same way as we did before for the output parameters, and we will autogenerate them and change some field names. In the case of input parameters, we will have to add them manually, as the autogeneration tool often fails to work properly. Take the following steps:

1. Click on **Add New Input Mapping** on the Edit query window.
2. Add the following information:

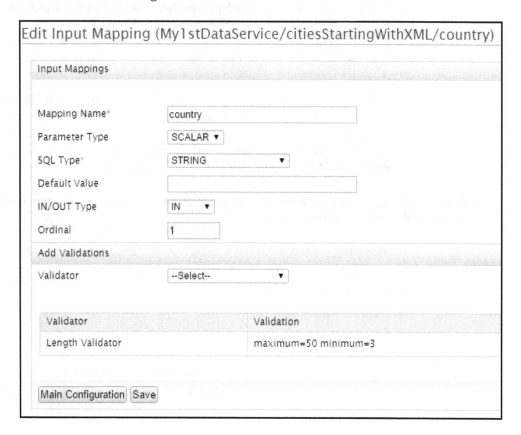

- **Mapping Name**: This is the name for the mapping; this will be the name of the parameter in the SOAP operation if we autogenerate the SOAP operation parameter. In this case, we set the name to `country`.
- **Parameter type**: The options here are SCALAR and ARRAY. We choose **SCALAR**.
- **SQL Type**: Here, we choose one SQL type of the parameter, which will also help us with the type validation of the parameter. We choose **STRING**.
- **Default Value**: Here, we can set a default value for the parameter for the cases where it is not sent.
- **IN/OUT type**: Here, we select whether it is an input, output, or input/output parameter in the query; we choose **IN**.
- **Ordinal**: This is the ordinal of the parameter in the SQL query we are setting with the input parameter we are defining; here, we choose `1`.
- **Validator**: We can set a validator for this input parameter. There are some built-in validators, such us length validator or long-range value validator. We choose **Length Validator** and set `3` and `50` for the **minimum** and **maximum** values, and we also click on **Add validator**. We can add as many validators as we need.

3. We now add the input parameter for the population, so we repeat the previous steps with the following information:

   - **Mapping Name**: `Population`
   - **Parameter Type**: `SCALAR`
   - **SQL Type**: `INTEGER`
   - **Default Value**: `blank`
   - **IN/OUT type**: `IN`
   - **Ordinal**: `2`
   - **Validator**: We choose **Long Range Validator** and set `1` and `999999999` for the minimum and maximum values, and we click on **Add validator**.

4. We click on **Save**, and then click on **Main Configuration** to return to the query edit window:

Input Mappings			
Mapping Name	**Parameter Type**	**Type**	**Action**
country	SCALAR	STRING	Edit Delete
population	SCALAR	INTEGER	Edit Delete

Finally, we click on **Save** and add the new query to the service.

Adding new queries for inserting data

This time, we will create a query for adding a new row to the city table, and the result will be the autogenerated primary key. We will have three input parameters, as we are using an insert statement and a single output parameter. We will create a new query with the following information:

- **Query ID**: `insertCity`
- **Datasource**: **MySQL**
- **Query**: `INSERT INTO city (Name, CountryCode, District, Population) VALUES (?,?,?,?)`
- **Input Mappings**:

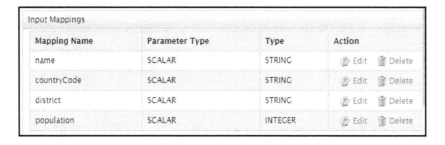

Input Mappings			
Mapping Name	**Parameter Type**	**Type**	**Action**
name	SCALAR	STRING	Edit Delete
countryCode	SCALAR	STRING	Edit Delete
district	SCALAR	STRING	Edit Delete
population	SCALAR	INTEGER	Edit Delete

We will set the ordinal number of each mapping according to the position of the '?' in the query, starting from 1.

- **Return Generated Keys**: This should be checked. This option allows us to insert values in a table with autoincrement columns. The data service will generate an autoincrement value; it will insert it in the column and return the value in the service response. When checking this, the window will automatically generate the following response:

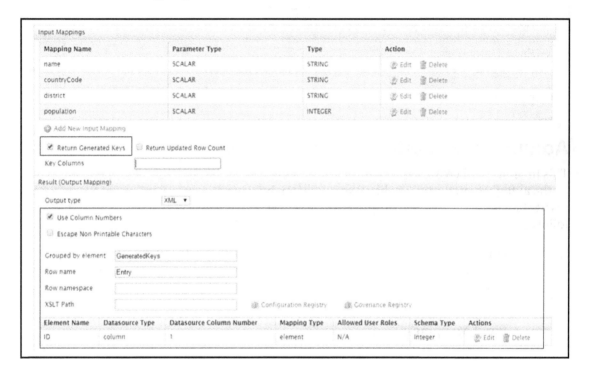

In the output mapping section, we can modify the output element to make it match the key columns. In this case, we need just one return element for the column ID.

- We finally click on **Save**.

Now we have added the new query to the data service.

Adding new queries for updating data

Sometimes, we also need to update the data in our tables, so we will now learn how to do that and return the updated results. We will generate a query with the following information:

- **Query ID:** `updateCity`
- **Datasource: MySQL**
- **Query:** `UPDATE city SET Name=?, CountryCode=?, District=?, Population=? WHERE ID=?`
- **Input Mappings:**

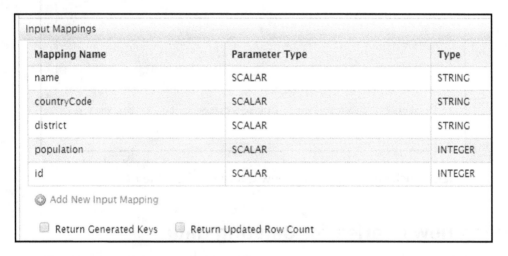

Mapping Name	Parameter Type	Type
name	SCALAR	STRING
countryCode	SCALAR	STRING
district	SCALAR	STRING
population	SCALAR	INTEGER
id	SCALAR	INTEGER

Add New Input Mapping

☐ Return Generated Keys ☐ Return Updated Row Count

We will set the ordinal number of each mapping according to the position of the '?' in the query, starting from 1.

- **Return Updated Row Count**: This should be checked. As with returning the generated keys for the input case, checking this will autogenerate the output mapping for returning the updated number of rows:

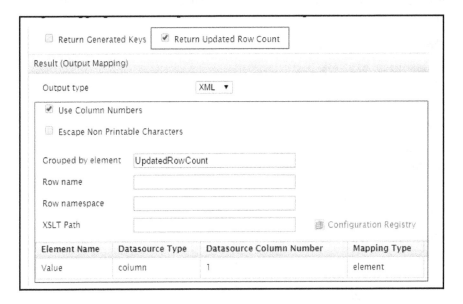

- Finally, click on **Save**, and the new query will be added.

Adding new queries for deleting data

This scenario closes the set of operations to manage a table. Here, we will learn how to delete a row from a table. This is a simple scenario, as we just need one input parameter for the primary key. Then, we will add a new query with the following information:

- **Query ID**: deleteCity
- **Datasource**: MySQL
- **Query**: DELETE FROM city WHERE ID=?
- **Input Mappings**:

Input Mappings		
Mapping Name	**Parameter Type**	**Type**
ID	SCALAR	INTEGER

- Finally, click on **Save**, and the new query will be added.

Now we have all the operations added to our service, as shown in the following screenshot:

Adding operations

In this step, we will add as many operations as we need for our data service:

Every operation will be a SOAP operation of the service, so in this step, we will configure the SOAP version of the service. From the query list, we will click on **Next** and go to the **Operations** list:

We will click on **Add New Operation,** and then the following window will appear for us to add the operation:

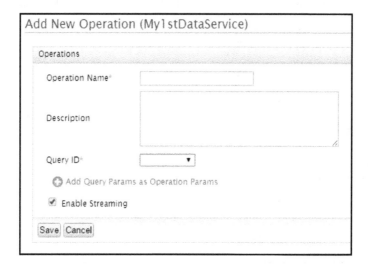

We just need the following listed items:

- **Operation Name:** This is the name for the SOAP operation. Here, we will type `citiesXML`.
- **Description:** This is a description of the operation; for instance, `This operation returns 10 cities`.
- **Query ID:** Here, we select the query that will retrieve the data to be returned by the operation. Here, we will choose the `citiesXML` operation.
- **Enable Streaming:** We keep this checked.

We can automatically generate the operation parameters from the query parameters by clicking on **Add Query Params as Operation Params**. However, in this case, it will have no effect as the query does not have input parameters. In most cases, they are autogenerated when selecting the **Query ID**.

We will now click on **Save** and return to the operation list.

We will generate SOAP operations for all our queries, but the `cityJSON` query will be exposed as a REST service instead of a SOAP service. So, we will repeat the steps described earlier for the rest of the queries, and finally, we should have the following list of operations:

Depending on how complex the services are, the built-in tool for trying the services might not work properly. For that reason, you can find a SoapUI project called `My1stDataservice-SoapUIProject.xml` for testing these services, including SOAP 1.1 and 1.2 operations, in this chapter's resources:

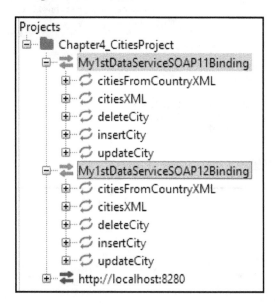

Adding resources

In the final step, we will add as many REST resources as we need for our data service:

From the operation's list, we will click on **Next** and proceed to the **Resources** list:

We will click on **Add New Resource** and add the following information:

- **Resource Path**: Here, we type a name for the path of the resource. We will set it to `cities`.
- **Description**: This is the description for the resource; for instance, `This resource will return 10 cities in JSON format`.
- **Resource Method**: This is the REST resource method for the resource. The typical methods are available: `GET`, `PUT`, `POST`, and `DELETE`. We will choose **GET**.
- **Query ID**: This is the query that retrieves the data that will be returned by the resource. In this case, we select the query that returns the data in the JSON format, that is, `citiesJSON`.
- **Enable Streaming**: We keep this checked. This means that the resulting set of a query is written to wire the results directly instead of building up and storing the complete result in memory.

We will now click on **Save** and return to the resources list:

Finally, we will click on **Finish** , and in a few seconds, our service will appear in the service list of WSO2 EI, as follows:

You must keep in mind that to try this kind of REST JSON service, you must use more specific software, such as SoapUI, since we have to add this property to the header of the request, `Accept: application/jsonj`.

In addition, this cannot be set using the WSO2 EI built-in testing feature. You can find a SoapUI project for testing this REST service, as well as the rest of them, called `My1stDataservice-SoapUIProject.xml` in this chapter's resources:

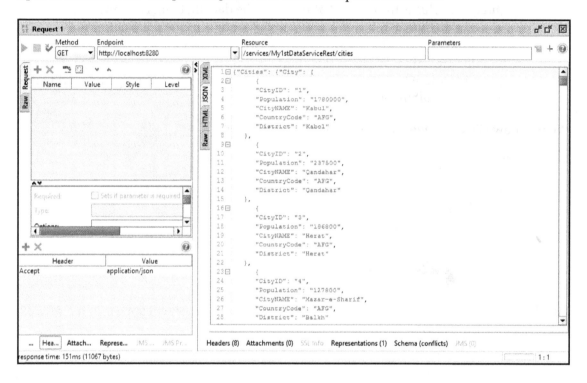

Creating CRUD data services

WSO2 EI gives us another feature that allows us to create web services for managing tables in our database. This is an SOAP data service with operations for inserting, deleting, updating, or selecting rows in one or several tables. This can only be performed using the Management Console, under **Services** | **Data Service** | **Generate**. You just have to follow these steps:

1. Select a data source and a database name:

2. Choose the table or tables you want to manage with the data service:

3. Choose whether you want a single data service for all the tables or a data service per table. Enter a namespace for the data service:

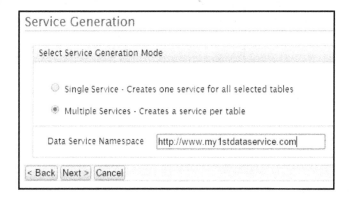

4. Then the data service will be created, as follows:

You will see the new data service in the service list:

The operations generated are as follows:

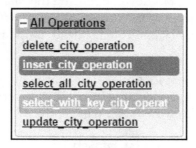

You may have noted that there are two `select` operations. One of them, called `select_all*`, retrieves all data in the table. The other one, `select_with_key*`, will retrieve data using the primary key of the table as a filter.

As you can imagine, customization has been sacrificed in favor of speed, so the final data service may not match all of your needs. Even so, you can take advantage of this powerful feature, and you can use it to create your initial data service, over which you can start working, and customize it to fit your needs, with most of the legwork done.

Creating data services using WSO2 EI Tooling

As you may remember, we have already learned how to create data services using the WSO2 EI Tooling, but we did not cover this topic in detail. Although we covered certain topics in depth in this chapter, we did not use WSO2 EI Tooling; instead, we used the WSO2 EI Management Console. You may be wondering why.

The reason is that the Management Console wizard is more user-friendly than WSO2 EI Tooling, and it also gives you more facilities, such as autogeneration for the output mappings. In contrast, the best practice is to use WSO2 EI Tooling, so what do we do?

The response is easy--take the best of both choices. Build your project and data service skeleton using WSO2 EI Tooling, but develop it using the Management Console wizard. This allows you to quickly apply and test your modifications. Once you have achieved the final functionality in your data services, you just need to update your data service skeleton in Eclipse.

You can easily update the data service skeleton in Eclipse by copying the code of the data service. You can access the data service code from the data services dashboard and clicking on **Edit Data Service (XML Edit)**, where you will get the XML code of the data service:

This is the XML of the data service:

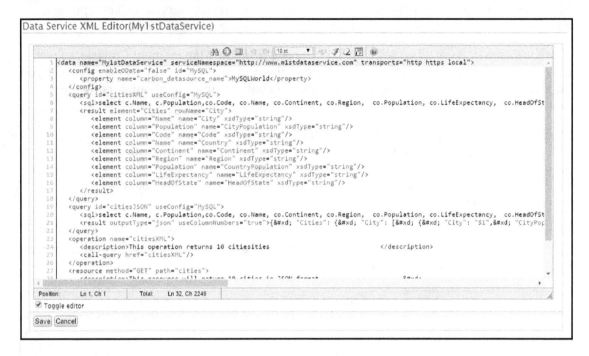

You just need to copy that XML and paste it into the code tab of your data service in WSO2 EI Tooling, as follows:

You also need to ensure that both services--the skeleton in Eclipse and the one created in the Management Console have the same name. This way, your data service will be updated, and you will be able to generate a carbon file to deploy it in other environments.

There is a known issue when setting a source code from the Management Console, so we have to avoid adding descriptions to the operations and resources in our data service. If you do, when you copy the code and try to save it, you will get an error about parsing the `description` tag.

Obviously, you can work with the Eclipse IDE and deploy and test each version you get, if you prefer to. The wizard for the data services may not be as user-friendly as the management console one, but the structure and procedure are quite similar. So, we can set the following mapping between the required steps in order to create a data service in the Management Console and in WSO2 EI Tooling.

Starting from the data service skeleton we created in Chapter 2, *Developing Integration Projects with WSO2EI Tooling*, we can create data sources, queries, operations, and resources by right-clicking on the data service:

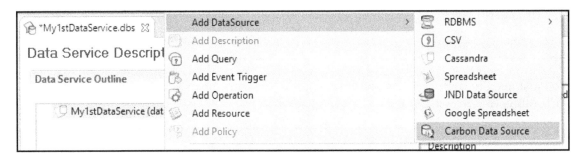

As you can see in the preceding screenshot, we have all the steps available in the right-click. This way, we create all that we need by following the order we learned in this chapter. The final data service may look like the following screenshot in WSO2 EI Tooling:

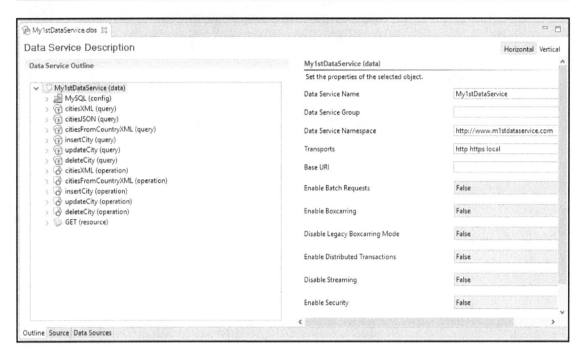

You will find the resources of the data service project for this data service in this chapter. Currently, at the time of writing this book, we have discovered some issues when creating a data service that contains resources using WSO2 EI Tooling. For that reason, in this chapter resource, you will find a workspace for WSO2 EI Tooling and a data service called **My1stDataService** where you can find all of these operations, except the `citiesJSON`.

Additionally, you can find another data service called `My1stDataServiceRest` containing all operations, including the REST one. It must be uploaded using the Management Console from **Services** | **Data Service** | **Upload** so that it works properly.

In the subsequent chapters, we will learn more about integration, as well as how to perform integration with the **Virtual File System** (**VFS**) in our services.

Summary

In this chapter, we learned how to build the data services needed for fetching the data required in our service orchestration. Additionally, we learned some tips to save some time when developing and testing our data services.

In the next chapter, you will learn how to transform the message received in the services.

5
Transforming the Content of the Payload

In the earlier chapters, you learned how to create different types of services in the **Enterprise Integrator (EI)** server. In this chapter, we will focus on the payload of the messages and the different ways that the EI offers us to modify it or get information. When we talk of payload, we can translate it to the body of the messages that will get the most important information for the logic of our services and requirements.

In this chapter, we will cover different topics related to the payload of the content:

- Creating new content
- Changing the format of the content
- Enriching the message
- Message conversion

To do this, we will cover the following WSO2 tools:

- XSLT Mediator
- FastXSLT Mediator
- Message Types
- Payload Factory Mediator
- Enrich Mediator
- XQuery Mediator
- Script mediator

Creating new content

In this use case, the message doesn't have a current payload, and we need to create the content of the message. We can affront this use case when we have a REST service that is only triggered with the URL endpoint with the parameters, but also needs a payload to consume a backend service. Another use case can be the inverse process, in which the backend service doesn't have a response, but our service needs to reply with a message for the client that makes the request.

In both scenarios, we can use different WSO2 tools, such as PayloadFactory mediator, Enrich mediator, or Script mediator, although the most simple and easy to use is the PayloadFactory mediator.

The PayloadFactory mediator

The PayloadFactory mediator defines new content for the payload, configuring a template of the new message inside the `<format>` tag and the dynamic values inside the `<args>` tag.

Here's the syntax:

Here, keep the following in mind:

- `media-type` is an attribute that defines the format of the generated message
- The `arg` can be a static or dynamic value with `xpath` or `json` expressions

Inside the template message that is placed in the `<format>` tag, we can add a dynamic argument that will be mapped with the arguments located in the `<args>` XML object. In order to do that, we need to place a `$n` element in each dynamic value, where n is a number starting with one and incrementing with each variable, for example $1, $2, and so on. Then, we need to place the arguments in the same order to inject them into the message.

For example, we have a REST service that will receive the origin and destination airport and a date for a flight and will return information on the different companies and times that you can choose.

WSO2 EI service:

REQUEST	RESPONSE

ENDPOINT:
/flights/get
URL PARAMETERS:
from=London
to=Liverpool
date=15/12/2017
	`<flights>`
	`<flight>`
	`<company>PacktAir</company>`
	`<time>10:30</time>`
	`<price>£ 300</price>`
	`</flight>`
	`</flights`

Backend service:

REQUEST	RESPONSE

`<flight>`
`<from>London</from>`
`<to>Liverpoo</to>`
`<date>15/12/2017</date>`
`</flight>`
	`<flights>`
	`<flight>` `<company>PacktAir</company>`
	`<time>10:30</time>`
	`<price>£ 300</price>`
	`</flight>`
	`</flights>`

So in our service, we don't have a payload in the request, but the backend service is waiting for a payload with the information related to the flight. In this scenario, we need to use the PayloadFactory mediator, as follows:

```
<api xmlns="http://ws.apache.org/ns/synapse" name="flights"
                                        context="/flights">
  <resource methods="POST" uri-template="/get?from={from}&
                                 to={to}&date={date}">
    <inSequence>
      <payloadFactory media-type="xml">
        <format>
          <flight>
            <from>$1</from>
            <to>$2</to>
            <date>$3</date>
          </flight>
        </format>
        <args>
          <arg evaluator="xml" expression="get
                      property('uri.var.from')"></arg>
          <arg evaluator="xml" expression="get
                      property('uri.var.to)"></arg>
          <arg evaluator="xml" expression="get
                      property('uri.var.date)"></arg>
        </args>
```

```
    </payloadFactory>
  [...]
```

As we can see in the preceding example, we are getting the URL parameters of the incoming request and generating an XML payload with those parameters. The list of arguments is in the same order that the $n parameters appear in the message template, so $1 references the first argument, that is, $2 references to the second argument, and so on. In the previous chapters, we learned how to get the URL parameters using the get-property('uri.var.paramName') function.

Script mediator

With Script mediator, we can use different scripting languages to process the payload, such as JavaScript, Groovy, or Ruby languages. The script code can be embedded in our service (API, proxy, sequence, and so on) or can be stored in a file inside the registry.

Syntax inline script:

```
<script language="js | groovy | rb">
  <![CDATA[
    (code of the script)
  ]]>
<script/>
```

Syntax registry store script:

```
<script key="string" language="js | groovy | rb"
                          [function="function name"]>
    <include key="string"/>
</script>
```

Here, keep these things in mind:

- Language can be js for JavaScript, groovy for Groovy, and rb for Ruby scripting languages
- Function is the name of the function to execute inside the scripting file specified in the key attribute

To see Script mediator in detail, take a look at Chapter 3, *Building Web Services*.

In the same example, we can replace the PayloadFactory mediator for Script mediator, as follows:

```
<api xmlns="http://ws.apache.org/ns/synapse" name="flights"
context="/flights">
  <resource methods="POST"
        uri-template="/get?from={from}&to={to}&date={date}">
    <inSequence>
      <script language="js">;
        <![CDATA[
        var from = mc.getProperty("uri.var.from");
        var to = mc.getProperty("uri.var.to");
        var date = mc.getProperty("uri.var.date");
        mc.setPayloadXML(
            <flight>
            <from>{from}</from>
            <to>{to}</to>
            <date>{date}</date>
          </flight>
        );
        ]]>
      </script>
  [...]
```

In this example, we get the content of the URL parameters directly inside the script using the mc.getProperty("uri.var.paramName") function. Then, we set the payload with the desired XML message using the mc.setPayloadXML(newPayload) function.

Change the format of the content

We follow this use case when we already have content in the payload, but it might not be in the format that we need; for example, when our service receives a request in a specific format but the backend is waiting for a different format, or the backend sends us a message and we need to modify it to format the response to the client.
The best way to do this is with the use of Message type.

Message type

Message type is a synapse property that defines the message format of the current payload. Here's the syntax:

```
<property name="messageType" value="string" scope="axis2"/>
```

In our flight example, we will change the response of the EI service to return the same information of the backend, but in the JSON format. So, the only change that we need to make is to configure the `messageType` property in the out sequence of our service to change the format of the payload to JSON:

```
<property name="messageType" value="application/json"
                            scope="axis2"></property>
```

RESPONSE OF THE BACKEND	RESPONSE OF THE EI SERVICE
```<flights> <flight> <company>PacktAir</company> <time>10:30</time> <price>£ 300</price> </flight></flights>```	```{"flights": {"flight": {"company": "PacktAir","time": "10:30", "price": "£ 300"}}}```

The XQuery mediator

The XQuery mediator allows us to make XQuery transformations over the payload.

This is the syntax:

```
<xquery key="string" [target="xpath"]>
    <variable name="string" type="string" [key="string"]
    [expression="xpath"] [value="string"]/>?
</xquery>
```

For the next example, we will do the inverse transformation of the same message; we will process a response from the backend in the JSON format and transform it to the XML format before sending it to the client.

RESPONSE OF THE BACKEND	RESPONSE OF THE EI SERVICE

`{`
`"flights": {`
`"flight": {`
`"company": "PacktAir",`
`"time": "10:30",`
`"price": "£ 300"`
`}`
`}`
`}`
	`<flights>`
	`<flight>`
	`<company>PacktAir</company>;`
	`<time>10:30</time>`
	`<price&gt;£ 300</price>`
	`</flight>;`
	`</flights>`

In the out sequence, we need to place the XQuery mediator:

```
<xquery key="gov:/xquery/flights.xq">
  <variable name="payload" type="ELEMENT"/>
</xquery>
[...]
```

The `flights.xq` file will be saved in the registry with the following transformation:

```
<x>;
  <![CDATA[
    declare variable $payload as document-node() external;
    <flights>
      <flight>
        <company>{$payload//company/child::text()}</company>
        <time>{$payload//time/child::text()}</time>
        <price>{$payload//price/child::text()}</price>
      </flight>
    </flights>
  ]]>;
</x>
[...]
```

Enrich the message

The difference in this use case from the earlier ones is that in this case, we already have a message that is in the correct format, but doesn't have the structure we need. For example, when we need to add information before sending the message to the backend, or when the response of the backend is similar to the response we need to reply to the client.

For modifying the content of the message, we can use Enrich mediator, Script mediator, XSLT mediator, FASTXSLT mediator, XQuery mediator, or Smooks mediator.

The Enrich mediator

The Enrich mediator can process the current payload for performing different actions such as replacing or adding child or sibling to a specific target of the message, such as envelope, body, or property.

The following is the syntax:

```
<enrich>
    <source [clone=true|false]   [type=custom|envelope|body|property|inline]
        xpath="" property="" />
    <target [action=replace|child|sibiling]
    [type=custom|envelope|body|property|inline]
        xpath="" property="" >
</enrich>
```

Keep the following in mind with regards to the preceding syntax:

- Clone configure is when the message will be cloned or used as a reference (false, by default)
- The `Soucrce` tag has the information to add to the payload
- The `Target` tag is where the information of the source tag must be placed

In the preceding flight sample, the backend service now needs a new parameter with the information of the current time. For this modification, we will use the Enrich mediator:

REQUEST BACKEND SERVICE	RESPONSE BACKEND SERVICE
`<flight>        <currentDate>2017.12.15<currentDate>` `<from>London</from>` `<to>Liverpool</to>` `<date>15/12/2017</date>` `</flight>`	`<flights>` `<flight>            <company>PacktAir</company>` `<time>10:30</time>` `<price&gt;£ 300</price&gt;` `</flight>` `</flights>`

Take a look at the following code snippet:

```
<api xmlns="http://ws.apache.org/ns/synapse" name="flights"
                                         context="/flights">
  <resource methods="POST"
        uri-template="/get?from={from}& to={to}&date={date}">
    <inSequence>
      <enrich>
      <source clone="false" type="inline">
        <currentDate xmlns=""></currentDate>
      </source>
      <target action="child" type="custom"
                                     xpath="//flight">
      </target>
      </enrich>
      <property name="date" scope="default"
      expression="get-property('SYSTEM_DATE','yyyy.MM.dd')" />;
      <enrich>
        <source clone="false" type="property"
                                   property="date"/>
        <target action="child" type="custom"
                                 xpath="//currentDate">
        </target>
      </enrich>
    [...]
```

In this example, we basically need to add a new child of the `<flight>` tag containing the current date. In the beginning of the service, we have the request message that is as follows:

```
<flight>
    <from>London</from>
    <to>Liverpool</to>
    <date>15/12/2017</date>
</flight>
```

Then, with the first Enrich mediator, we add a child of the `<flight>` element that will contain the inline specifying the XML element; after that the message is the following:

```
<flight>
  <currentDate></currentDate>
    <from>London</from>
    <to>Liverpool</to>
    <date>15/12/2017</date>
</flight>
```

Now we have the correct message structure, but we need to add a value to the `<currentDate>` element. To do that, we use the second Enrich mediator that is a little different from the previous one. In this Enrich mediator, we don't specify the content inline; we specify the name of the property that contains the information to inject into the code:

```
<flight>
   <currentDate>2017.12.15</currentDate>
   <from>London</from>
   <to>Liverpool</to>
   <date>15/12/2017</date>
</flight>
```

Message transformation

In this case, we have a payload, but unlike what we had in the previous use case, the content is not at all similar to the payload we need. For that reason, we cannot use the Enrich mediator and must use the XSLT, FASTXSLT, XQuery, Smooks, or Script mediator.

 In fact, we can use the Enrich mediator, but it will be less efficient than the other WSO2 toolings that we commented on.

The XSLT mediator

With this mediator, we can perform transformations over the XML message using the XSLT language. It is useful for complex transformations, or those in which the payloads change too much and it's not possible to change the message using other tools such as the Enrich mediator.

This is the syntax:

```
<xslt key="string" [source="xpath"]>
    <property name="string" (value="literal" |
                                      expression="xpath")/>*
    <feature name="string" value="true| false" />*
    <resource location="string" key="string"/>*
</xslt>
```

In the next example, we will receive an XML payload in our service, but the backend service is waiting for a completely different payload.

In the sequence, we need to place the XSLT mediator:

REQUEST EI SERVICE	REQUEST BACKEND SERVICE
```<flight> <from>London</from> <to>Liverpool</to> <date>15/12/2017</date> </flight>```	```<getflights> <origin>London</origin> <destination>Liverpool</destination> </getflights>```

The `flights.xq` file will be saved in the registry with this transformation:

```
<xslt key="gov:/xslt/flights.xslt">
</xslt>

[...]
```

The `flights.xq` file will be saved in the registry with this transformation:

```
<?xml version="1.0" encoding="UTF-8"?>
<xsl:stylesheet xmlns:xsl="http://www.w3.org/1999/XSL/Transform"
version="2.0">
<xsl:output method="xml" indent="yes" encoding="utf-8"/>
<xsl:template match="/">
 <getflights>
   <origin>
     <xsl:value-of select="//from/text()" />
   </origin>
    <destination>
     <xsl:value-of select="//to/text()" />
    </destination>
   </getflights>
</xsl:template>
```

The FastXSLT mediator

The FastXSLT mediator is similar to the previous XSLT mediator; it uses the XSLT language to apply a transformation over the XML payload, but this mediator applies the transformation to the message stream, and not over the XML message payload like the previous mediator. For that reason, this mediator is faster, but conversely, we can't configure the source, properties, features, or resources.

Let's look at the syntax:

```
<fastXSLT key="string"/>
```

Summary

In this chapter, we learned how to work with the payload of messages to adapt it to our requirements. We saw the use of different tools in relation to the target that we need to cover, because if we want to create a new payload, we'll use the PayloadFactory mediator. Meanwhile, if we want to change small things in the payload, we will use the Enrich mediator instead.

As we saw in the chapter, we can easily modify the content of the payload using the PayloadFactory mediator or the Enrich mediator without needing to have advanced knowledge of transformation languages such as XSLT or XQuery. However, these languages will be useful when we have complex transformations, and we want to use the XSLT/FastXSLT or XQuery mediator.

In the next chapter, we will see the different techniques and tools that we have for adding conditional routing to our services. This will give us the opportunity to create more complex and intelligent services that can use different methods based on the context, payload, header, and so on.

6
Conditional Route

By now, we are familiar with the theory of service-oriented architecture and how to perform integration of different systems in an environment. We also have the technical knowledge for configuring the Enterprise Integrator server and developing different types of services depending on our requirements. Finally, in the last chapter, we will go further into the payload of the messages and the different tools, mediators, and languages that we can use to get, create, replace, modify, and change the format.

As you can see, we started from the simplest and generic topics and with every chapter, we are focusing on more specific and complex topics, so it's important that you take the time to go through the main ideas of every chapter, and read again if needed before starting a new and more complex chapter. The best way to learn all those concepts is by playing with our EI server and letting our imagination run wild with different scenarios and integrations.

In this chapter, we take a step forward to focus on advanced processing of the services. The target is to make more advanced services that can make decisions and perform different actions based on the payload, the user who makes the request to the service, the endpoint, and the parameters.

To do that, we will cover the following WSO2 tools:

- Validate mediator
- Filter mediator
- Switch mediator
- Conditional router mediator
- Rule mediator

All this tooling allows us to process the incoming requests to our service (proxy, API, inbound endpoint, and so on) and check some information such as URL, payload, and parameters against regex expressions or rules. Depending on the result of this evaluation, we can route the service to one or the other sequence and perform different actions in each one, depending on our requirement for that specific message:

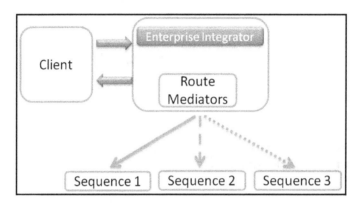

Checking the payload content

When we have a service, we usually work with a lot of different payload structures in the service workflow: incoming requests, calls to a backend, error messages, responses of the backend, and so on. We need to ensure that every one of these messages have the correct format, because our service will get an error otherwise; so, part of the job when we develop a service is to check those messages.

If we don't check those messages, we'll get an unhandled exception, and the final client will be waiting for the response of the service until we get a timeout without any type of response for our service. Also, the service won't be processed (or at least, not completely) so this is not a good solution.

If we check those messages, we can leave the normal processing when the messages are good; however, in other cases, we can perform an action to control the exception and give a workaround, solve it, store the problem in a database/business queue to be checked by an administrator, notify someone by email to check and solve the problem, print the error in the logs, give a descriptive error to the client that makes the request, and so on.

For that purpose, we have the validate mediator that validates the current XML or JSON payload against a defined schema and performs an action if the message is incorrect.

Validating XML

This mediator will evaluate the content inside the `soapBody` tag by default, but we can also specify an XPath expression for evaluating a concrete part of the payload. The validation is done against an XML schema, which is a **World Wide Web Consortium** (**W3C**) recommendation to define the elements in XML documents. The schema file has a `.xsd` extension, and we can configure the structure that the document should match, for example, the mandatory parameters, the order of the elements, and so on.

This is the syntax:

```
<validate [source="xpath"]>
   [<property name="validation-feature-id" value="true|false"/>*]
   [<resource location="string" key="string"/>+]
   <schema key="string"/>+
   <on-fail>
      mediator+
   </on-fail>
</validate>
```

Here, take the following into consideration:

- `Source` is the xpath expression for the message to evaluate
- The properties specify whether those features are active or inactive
- The resources include other files needed for the schema file
- Schema references the XSD file for validating the message
- The `on-fail` tag has the mediator to execute in case the message is not correct

In the next example, we will validate all the content of the payload over the `XMLSchema.xsd`& XSD file and if the current message is not correct, create a log with the description of the error, format a SOAP fault message, and send it back to the client that makes the request to the service:

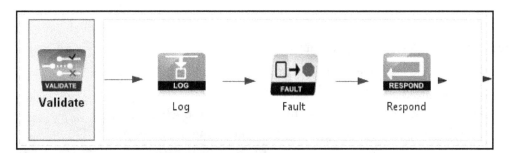

The validation is doing with the following source code:

```
<validate>
    <!-- Specify the XSD schema -->
    <schema key=" conf:/XMLSchema.xsd"/>
    <on-fail>
        <!-- Log the error in the server log -->
        <log level="custom">
            <property name="ERROR" value="Invalid Request"/>
        </log>
        <!-- Create a SOAP Fault message -->
        <makefault>
            <code value="tns:Receiver"
            xmlns:tns="http://www.w3.org/2003/05/soap-envelope"/>
            <reason value="Invalid Request"/>
        </makefault>
        <!-- Return message to the client -->
        <respond/>
    </on-fail>
</validate>
```

Validating JSON

In the same way, we can use the validate mediator to validate a complete JSON payload or a specific path over a JSON schema.

Here's the syntax:

```
<validate [source="JSONPath"]>
    [<resource location="string" key="string"/>+]
    <schema key="string"/>+
    <on-fail>
        mediator+
    </on-fail>
</validate>
```

Here, keep the following things in mind:

- `Source` is the JSONPath expression for the message to evaluate. When it is not configured, all of the payload will be evaluated.
- The resources include other files needed for the schema file.
- Schema references the JSON file for validating the message.
- The `on-fail` tag has the mediator to execute in case the message is not correct.

Following the preceding example, we will log and create a descriptive response message to send back to the client:

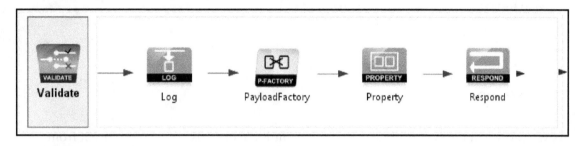

This is the source code for the JSON validation:

```
<validate source="json-eval($.rootElement)">
    <!-- Specify the JSON schema -->
    <schema key=" conf:/JSONSchema.json"/>
    <on-fail>
        <!-- Log the error in the server log -->
        <log level="custom">
            <property name="ERROR" value="Invalid Request"/>
        </log>
        <!-- Create a error message -->
        <payloadFactory media-type="json">
            <format>{"Error":"Invalid Request"}</format>
        </payloadFactory>
        <!-- Configure the HTTP code of the response -->
        <property name="HTTP_SC" value="500" scope="axis2"/>
        <!-- Return to the client -->
        <respond/>
    </on-fail>
</validate>
```

Boolean filtering

In our services, we can check boolean conditions in a simple way using the filter mediator, which performs actions such as the `if else` structure that we found in most of the programming languages. Once more, we can use this mediator for XML or JSON messages.

The following is the syntax:

```
<filter (source="[XPath|json-eval(JSONPath)]" regex="string") |
xpath="[XPath|json-eval(JSONPath)]">
   <then [sequence="string"]>
     mediator+
   </then>
   <else [sequence="string"]>
     mediator+
   </else>
</filter>
```

As we can see in the syntax, this mediator has multiple options, and we can use it from different configurations. The `else` tag is optional, and we can specify the logical behavior inline or with an external sequence.

In the first example, we will filter the incoming message depending on the HTTP method of the request. Imagine that we have a REST API that exposes the same resource for GET and POST methods. We can use the filter mediator to check if the request was done over the GET or POST method, and get the value of the parameters because every method has its specific way to do that. In that case, we are adding the logical inline inside the filter mediator:

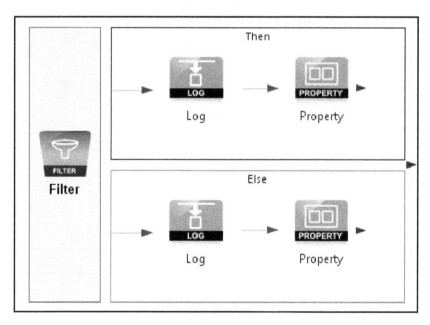

In the preceding figure, we can see that the different behavior depends on the HTTP method of the incoming request, which will execute the mediators inside then tags or the mediators inside else tags. In the following source code you can see different ways to get a parameter value depends on the HTTP method of the request.

```
<filter xpath="boolean($axis2:HTTP_METHOD = 'POST' )">
    <then>
        <log>
            <property name="Method" value="POST"></property>
        </log>
        <property name="flightID"
        expression="json-eval($.flightID)"/>
    </then>
    <else>
        <log>
            <property name="Method" value="GET"></property>
        </log>
        <property name="flightID"
        expression="$ctx:query.param.flightID"/>
    </else>
</filter>
```

In the next example, we will check whether a property is currently defined in the sequence; this will be useful for checking the mandatory parameters. Here, we are using the source and regex attributes instead of the xpath as in the preceding example, and the logical solution is stored in the external sequence, which can be reused for other services:

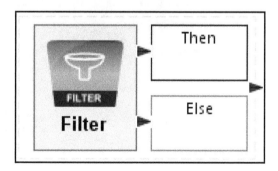

In this case, we don't have any mediators in the `then` or `else` tags, so the graphic editor will be shown empty. The mediators to execute when a request matches the filter condition is specified in a sequence called `invalidParams` stored in the registry in the `conf:/` path, and we don't have to set up any action when a request doesn't match the filter expression. This is the XML source code:

```
<filter source="boolean(get-property('flightID'))" regex="false">
<then sequence="conf:/invalidParams"></filter>
```

Also, we can check multiple parameters in the same filter mediator:

```
<filter source="boolean(get-property('flightID')) and boolean(get-property('date'))" regex="false">
```

Multiple filtering

In a lot of cases, we can cover our requirement with the filter mediator, but we can sometimes have more than two different parameters to compare. In this case, we need the switch mediator, which works similar to the filter mediator, but can handle N alternative cases.

We need to filter the payload by an XPath or JSONPath expression, and the string response will be checked against all the regex expressions of every `case` tag. When none of these cases match the condition, the mediator inside the `default` tag will be processed.

Let's look at the syntax:

```
<switch source="[XPath|json-eval(JSON Path)]">
  <case regex="string">
    mediator+
  </case>+
  <default>
    mediator+
  </default>?
</switch>
```

In the following example, we have a service that receives, among other information, the name of a country. With this name of the country gets its identified code and send it to a backend service. We need to create an expression to process the country name of the incoming message and use the switch mediator for creating the `case` tags with the code of the different country that we have, for storing the information of the code of each country:

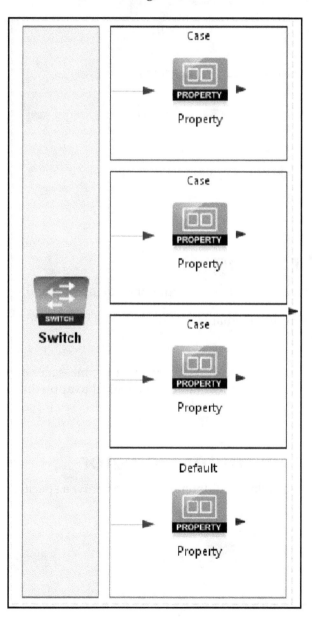

In the preceding image, we can see how to handle different options at the same time using the switch mediator. We can also do the same functionality using the filter mediator, but we need to use (at least) two mediators, with the inconveniences in the performance of the server. This is the source code associated:

```
<switch source="//Country/name">
  <case regex="Spain">
     <property name="code" value="ES"/>
  </case>
  <case regex="UK">
     <property name="code" value="GB"/>
  </case>
  <case regex="Germany">
     <property name="code" value="DE"/>
  </case>
  [...]
  <default>
     <property name="code" value="UNKNOWN"/>
  </default>
</switch>
```

Advanced routing

The Enterprise Integrator has two other mediators that are more powerful and complex:

- Conditional router mediator
- Rule mediator

These mediators allow us to create different rules for the messages and redirect the flow of the service to an existing sequence containing the logical to apply in every particular condition.

The conditional router mediator

With this mediator, we can define different rules and throw a specific sequence to process this request.

Let's look at the syntax:

```
<conditionalRouter continueAfter="(true|false)">
    <conditionalRoute breakRoute="(true|false)">
        <condition ../>
        <target ../>
    </conditionalRoute>+
</conditionalRouter>
```

Here, keep the following points in mind:

- `continueAfter` specifies whether the routing must continue when a child route is executed
- `breakRoute` configures whether a matching route will break the router
- Target contains the name of the sequence to execute

Inside the `condition` tag, we can use the information of the request to the service, such as headers, parameters, and URL, to check when a request must be over one condition or another. Also, we can configure multiple rules inside the condition using the `and`, `not`, and `or` expressions.

In the first example, we use a single condition that verifies that the service is `flight` and the operation is `get`. In order to do that, we need to check the URL of the request, as follows:

The graphical editor of the conditional router mediator doesn't give us too much information, but we can set up from the `properties` view as usual. The definition of the condition is defined as follows:

```
<conditionalRouter continueAfter="false">
<conditionalRoute breakRoute="false">
  <condition>
     <match xmlns="" type="url" regex="/flights/get.*"/>
  </condition>
  <target sequence="flights_IN_SEQ"/>
</conditionalRoute>
</conditionalRouter>
```

In the second example, we include a condition to verify that the request has a custom header called company with the value PacktAir:

```
<conditionalRouter continueAfter="false">
<conditionalRoute breakRoute="false">
  <condition>
     <and xmlns="">
        <match type="url" regex="/flights/get.*"/>
        <match type="header" source="company"
        regex="PacktAir"/>
     </and>
  </condition>
  <target sequence="PacktAir_IN_SEQ"/>
</conditionalRoute>
</conditionalRouter>
```

Now, we will add an or clause to match the request that has a parameter called company although not match the first rule:

```
<conditionalRouter continueAfter="false">
  <conditionalRoute breakRoute="false">
  <condition>
     <and xmlns="">
        <match type="url" regex="/flights/get.*"/>
        <match type="header" source="company"
        regex="PacktAir"/>
     </and>
     <or>
        <equal type="param" source="company" value="PacktAir"/>
     </or>
  </condition>
  <target sequence="PacktAir_IN_SEQ"/>
  </conditionalRoute>
</conditionalRouter>
```

For the last example, we also verify that the request doesn't include any specific parameter:

```
<conditionalRouter continueAfter="false">
  <conditionalRoute breakRoute="false">
   <condition>
      <and xmlns="">
         <match type="url" regex="/flights/get.*"/>
         <match type="header" source="company"
         regex="PacktAir"/>
      </and>
      <or>
         <equal type="param" source="company"
         value="PacktAir"/>
      </or>
      <not>
         <equal type="param" source="next24Hr"
         value="false"/>
      </not>
   </condition>
   <target sequence="PacktAir_IN_SEQ"/>
  </conditionalRoute>
</conditionalRouter>
```

The rule mediator

This mediator is similar to the previous one, but it offers us more options and processes, so we can handle complex scenarios that we can't achieve with the conditional router.

This is the syntax:

```
<rule>
   <ruleset>
      <source [ key="xs:string" ]>
         [ in-Lined ]
      </source>
      <creation>
         <property name="xs:string" value="xs:string"/>*
      </creation>
   </ruleset>

   <session type="[stateless|stateful]"/>*

   <facts>
      <fact name="xs:string" type="xs:string"
      expression="xs:string" value="xs:string"/>+
   </facts>
```

```
<results>
   <result name="xs:string" type="xs:string"
   expression="xs:string" value="xs:string"/>*
</results>

[<childMediators>
   <mediator/>*
</childMediators>]

</rule>
```

Here, keep the following points in mind:

- The `Ruleset` contains the list of rules to apply
- The `session` configures the type of session
- The `facts` are sent by the rule service client
- The `results` is the information after applying the rules
- The `ChildMediators` contains the logical to apply

In the next example, we will use the rule mediator to read the name of the country of the incoming request and then obtain the code associated with that country, in a similar way that we did earlier using the switch mediator:

```
<rule xmlns="http://wso2.org/carbon/rules">
   <source>soapBody</source>
   <target action="replace"
       resultXpath="//country::text()">$country</target>
   <ruleSet>
      <properties/>
      <rule resourceType="regular" sourceType="inline">
         <![CDATA[
            rule "Country ES" no-loop true
            when
               country: String()eval(country.equals("Spain"))
            then
                     update(drools.getWorkingMemory()
                     .getFactHandle(country),"ES");
            end
            rule "Country GB" no-loop true
            when
               country: String()eval(country.equals("UK"))
            then
                     update(drools.getWorkingMemory()
                     .getFactHandle(country),"GB");
            end
```

```
            rule "Country DE" no-loop true
            when
            country: String()eval(country.equals("Germany"))
            then
                    update(drools.getWorkingMemory()
                    .getFactHandle(country),"DE");
            end
        ]]>
    </rule>
</ruleSet>
<input wrapperElementName="flights">
    <fact elementName="country" type="java.lang.String"
    xpath="//country::text()"/>
</input>
<output wrapperElementName="flights">
    <fact elementName="country" type="java.lang.String"/>
</output>
</rule>
```

Summary

This chapter helped us know how to create more intelligent services that can route the flow over different ways, depending on the parameters, the URL, headers, and so on. In order to do that, we covered the use of five Enterprise Integrator mediators that are complementary to each other.

The first mediator that we learned to use is the validate mediator, which we will use to check the payload over a schema. This will be very useful when verifying that the incoming request to a service is well formed.

Then, we took a look at the filter and switch mediators, which we use to check the payload, or a part of it, over a regex expression. Evaluating the string response, we can perform different actions in our services with external sequences or inline mediators.

Ultimately, we saw the advanced conditional router and rule mediators, in which we can define a list of rules over the messages and customize the behavior of the service for that particular case.

In the next chapter, we will go over the quality of service configuration in depth to learn how to configure security in the services, apply throttling policies such as specifying a maximum number of requests that can be done for a user in a period of time, and how to use the cache for improving the performance in the servers, among other things.

7
Quality of Service

In the last chapter, we learned to create more advanced services that can perform different actions depending on some external information such as query parameters, input requests, body, or headers. `Chapter 6`, *Conditional Route,* was the last chapter of the series of chapters with the main purpose of adding functionality to the services. Now in this chapter, we will focus on the quality of services, in which we will discover how to configure our services with security, throttling, and caching in order to create more realistic services with better performance and real-world security scenarios. With the security configuration, we can set up 16 different scenarios for handling the basic principles of security: authentication, availability, confidentiality, integrity, and non-repudiation:

1. **Authentication**: The act of verifying that one user is really that user and is not trying to spoof another user.
2. **Availability**: The services must be available for the users when they are needed.
3. **Confidentiality**: The services are only available to the users who have the permissions to consume them.
4. **Integrity**: The data of the services cannot be modified in an unauthorized or undetected manner.
5. **Nonrepudiation**: The service consumer cannot deny having received a response from the service or deny the request to the service.

When we speak about throttling, it means the different policies to apply to the incoming requests to avoid heavy loads that can cause performance issues in the server and also restrict access to an IP address or domain of a service. For example, we can define a throttling policy for a traffic service, in which users of the same city can make 100 requests per hour, but the outside users can perform only 10 requests per hour. In this way, we are offering the same service to all the users, but we are giving priority to the users of the same city to obtain information about the traffic jams in their city.

Caching is a tool that helps WSO2 improve the performance of our services. The operation is simple--when the server receives a request, it checks whether the same request has already been triggered before processing it. If it has been triggered, the server responds with the same result of the previous request. So, the server does not need to perform all the logic in the service, and it's free to work with other services and requests as well.

Security

In this section, we will cover all the related stuff where we need to use security in our integrations, such as creating secured services or consuming a secured backend with different technologies.

Security scenarios

In this section, we will explain the different scenarios provided for WSO2 by default so as to handle all the security use cases. We need to use the WSO2 Tooling IDE to create the policies, and deploy and apply them to the services in the Enterprise Integrator server. In the previous version of Enterprise Service Bus, it was possible to configure some of these properties directly in the web console of each proxy, but this feature has been deleted from the portal for security reasons.

This 16 scenarios are the most commonly used in all environments; nevertheless, we can create our custom security policy if our requirements aren't covered by the previous one. The list of all of the integration scenarios can be found on the WSO2 official documentation page at: `https://docs.wso2.com/display/EI611/Security+Implementation`.

Scenario 1: UsernameToken

This is the simplest and most used scenario, in which the user sends the UsernameToken in the message, and it's validated against the user stores setting up in the EI server. This scenario provides us with an authentication and authorization security environment, because we can define the roles that will have permission to consume the final service:

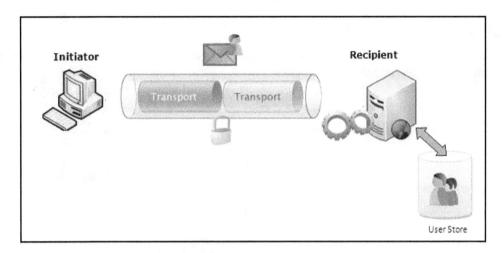

Scenario 2: Non-repudiation

In this scenario, the clients must have an X.509 certificate to sign the messages with its private key and then the receiver can check the client using the client's public key:

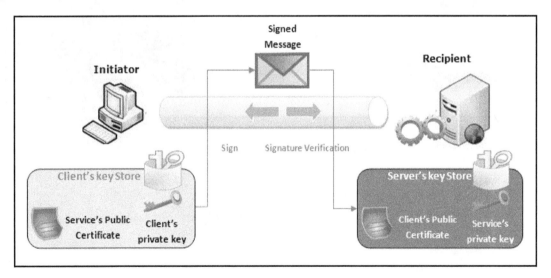

Scenario 3: Integrity

The client generates a symmetric key and sign the message with that key. Then, it encrypts the symmetric key with the service's public key and sends it inside the SOAP message. This way, the only one that can decrypt the symmetric key and check the signature of the message is the service, using their private key:

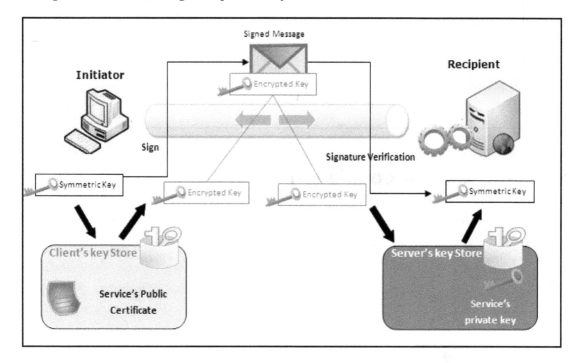

Scenario 4: Confidentiality

The client generates a symmetric key and encrypts the message with that key. Then, it encrypts the symmetric key with the service's public key and send it inside the SOAP message. The service decrypts the symmetric key using their private key, and with this symmetric key, decrypts the message:

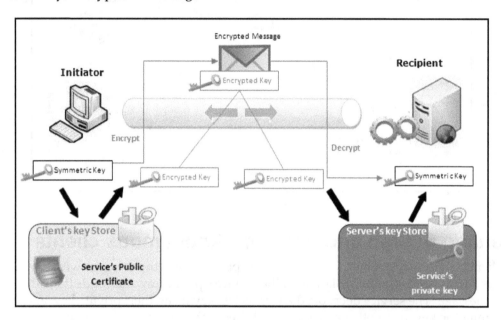

Scenario 5: Sign and encrypt - X509 authentication

The client encrypts the message using the service public key and signs it using their private key. The service decrypts the message using their private key and checks the signature over the client public key.

In this scenario, the client and the server needs to have the public certificate of the other part in their key store:

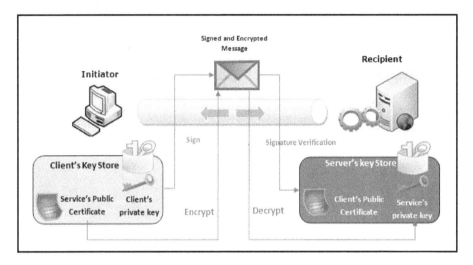

Scenario 6: Sign and encrypt - Anonymous clients

The client generates a symmetric key, and encrypts and signs the message with that key. Then, it encrypts the symmetric key with the service's public key and sends it inside the SOAP message. The service decrypts the symmetric key using their private key, and with this symmetric key, decrypts the message and checks the signature:

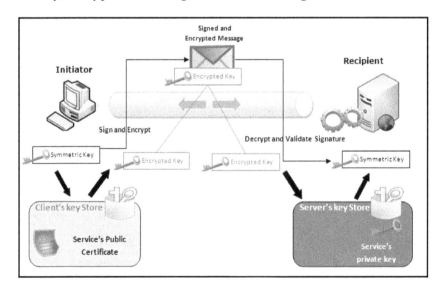

Scenario 7: Encrypt only - UsernameToken authentication

This scenario is a mix between the *Scenario 1: UsernameToken* and *Scenario 4: Confidentiality*. The client generates a symmetric key and encrypts the message with that key. Then, it encrypts the symmetric key with the service's public key and sends it inside the SOAP message. The service decrypts the symmetric key using their private key and with this symmetric key, decrypts the message. The user sends the UsernameToken in the message, and it's validated against the user stores setting up in the EI server:

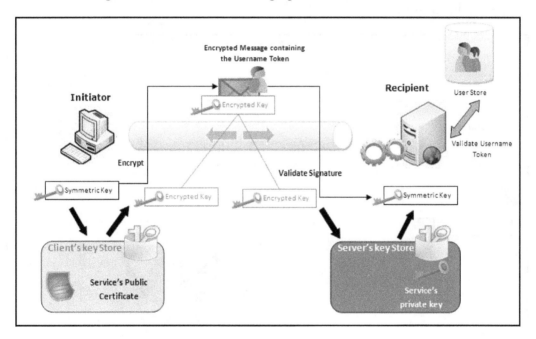

Scenario 8: Sign and encrypt - UsernameToken authentication

This scenario is a mix between the *Scenario 1: UsernameToken* and *Scenario 6: Sign and encrypt - Anonymous clients*. The client generates a symmetric key, and encrypts and signs the message with that key. Then, it encrypts the symmetric key with the service's public key and sends it inside the SOAP message. The service decrypts the symmetric key using their private key, and with this symmetric key, decrypts the message and checks the signature. The user sends the UsernameToken in the message, and it's validated against the user stores setting up in the EI server:

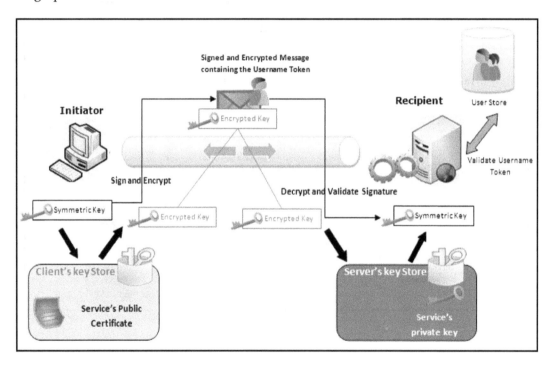

Scenario 9: Secure conversation - Sign only - Service as STS - Bootstrap policy - Sign and encrypt, X509 authentication

This scenario establishes a security context between the client and the service using the X.509 certificates. All the communication in the security context is signed using the keys from the security context:

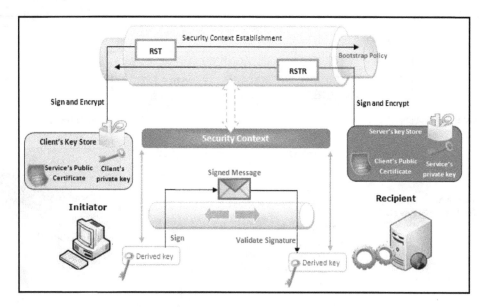

Scenario 10: Secure conversation - Sign only - Service as STS - Bootstrap policy - Sign and encrypt, anonymous clients

This scenario is equal to the previous one, with the only difference being that the messages inside the security context are encrypted instead of signed. With that difference, the environment is safer because the message is not visible to third parties:

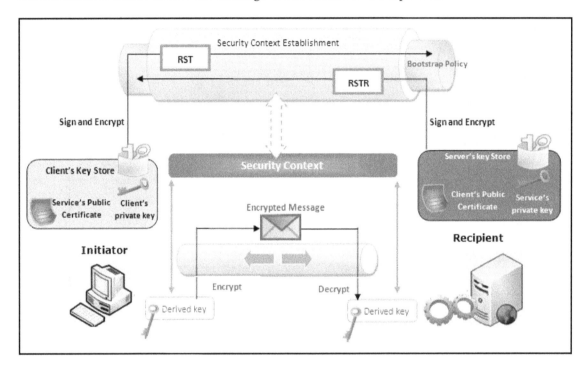

Scenario 11: Secure conversation - Sign and Encrypt - Service as STS - Bootstrap policy - Sign and encrypt, X509 authentication

This scenario, is a mix between scenario 9 and scenario 10, in which all the messages inside the security context are signed and also encrypted; for that reason, this scenario is the most complete of these three scenarios:

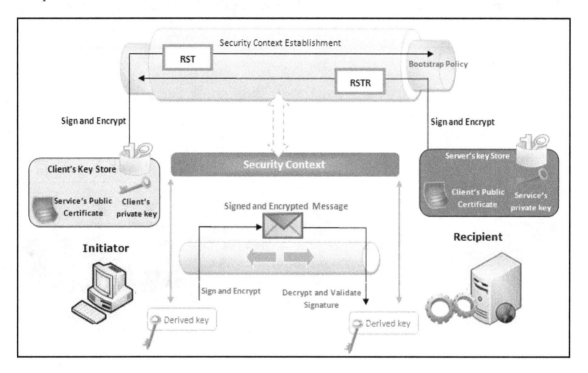

Scenario 12: Secure conversation - Sign only - Service as STS - Bootstrap policy - Sign and encrypt, anonymous clients

In this scenario we also have a security context between the client and the service, but the client doesn't have a X.509 certificate, so the context is established using a symmetric key.

All the communication in the security context is signed using the keys from the security context:

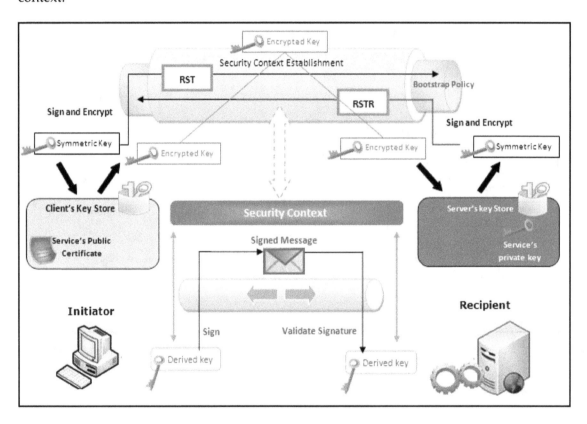

Scenario 13: Secure conversation - Sign and Encrypt - Service as STS - Bootstrap policy - Sign and encrypt, anonymous clients

This scenario is equal to the previous one, with the only difference being that the messages inside the security context are encrypted instead of signed:

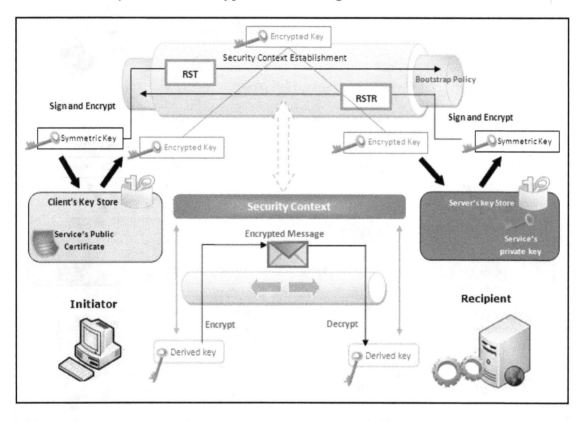

Scenario 14: Secure conversation - Encrypt only - Service as STS - Bootstrap policy - Sign and encrypt, UsernameToken authentication

This scenario is equal to the previous one, with the only difference being that the user is authenticated with the UsernameToken when establishing the security context:

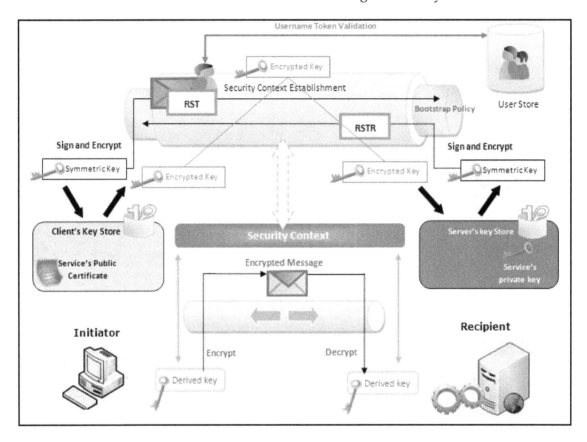

Scenario 15: Secure conversation - Sign and encrypt - Service as STS - Bootstrap policy - Sign and encrypt, UsernameToken authentication

This scenario is equal to the previous one, with the only difference being that the messages inside the security context are signed and encrypted instead of only encrypted:

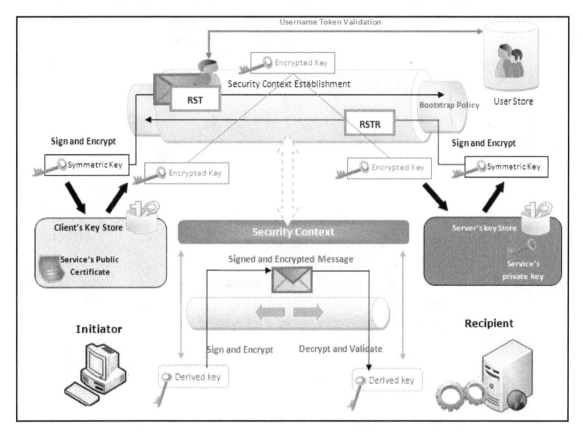

Scenario 16: Kerberos token-based security

For this scenario, we need a **Key Distribution Center** (**KDC**) and an authentication server to connect to our services. In the `<EI_HOME>/repository/conf/security` path, we found two configuration files named `krb5.conf`, with the KDC server configuration, and `jass.conf`, with authorization configuration:

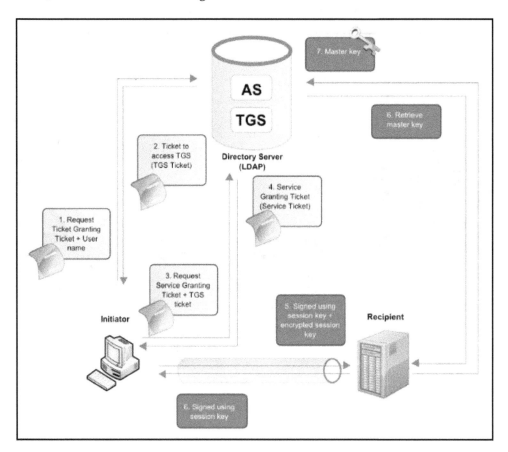

Securing the transport

The first thing that we need to configure when we want to provide security to our services is the transport layer, because our network can be vulnerable to evil attacks such as man in the middle, spoofing, poisoning, and so on.

For secure communication, we can use the **Secure Sockets Layer** (**SSL**) and **Transport Layer Security** (**TLS**) protocols that will encrypt the messages between the sender and receiver, restricting access to the information for a third, unauthorized party.

These protocols use the **Public Key Infrastructure** (**PKI**) scenario, in which the certificates are used to encrypt and sign the communication and have a secured way for the information.

Creating a certificate for the EI server

By default, all the WSO2 servers are configured with a certificate for localhost that is not bad for testing purposes in a local machine, but not enough for the other environments. If we don't create and configure a valid certificate in the server, the users will get an error for invalid certificate, which you can see in the following image:

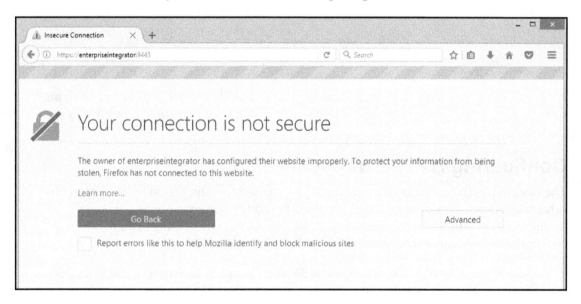

In order to create a valid certificate for the server, we will use the `keytool` program, which is the default program that provides us with Java inside the **Java Development Kit** (**JDK**) to work with keystores and certificates.

In the creation, we need to specify the algorithms, time of validity, password, and so on. In the following example, you can see the whole process to create a valid certificate.

Consider the following example:

```
$ keytool -genkeypair -alias EnterpriseIntegrator -keyalg RSA -keysize 2048
-sigalg SHA1withRSA -validity 365 -keypass wso2carbon -keystore
EnterpriseIntegrator.jks -storepass wso2carbon -ext
ku:c=digitalSignature,nonRepudiation,keyEncipherment,dataEncipherment

What is your first and last name?
  [Unknown]:  enterpriseintegrator
What is the name of your organizational unit?
  [Unknown]:  EI
What is the name of your organization?
  [Unknown]:  packtpub
What is the name of your City or Locality?
  [Unknown]:  Seville
What is the name of your State or Province?
  [Unknown]:  Andalusia
What is the two-letter country code for this unit?
  [Unknown]:  ES
Is CN=192.168.1.37, OU=EI, O=packtpub, L=Seville, ST=Andalusia, C=ES
correct?
  [no]:  yes
```

After executing this command, a keystore will be created in the same directory with the name `EnterpriseIntegrator.jks`, which will contain the private and public keys.

Configuring HTTPS transport

The next step is to configure this certificate just created for being used by the Enterprise Integrator server. In order to do that, we need to modify the `keystoreFile` and `keystorePass` properties in the `<WSO2_HOME>/conf/tomcat/catalinaserver.xml` configuration file inside the connector with the `9443` port.

 In general, all the changes in the configuration files need a restart in the server in order to be applied.

This certificate is self-signed, so we will need to add a trusted certificate in the browser to avoid the annoying message of error.

We need to add the created certificate to the `truststore.jks keystore`. The first step is to export the certificate with the same `keytool` program with the following command:

```
keytool -export -alias EnterpriseIntegrator -file EI.cer -keystore
EnterpriseIntegrator.jks -storepass wso2carbon
```

Then, import it in the `truststore.jks` with the command:

```
keytool -import -alias EnterpriseIntegrator -file EI.cer -keystore client-
truststore.jks -storepass wso2carbon
```

 The default path for the keystores in Enterprise Integrator is
`<WSO2_HOME>/repository/resources/security`.

The following file to configure is `<WSO2_HOME>/conf/axis2/axis2.xml`, in which we need to configure the HTTPS `transportReceiver` and `transportSender` with the new keystore.

Securing REST APIs

By default, Enterprise Integrator does not provide any authentication method for the REST APIs, so we need to create a Java program with the logic of the authentication, generate a `.jar` project, deploy to the server in the `<WSO2_HOME>/lib` folder, and configure the APIs to use this project like `handler`.

Basic authentication

In the basic authentication scenario, the consumer will send the `username` and `password` in the `Authorization` header of the request. This header has the `username:password` structure codified in the `base64` format. In the Java class, we get the credentials as follows:

```
String authHeader = (String) headersMap.get("Authorization");
String credentials = authHeader.substring(6).trim();
String decodedCredentials = new String(new
Base64().decode(credentials.getBytes()));
String userName = decodedCredentials.split(":")[0];
String password = decodedCredentials.split(":")[1];
```

In the API, we need to configure the handler with the Java package and class that contains the logic to perform the basic authentication, as in the next example:

```
<api xmlns="http://ws.apache.org/ns/synapse" name="flights"
context="/flights">
    <resource methods="POST" uri-template="/get?from={from}&
to={to}&date={date}">
        <inSequence>
            mediators...
        </inSequence>
    </resource>
    <handlers>
        <handler class="org.wso2.rest.BasicAuthHandler"/>
    </handlers>
</api>
```

 You can find the Maven project with the source code and the compiled JAR in the `resources` folder of the chapter.

Authentication against WSO2 Identity Server

The Enterprise Integrator has a mediator that allows us to check the credentials against the WSO2 Identity Server using the OAuth protocol. We will need to create and configure an OAuth application in the Identity Server and use the OAuth mediator in our services; then, when we get a request with the **Authorization** header, the server will send a request to the Identity Server and check whether the credentials provided are correct.

The syntax of the mediator is simple:

```
<oauthService remoteServiceUrl="" username="" password=""/>
```

Here, note the following:

- `remoteServiceUrl` is the URL of the Identity Server

- `username` and `password` are the credentials to log into the WSO2 Identity Server

Consider this example:

```
<oauthService xmlns="http://ws.apache.org/ns/synapse"
remoteServiceUrl="https://localhost:9443/services" username="admin"
password="admin" />
```

Securing SOAP Proxies

For creating a secured SOAP Proxy, we need to use the WSO2 EI Tooling and configure three different projects, each one with its concrete functionality:

- **ESB Config Project**: This project will contain the proxy definition
- **Registry Resources Project**: Will get the security policy
- **Composite Application Project**: This is the project to create the `.car` file deployable to the server

The process to create the policy is to select a **Registry Resource** in the Developer Studio dashboard, and then configure the policy over a WS-Policy template:

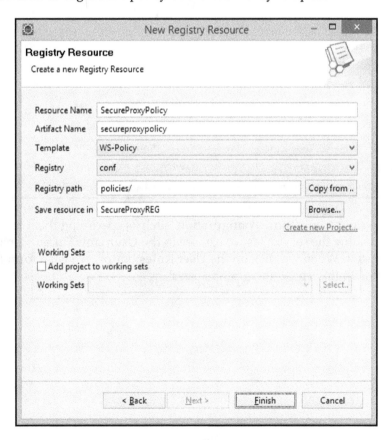

This policy will give us a wizard drive menu to select and configure the security scenario to apply to the policy:

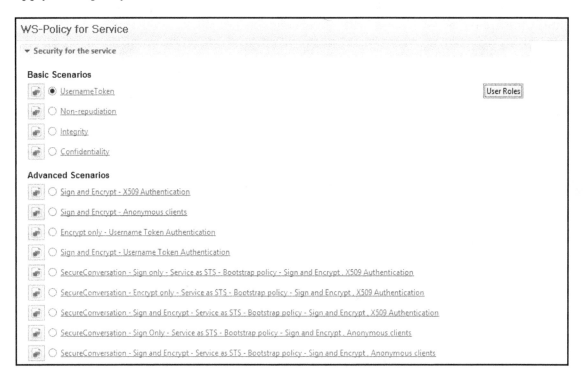

Some of the scenarios require more configuration, such as specifying the roles that have permission to consume the service, as we can see in the **UsernameToken** scenario of the preceding screenshot. When we click on the **User Roles** button, we get a form for getting the remote roles of an Enterprise Integrator server:

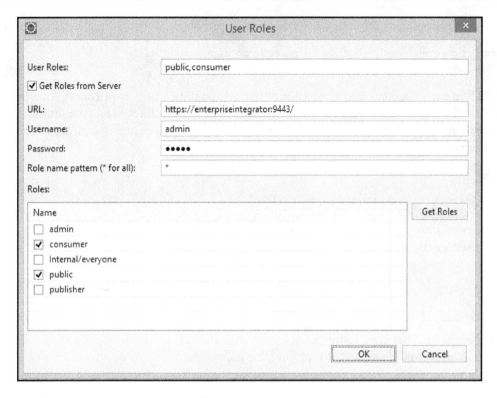

In the proxy, we need to configure two properties:

- **Security Enabled**: Set to `true`
- **Service Policies**: Set the path to the previous policy

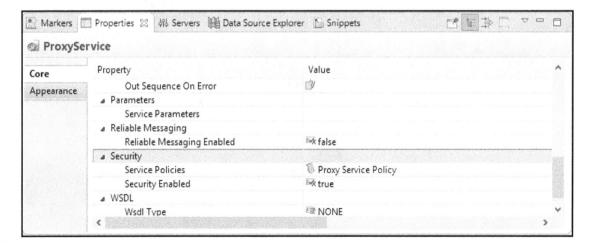

This configuration adds the following code to our proxy:

```
<policy key="conf:policies/SecureProxyPolicy.xml"/>
<enableSec/>
```

The last thing we need to do is to configure the composite carbon application with the proxy and the policy, generate the `.car` file, and deploy it to the server. Automatically, the server will get the policy definition inside the registry and the proxy is secured at the time of deployment.

Invoking secure backend

In this section, our service can be secured or it can't, it doesn't matter, the focus here is the backend server that we want to consume. The backend service can be secured in different ways, so let's take a look.

Basic-auth authentication

To invoke a secure backend using a basic authentication, we need to send a header called `Authorization` in the request, containing the username and password joined with : and encoded in `Base64`:

```
<!-- Define the username -->
<property name="username" value="USERNAME_OF_BACKEND" scope="default"
type="STRING" xmlns="http://ws.apache.org/ns/synapse"/>

<!-- Define the password -->
<property name="password" value="PASSWORD_OF_BACKEND" scope="default"
type="STRING" xmlns="http://ws.apache.org/ns/synapse"/>

<!-- Configure the header with the above parameters -->
<property expression="fn:concat('Basic ',
base64Encode(fn:concat($ctx:username,':',$ctx:password)))"
name="Authorization" scope="transport" type="STRING"
xmlns="http://ws.apache.org/ns/synapse"/>
```

OAuth authentication

For OAuth authentication, the process is similar to the previous one, with the difference being that we need to send the token instead of the credentials:

```
<!-- Define the Oauth token -->
<property name="token" value="OAUTH_TOKEN" scope="default" type="STRING"
xmlns="http://ws.apache.org/ns/synapse"/>

<!-- Configure the header with the above parameters -->
<property expression="fn:concat('Bearer ',$ctx:token)" name="Authorization"
scope="transport" type="STRING" xmlns="http://ws.apache.org/ns/synapse"/>
```

Getting a token from the WSO2 API manager

We can get this OAuth token from the WSO2 API manager server if we want to perform a request to an API deployed in that server. This server has some useful web services that we can invoke from the Enterprise Integrator server; one of these services returns us a valid token. We will need a valid consumer key and consumer secret to generate a token:

```
<!-- Required properties -->
<property value="XXXX" name="CONSUMER_KEY" scope="default" type="STRING"/>
<property value="YYYY" name="CONSUMER_SECRET" scope="default"
type="STRING"/>
<property
expression="fn:concat($ctx:CONSUMER_KEY,':',$ctx:CONSUMER_SECRET)"
name="accessTokenKey" scope="default" type="STRING"/>
<property expression="base64Encode($ctx:accessTokenKey)"
name="encodedAccessTokenKey" scope="default" type="STRING"/>
<property expression="fn:concat('Basic ',$ctx:encodedAccessTokenKey)"
name="Authorization" scope="transport" type="STRING"/>
<property name="ContentType" scope="axis2" type="STRING"
value="application/x-www-form-urlencoded"/>
<send>
    <endpoint>
        <http method="post" uri-
template="http://<AM_HOST>:<AM_PORT>/token?grant_type=client_credentials"/>
    </endpoint>
</send>
```

The response of the service will have the following message format:

```
{"token_type":"Bearer","expires_in":2061,"access_token":"ca19a540f544777860
e44e75f605d927"}
```

We can parse the preceding message format using an XPath expression:

```
<property expression="//*[local-name()='access_token']" name="accessToken"
scope="default" type="STRING" />
<property expression="//*[local-name()='expires_in']" name="expiresin"
scope="default" type="STRING" />
```

WS-Security

When we have a secure SOAP backend service, we need to specify the policy to apply the required security and then configure the endpoint to use this policy in the communication flow:

```
 <!-- Define the security policy -->
<localEntry key="securityPolicy" src="path/to/policy"/>

<!-- Define the security policy -->
<send>
<address uri="http://enterpriseintegrator:8280/ flights/list"
format="soap11">
    <enableAddressing/>
    <enableSec policy="securityPolicy"/>
</address>
</send>
```

In the out sequence, we must delete the security header:

```
<header
xmlns:wsse="http://docs.oasis-open.org/wss/2004/01/oasis-200401-wss-wssecur
ity-secext-1.0.xsd" name="wsse:Security" action="remove"/>
```

Throttling

The WSO2 Enterprise Integrator has a mediator called `throttle` that is useful to restrict the use of the services or give priority to specific groups of users defined by IP addresses or domains.

Here's the syntax:

```
<throttle [onReject="string"] [onAccept="string"] id="string">
    (<policy key="string"/> | <policy>..</policy>)
    <onReject>..</onReject>?
    <onAccept>..</onAccept>?
</throttle>
```

We can divide the mediator into three sections:

- **Policy definition**: Here's where we define the policies to apply to the incoming requests. The policies can be written in-line or referred in the registry.
- **On rejection**: When a request does not follow the rules defined in the policy, the mediators in this section will be triggered. In this section, we usually send a descriptive message to the consumer or store the invalid request in a database for later analysis.
- **On acceptance**: This section contains the mediators to execute when the incoming request is good; it means that they follow the configured policies. We can define these mediators in-line or specify an external sequence, in the acceptance and rejection section as well.

In the following example, we will set up a restriction for the IP `192.168.1.37` to send only five requests per minute to the proxy:

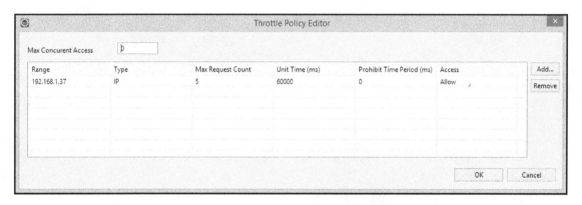

To test the throttling mediator, we will print a message in the log that will tell us whether the incoming request was for the on acceptance or rejection section. The sample throttling mediator is as follows:

```
<throttle id="testingThrottling">
    <policy>
        <wsp:Policy wsu:id="WSO2MediatorThrottlingPolicy"
        xmlns:wsp="http://schemas.xmlsoap.org/ws/2004/09/policy"
        xmlns:wsu="http://docs.oasis-open.org/wss/2004/01/oasis-
        200401-wss-wssecurity-utility-1.0.xsd">
            <throttle:MediatorThrottleAssertion
            xmlns:throttle="http://www.wso2.org/products
            /wso2commons/throttle">
<throttle:MaximumConcurrentAccess>0
                </throttle:MaximumConcurrentAccess>
```

```
                <wsp:Policy>
                   <throttle:ID throttle:type="IP">192.168.1.37
                      </throttle:ID>
                   <wsp:Policy>
                      <throttle:Control>
                         <wsp:Policy>
                            <throttle:MaximumCount> 5
                            </throttle:MaximumCount>
                            <throttle:UnitTime> 60000
                            </throttle:UnitTime>
                            <throttle:ProhibitTimePeriod> 0
                            </throttle:ProhibitTimePeriod>
                         </wsp:Policy>
                      </throttle:Control>
                   </wsp:Policy>
                </wsp:Policy>
             </throttle:MediatorThrottleAssertion>
          </wsp:Policy>
      </policy>
      <onReject>
         <log>
            <property name="Throttle" value="onReject"/>
         </log>
      </onReject>
      <onAccept>
         <log>
            <property name="Throttle" value="onAccept"/>
         </log>
      </onAccept>
   </throttle>
```

Now when we make some request to the service, we can see the following log, which has changed the mediation sequence after the first five requests:

```
INFO - LogMediator Throttle = onAccept
INFO - LogMediator Throttle = onAccept
INFO - LogMediator Throttle = onAccept
INFO - LogMediator Throttle = onAccept
INFO - LogMediator Throttle = onAccept
INFO - AccessRateController You cannot access this service since you have
exceeded the allocated quota.
INFO - LogMediator Throttle = onReject
```

Caching

The main objective of the cache mediator is to prevent the server from wasting time, and from overload by processing a request that has already been received and processed in advance.

Let's look at the syntax:

```
<cache [id="string"] [hashGenerator="class"] [timeout="seconds"]
[scope=(per-host | per-mediator)] collector=(true | false)
[maxMessageSize="in-bytes"]>
   <onCacheHit [sequence="key"]>
     (mediator)+
   </onCacheHit>?
   <implementation type=(memory | disk) maxSize="int"/>
</cache>
```

When the service receives the same request processed earlier, it executes the onCacheHit sequence, which can be defined online or referred to from an existing sequence.

To use the cache mediator, we need to configure two places for the services:

- **In sequence**: To check the requests: collector="false"
- **Out sequence**: To store the result of the service: collector="true"

In the next example, we will use a cache mediator inside the API to store the result and improve the performance of the server:

```
<api xmlns="http://ws.apache.org/ns/synapse" name="flights"
context="/flights">
   <resource methods="GET" url-mapping="/list">
      <inSequence>
         <log>
            <property name="inSequence" value="***"/>
         </log>
         <cache scope="per-host" collector="false"
         hashGenerator="org.wso2.carbon.mediator.cache
         .digest.DOMHASHGenerator" timeout="20">
            <onCacheHit>
               <log>
                  <property name="message cached" value="***"/>
               </log>
               <respond/>
            </onCacheHit>
            <implementation type="memory" maxSize="100"/>
         </cache>
```

```
            <payloadFactory media-type="xml">
                <format>
                    <flights xmlns="">
                        <flight>
                            <company>PacktAir</company>
                            <time>10:30</time>
                            <price>£ 300</price>
                        </flight>
                    </flights>
                </format>
                <args/>
            </payloadFactory>
            <loopback/>
        </inSequence>
        <outSequence>
            <log>
                <property name="outsequence" value="***"/>
            </log>
            <cache scope="per-host" collector="true"/>
            <respond/>
        </outSequence>
    </resource>
</api>
```

All the requests to that API will return the same flight in the XML format:

```
<flights>
    <flight>
        <company>PacktAir</company>
        <time>10:30</time>
        <price>£ 300</price>
    </flight>
</flights>
```

However, if we take a look at the console log output, we will realise that the first request prints these logs:

```
INFO - API Initializing API: flights
INFO - LogMediator MessageID: urn:uuid:78c60ea1-7d57-4363-b0a1-
cc5b17144802, Direction: request, inSequence = ***
INFO - LogMediator MessageID: urn:uuid:78c60ea1-7d57-4363-b0a1-
cc5b17144802, Direction: response, outsequence = ***
```

This means that the service is processing the request, because we can see the log in the in sequence and the out sequence. Nevertheless, for the following request, the output log will show this:

```
INFO - LogMediator MessageID: urn:uuid:9e9d464a-3c49-48c2-977f-
a71f551fe154, Direction: request, inSequence = ***
INFO - LogMediator MessageID: urn:uuid:9e9d464a-3c49-48c2-977f-
a71f551fe154, Direction: response, message cached = ***
```

This means that the service is not processing the mediators, and is just returning the same payload as for the previous response. You can see the `message cached` log instead of `outsequence`.

Summary

In this chapter, we learned how to work with security of the services in two different roles: one to consume secure backend services over basic, OAuth, and WS-Security authentication, and the other to expose our services with security and not be available to all the users. In that way, we created a certificate and configured our server to use for the HTTPS communication over SSL/TLS to provide more security in the transport layer, and go deep in setting up the APIs and Proxies. One important thing is to have all the scenarios that WSO2 provides us with to configure the services clearly, because we will need to use one of them based on our requirement.

In this chapter, we introduced the throttle mediator that allows us to create complex policies based on IP addresses and domains, and we can set up the maximum number of requests that can be performed in a specific unit time, or even block all the requests; for example, expose a financial service only for the financial team and not for the commercial team.

The cache mediator is another advanced mediator that is really easy to use and can provide us a lot of benefits over the performance of the servers. It is always a good idea to use this mediator in complex services that take a long time in processing requests. They have many requests, although only in peaks, and the response doesn't have changes.

In the next chapter, we will learn how to schedule tasks in the Enterprise Integrator, that is common feature in SOA environments to execute daily heavy processes in the night when the servers are idler, instead of executing them in the day where the performance can affect the final users.

8
Tasks Scheduling

In this chapter, we will focus on the options we have for scheduling tasks inside the Enterprise Integrator server. The task scheduler is an important mechanism in integration scenarios because it gives us the opportunity to perform some actions automatically and at specific times. It will be very useful for launching big services that consume huge amounts of the server's resources; however, it will not be possible to execute it when there are final users consuming other services on the same server, because the server will have low performance. To remedy this, we can create a scheduled task for these types of service and execute it when the server is idle, at midnight for example.

In the Enterprise Integrator, we have three different types of scheduled tasks:

- DSS task
- ESB task
- Custom task

In this chapter, we will see the differences between them and the occasions where we need to use one or the other. **Data Services Server (DSS)** tasks are for scheduling the data services in the schedule system that we have in the old Data Services Server of WSO2. With ESB tasks, we can schedule tasks for proxy services, sequences, and endpoints, like we did in the **Enterprise Service Bus (ESB)** server.

We can also create a custom task implementation that will perform a specific action when it is executed. We will look at the steps needed to develop, deploy, and use it in the Enterprise Integrator server.

In this chapter, we will cover the following topics:

- Standalone server configuration
- Clustered environment configuration
- Integration services schedule tasks
- Data services scheduled tasks
- Custom task creation

Configuring the server

For using the tasks, the EI server uses a configuration file called `tasks-config.xml`, stored in the `<EI_HOME>/conf/etc` directory. This file is pre-setup with the default values for a basic usage of this feature. In this section, we will take a look at the options that we can configure inside this file and the different values, depending on the environment and the requirements we have.

Setting the server mode

The first property to configure in this file is under the `taskServerMode` tag, which specifies the mode of the Enterprise Integrator server. We can set the value of this property to the following options:

- `STANDALONE`: The Enterprise Integrator is running in a simple server instance. For example, when we download the server and start it without more configurations, we are using a standalone architecture. In this option, the tasks will be managed locally.
- `CLUSTERED`: In this case, we have a set of servers that work together for better performance and scalability, which is called a cluster environment. When we configure the tasks for a clustered environment, the tasks will be rescheduled to another server when a server fails.
- `AUTO`: This is the default option configured in the file. The server checks at start up whether clustering is enabled in the system for setting up the `CLUSTERED` or `STANDALONE` mode.

Configuring a clustered task server

Only when we have configured a `clustered` task mode, as mentioned in the previous step, can we set up the parameters that we will focus on in this section.

The `<taskServerCount>` tag is an integer field used to specify the total number of servers that comprise the cluster environment. The tasks will be waiting until the total number of servers configured in this property are active before scheduling it. In other cases, all the tasks will be scheduled in the first server that starts.

The next property to configure is `<defaultLocationResolver>`, which can handle the procedure for scheduling the tasks between all the nodes of the cluster. We can choose from the following options:

- `RoundRobinTaskLocationResolver`: The tasks are scheduled using a round robin algorithm; it means the tasks are distributed proportionally between all the servers.

- `RandomTaskLocationResolver`: With a random algorithm, the tasks are allocated under the nodes. With this configuration, it's possible that some servers are busier than others.

- `RuleBasedLocationResolver`: We can define a list of rules to allocate tasks based on their type and name.

Consider the following example:

```
<defaultLocationResolver>
    <locationResolverClass>
    org.wso2.carbon.ntask.core.impl.RuleBasedLocationResolver
    </locationResolverClass>
    <properties>
        <property name="rule-1">
            HIVE_TASK,HTTP_SCRIPT*,192.168.1.*
        </property>
        <property name="rule-2">
            HIVE_TASK,.*,192.168.2.*
        </property>
    </properties>
</defaultLocationResolver>
```

In this example, we defined two rules, named `rule-1` and `rule-2`, which will be processed sequentially; so, if the first rule matches, it will be triggered without processing the second one.

The properties will have the following structure:

```
<property name="rule name">
task type pattern, task name pattern, address pattern of the server node
<property>
```

Scheduling integration services

This scheduled task is based on the Enterprise Service Bus server tasks, with which we can schedule different artifacts, such as sequences, proxy services, or endpoints. The wizard in the Enterprise Integrator management console is located in the following path:

Main | **Manage** | **Service Bus** | **Scheduled Tasks**:

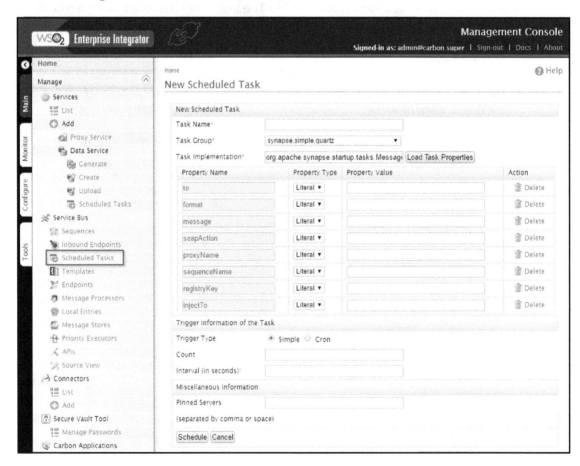

We have three different ways of scheduling a task in the Enterprise Integrator server:

1. Specifying the delay between executions in the `interval` attribute and, optionally, the number of times that it should be executed in the `count` attribute:

```
<task name="IntervalTask"
class="org.apache.synapse.startup.tasks.MessageInjector">
 <trigger interval="3" count="5"/>
</task>
```

This task will be executed 5 times every 3 seconds .

2. Using a `cron` expression:

```
<task name="CronTask"
class="org.apache.synapse.startup.tasks.MessageInjector">
 <trigger cron="0 0 8 * * ?"/>
</task>
```

This task will be executed once a day at 08:00 AM. At: http://www.quartz-scheduler.org/documentation/quartz-2.x/tutorials/crontrigger.html, we can find a `cron` tutorial with examples useful to learn how to compose the expressions.

3. Execute the task only once at server startup, using the `once` attribute:

```
<task name="OnceTask"
class="org.apache.synapse.startup.tasks.MessageInjector">
 <trigger once="true"/>
</task>
```

This task will be executed only once after the server starts.

This is the syntax:

```
<task class="string" name="string" [group="string"]
[pinnedServers="(serverName)+"]>
    <property name="string" value="String"/>
    <property name="string"><somexml>config</somexml></property>
    <trigger (
        [[count="int"]? interval="int"]   |
        [cron="string"]                   |
        [once=(true | false)]
    )/>
</task>
```

Keep these things in mind:

- `class`: This is the implementation class of the task. In this attribute, we can set our custom task implementation, use third-party libraries, or use the default one, that is, `org.apache.synapse.startup.tasks.MessageInjector`, which injects a message into the synapse environment. When the task is triggered, the default implementation can send a specified message into a proxy service or sequence to perform the task action.
- `name`: This is a unique name to identify the task.
- `group`: The group name for grouping tasks. The default is `synapse.simple.quartz`.
- `pinnedServers`: This is a list of WSO2 Enterprise Integrator servers to schedule this task.
- trigger:
  - `simple`: We can configure the `interval` and `count` attributes to specify the delay and the number of times that the task must be triggered, respectively.
  - `cron`: A `cron` expression to launch the task.
  - `once`: A boolean attribute to execute the task only once at server startup.

In the management console the task looks as follow:

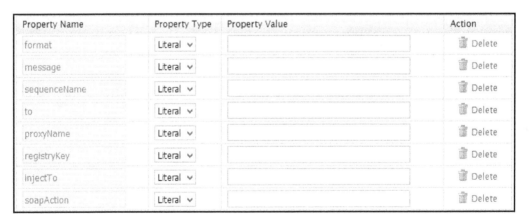

Property Name	Property Type	Property Value	Action
format	Literal ⌄		🗑 Delete
message	Literal ⌄		🗑 Delete
sequenceName	Literal ⌄		🗑 Delete
to	Literal ⌄		🗑 Delete
proxyName	Literal ⌄		🗑 Delete
registryKey	Literal ⌄		🗑 Delete
injectTo	Literal ⌄		🗑 Delete
soapAction	Literal ⌄		🗑 Delete

When we use the default task implementation, we can configure the following properties:

- **format**: Format of the message, for example, soap11, soap12, pox, get, and so on.

- **message**: Payload to inject to the synapse layer. It's mandatory to specify one message, although we don't need it in the backend service.
- **sequenceName**: Name of the sequence to inject the message. It will only be used when the `injectTo` property is configured as `sequence`.
- **to**: Specifies the endpoint address.
- **proxyName**: Name of the proxy to inject the message. It will only be used when the `injectTo` property is configured as `proxy`.
- **registryKey**: Path to the registry artifact to inject the message.
- **injectTo**: Configure where the message will be injected. The available options are `sequence`, `proxy`, and `main`.
- **soapAction**: Configure the SOAP action header when the task is consuming a soap endpoint in the `to` property.

Scheduling data services

In the same way that we saw in the preceding section when we were scheduling integration services, we have another option for scheduling data services. This wizard allows us to create and configure tasks specifically for data services, where we can specify which operation will be processed. This wizard for scheduling data services is the same wizard that we used in the old Data Services Server, and in the Enterprise Integrator server, it is located under **Main** | **Manage** | **Services** | **Add** | **Data Service** | **Scheduled Tasks**:

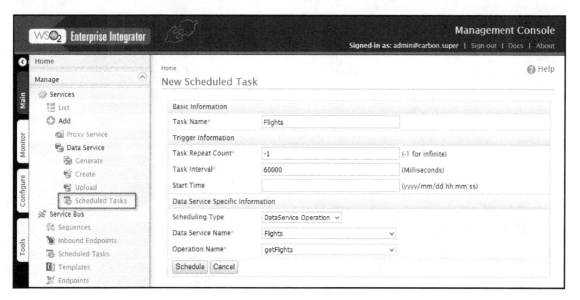

Here, consider the following:

- **Task Name***: Identifier of the scheduled task.
- **Task Repeat Count***: Number of times that the service will be executed without regard for the first invocation.
- **Task Interval***: Time between the different executions.
- **Start Time**: Time to launch the first execution. When we don't specify, this parameter will be processed just after creating the task.
- **Scheduling Type**:
    - **DataService Operation***: For invoking an existing data service operation.
    - **DataService Task Class***: For invoking a custom task class.

Custom tasks

We can also create and schedule our custom task implementations. In this section, we will explain the process of scheduling our custom task implementations.

The first step for creating a custom task is to make a Java program that will handle the logic of the task. The Java class should implement the `org.apache.synapse.task.Task` interface that has a single method called `execute()` with the logic of the procedure that will be to shoot every interval or `cron` expression matches.

Also, our task should implement the `ManagedLifecycle` interface that will be used by the creation and deletion workflow. This interface has two methods:

- `init(SynapseEnvironment)`: This will be executed in the creation of the task
- `destroy()`: This will be executed before deleting it

Our custom task implementation will have the following structure:

```
public class CustomTask implements Task, ManagedLifecycle {
    private Log log = LogFactory.getLog(CustomTask.class);
    private SynapseEnvironment synapseEnvironment;
    public void init(SynapseEnvironment synapseEnvironment){
        log.debug("CustomTask init");
        this.synapseEnvironment = synapseEnvironment;
    }
    public void destroy() {
        log.debug("CustomTask destroy");
    }
```

```
    public void execute() {
        log.debug("CustomTask execute");
    }
}
```

It is possible that we might need to use some parameters for scheduling the task, so EI gives us the opportunity to have two different types of input parameters: String and OMElement (which will be shortly explained); these will be initialized at configuration time in the management console:

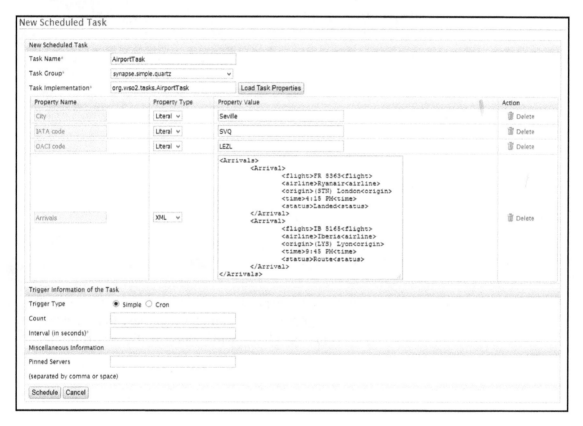

The OMElement comes from Apache Axiom, which is an object model used for XML structured text. In order to define and use those properties, we need to create Java attributes with the `getters` and `setters` methods. Then, when we click on the **Load Task Properties** button in the scheduled task, we will find all of these properties; some of them may be mandatory and others may be optional. In the preceding example, we defined three string input parameters called `city`, IATA code, and OACI code, and one XML input parameter called `arrivals`. These parameters will be handled in the Java program as follows:

```
private String city;
private OMElement arrivals;

//city
public String getCity() {
   return city;
}

public void setCity(String city) {
   this.city = city;
}

//arrivals
public OMElement getArrivals() {
   return arrivals;
}

public void setArrivals(OMElement arrivals) {
   this.arrivals = arrivals;
}
```

Once we have developed the logic of the task, we need to compile and create the `.jar` file that we will put in the EI server in the `<EI_HOME>/lib` path. It's necessary to restart the server before using the custom task because the library will be loaded at server runtime.

Summary

In this chapter, we learned how to use scheduled tasks in the Enterprise Integrator server, which is a powerful way of launching periodic jobs or complex jobs that require a large amount of resources to be processed by the server. We saw that there are three ways to schedule tasks in the EI server: one for data services, another for integration artifacts, such as sequences, proxy services, and endpoints, and a custom task implementation that we can develop from a Java project and can deploy in the server to extend the functionality.

The next chapter is focused on how to use the logging in the Enterprise Integrator. We will learn how to configure the Log4j engine that brings the server, how to use it for logging the envelope, payload, and properties, how to log inside the script mediator, and so on.

9

WSO2 Enterprise Integration Logging

In the earlier chapters, we learned how to create a task and build services and data services as well as how to implement the logic of our services. In this chapter, we will complement this knowledge with some new knowledge that is the basis for being a developer. This is to trace the logic of our services and tasks. We will cover the following topics in this chapter:

- Logging the Envelope
- Logging the payload
- Logging part of the payload
- Logging custom properties
- Logging custom strings
- Logging within script mediator
- Logging levels
- Logging per API and per Proxy Service

General enterprise integration logging

We have several ways to log what is going on in WSO2 EI. As you may know, WSO2 EI is a Java application underneath, and as is typical in this type of application, it uses `log4j` for logging purposes.

You can configure this `log4j` logging. On the one hand, you can manually edit the configuration file you can find in `<EI_HOME>/conf/log4j.properties`. As you can imagine, you can modify the `log4j.properties` configuration file to suit your needs.

On the other hand, you can change this configuration through the management console. When you do this, the changes are persisted in the registry so that they are available after restarting the server and overwrite the configuration in the `log4j.properties`. You can find the logging configuration window in the Configure/Logging window, once signed into the Management Console.

The log files are placed in the `<EI_HOME>/repository/logs/` folder by default. Here, we will find the following type of log files by default:

- `audit.log`: This is the log file where the audit log generated by our components will be stored.
- `http_access_management_console.log`: In this log, you can check the basic information of each HTTP access to WSO2 EI.
- `patches.log`: In this file, WSO2 EI will register the log information when any patches are installed.
- `tm.out`: This log file is for Atomikos transaction logs.
- `wso2carbon.log`: This is the main log file of WSO2 EI, and this is the file you can see when you access or log into the management console. This is the log that will be checked most of the times.
- `wso2carbon-trace-messages.log`: This log file used to be empty, and it seems to be an appender inherited from carbon core that is not used by WSO2 EI.
- `wso2-ei-errors.log`: In this file, we can find all warning and error messages from `wso2carbon.log`.
- `wso2-ei-service.log`: In this file, you will find the specific log from the proxy services deployed in WSO2 EI. This is a way to extract the service logging entries from the general log (`wso2carbon.log`).

- `wso2-ei-trace.log`: In here, we find more detailed information about the steps performed in our sequences, mediators, or services when tracing has been enabled on them. This is quite a useful log, and you can enable this for your services in the quality of service configuration in the service dashboard:

- In the case of sequences, you can enable it in the sequence list in the Management Console:

By default, all these files are configured as daily rolling log files, so you will probably find some of these log files that have the date attached to the name.

In addition to this set of log files, you can find in the filesystem, you can access the log in the Management Console in Monitor/System Logs. In this case, the log shown is the `CARBON_MEMORY logger`, in which configuration is also set in the `log4j.properties` files.

Logging the orchestration

Once we know how to configure the logging feature and where to find the log files, we are ready to learn how to trace our service orchestration to help us during the development stage.

There are two ways to trace our flow:

- Using the log mediator in our sequences or proxies
- Using the script mediator

Log mediator

This mediator allows you to log all kinds of information related to your service. It is the option you will use most times. This mediator is added to your sequence flow just like any other mediator, and you can find it in the **Core** section when editing the sequence through the Management Console:

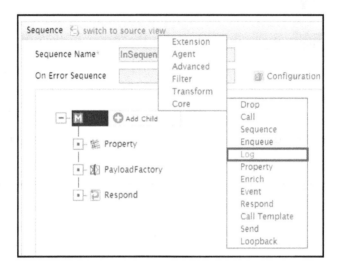

Alternatively, you can find it in the mediator list in the WSO2 EI Tool:

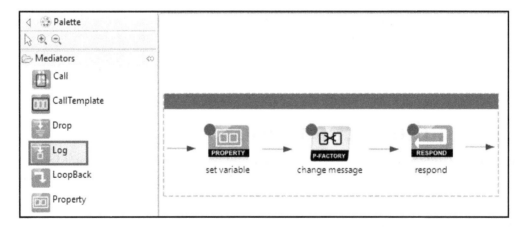

We will use the **Log** configuration window from the Management Console for teaching and learning purposes since this wizard is more user-friendly than the Eclipse **Property** tab.

When we add the **Log** mediator, we can configure the following information:

- **Log Category**: This is the `log4j` category. As you may know, the available options are TRECE, DEBUG, INFO, WARN, ERROR, and FATAL.
- **Log level**: Here, we choose how much information about the payload is written to the log. The options are as follows:
  - Full: The following properties will be shown:
    - **To**
    - **WSAction**
    - **SOAPAction**
    - **MessageID**
    - **Direction**
    - **Envelope**

    If you check the log, the information written will look like this:

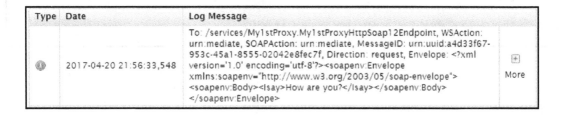

- Simple: In this case, the message Envelope will be omitted:
  - **To**
  - **WSAction**
  - **SOAPAction**
  - **MessageID**
  - **Direction**

This log entry will look as illustrated:

Type	Date	Log Message	
ⓘ	2017-04-20 21:57:47,802	To: /services/My1stProxy.My1stProxyHttpSoap12Endpoint, WSAction: urn:mediate, SOAPAction: urn:mediate, MessageID: urn:uuid:3f06cb87-906c-40b8-ac32-2d4f5c4a0b76, Direction: request	⊞ More

- Headers: In this case, just the header from the Envelope will be shown for the following request with header content:

The log shown is as follows:

Type	Date	Log Message	
ⓘ	2017-04-20 21:41:57,224	myHeader : This is the header!	⊞ More

- Custom: When choosing this option, no information about the payload will be shown in the log. The only information written in the log will be the properties added:

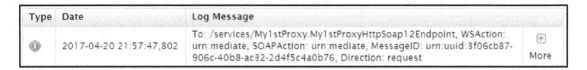

Type	Date	Log Message	
ⓘ	2017-04-20 21:57:47,802	To: /services/My1stProxy.My1stProxyHttpSoap12Endpoint, WSAction: urn:mediate, SOAPAction: urn:mediate, MessageID: urn:uuid:3f06cb87-906c-40b8-ac32-2d4f5c4a0b76, Direction: request	⊞ More

- **Log Separator**: This will be the characters used to separate each property added to the log entry. By default, the separation string is , as you can see in the preceding screenshot.
- **Properties**: We can add any custom content by adding new properties whose content is the value we want to trace. We can trace static values such as strings, or we can trace context property values. As many properties as desired can be added.

Adding log properties

Besides the message or the header properties, we usually need to log the value of the property we have previously set using any expression, or log a specific part of the message:

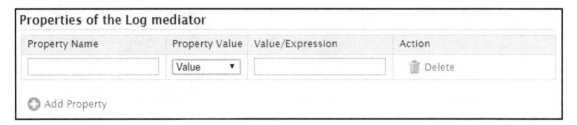

Properties of the Log mediator			
Property Name	Property Value	Value/Expression	Action
	Value ▾		🗑 Delete
⊕ Add Property			

To achieve this, we just need to click on **Add Property** to add as many properties as you need to the log mediator, in which values will be written to the log. We can also set values for these properties in different ways:

- String values: We can add properties to a string, for instance, step 1. In this case, we add the following information:
  - **Property Name**: Name of the property that will be written in the log, for instance, `flow`
  - **Property Value**: We set this option to **Value** to make it a string

- **Value/Expression**: The static string you want to show, for instance, `step 1`

So, the log entry will look like this:

Type	Date	Log Message	
ⓘ	2017-04-21 19:27:32,087	flow = step 1	⊞ More

- Dynamic values: This way, we can set a XPath expression that is performed over the message, or the value of a property we have previously set to the log property. In both cases, the information we have to add is as follows:
    - **Property Name**: Name of the property that will be written in the log.
    - **Property Value**: We set this option to **Expression** to make it a dynamic value.
    - **Value/Expression**: In this case, the expression whose result we want to show. We have several options in this case:
    - XPath expression: We can use a XPath expression that is performed over the message. You will have to previously add all namespaces required in your XPath expression using the **Names Space Editor**:

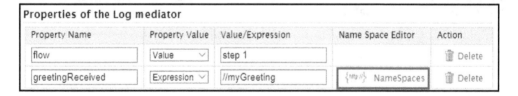

Properties of the Log mediator				
Property Name	Property Value	Value/Expression	Name Space Editor	Action
flow	Value ⌄	step 1		🗑 Delete
greetingReceived	Expression ⌄	//myGreeting	{http://} NameSpaces	🗑 Delete

You will be able to log any part of the message using a XPath expression. For example, for the `greetingReceived` property set in the preceding screenshot, consider that we send the following message:

```
<soapenv:Envelope xmlns:soapenv="http://schemas.xmlsoap.org/soap/envelope/">
    <soapenv:Body>
        <myGreeting>How are you?</myGreeting>
    </soapenv:Body>
</soapenv:Envelope>
```

The log entry generated will finally be as illustrated:

Type	Date	Log Message	
ⓘ	2017-04-21 20:00:24,130	flow = step 1, greetingReceived = How are you?	⊞ More

- A property value: We can inject the value of an existing property to the log property using the `get-property('propertyName')` expression. For instance, consider the following log property defined:

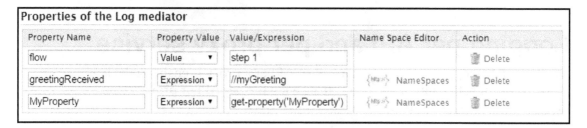

Properties of the Log mediator

Property Name	Property Value	Value/Expression	Name Space Editor	Action
flow	Value ▾	step 1		🗑 Delete
greetingReceived	Expression ▾	//myGreeting	{⟨hts⟩} NameSpaces	🗑 Delete
MyProperty	Expression ▾	get-property('MyProperty')	{⟨hts⟩} NameSpaces	🗑 Delete

The entry log will look like this:

Type	Date	Log Message	
ⓘ	2017-04-21 20:16:18,595	flow = step 1, greetingReceived = How are you?, MyProperty = This is a property value	⊞ More

Script mediator

There are times when the fastest or easiest way (or both) to perform an operation is using a script instead of using several mediators in your service sequence. Then, you will probably need to log some information to check whether the script is working properly, especially when it gets a little complex.

You can write this script using JavaScript, Groovy, or Ruby. We will focus on JavaScript because it is widely spread and there are tons of resources. So, when you need to log inside a JavaScript code, you can do it this way:

```
var log = mc.getServiceLog();
log.info("Logging inside Script Mediator");
```

You just need to retrieve the ServiceLog from the message context and use the level of log desired for the logging. In this example, we used the info level. The class of the ServiceLog fetched from the context is org.apache.commons.logging.Log, so you can check this class to take advantage of it.

When logging that way, you will be able to see an entry log as follows:

Type	Date	Log Message	
ⓘ	2017-04-21 21:05:42,976	Logging inside Script Mediator	⊞ More

Logging per API and per proxy service

Another way of logging information in a Rest API or a proxy is enabling the logging per API or proxy functionality, which will create a log file per API or proxy where all information logged is written.

To enable logging per API, we just need to configure the API_LOGGER category of the log4j.properties. We will assume that our rest API is called myFirstRestAPI. Then, we just follow these steps:

1. Open $EI_HOME/conf/log4j.properties.
2. Add the following section for the INFO level in the API_LOGGER category:

```
log4j.category.API_LOGGER=INFO, API_APPENDER
log4j.additivity.API_LOGGER=false
log4j.appender.API_APPENDER=org.apache.log4j.RollingFileAppender
log4j.appender.API_APPENDER.File=${carbon.home}/repository/logs/${instance.
log}/wso2-ei-api${instance.log}.log
log4j.appender.API_APPENDER.MaxFileSize=1000KB
log4j.appender.API_APPENDER.MaxBackupIndex=10
log4j.appender.API_APPENDER.layout=org.apache.log4j.PatternLayout
log4j.appender.API_APPENDER.layout.ConversionPattern=%d{ISO8601} [%X{ip}-
%X{host}] [%t] %5p %c{1} %m%n</pre>
```

This will write the information logged using the log mediator in our API in the file $EI_HOME/repository/logs/wso2-ei-api.log when using info level.

3. Add the following section for the DEGUG lever in the API_LOGGER category. We will suppose that our rest API is called:

```
log4j.category.API_LOGGER.myFirstRestAPI =DEBUG, TEST_API_APPENDER
log4j.additivity.API_LOGGER.myFirstRestAPI=false
log4j.appender.TEST_API_APPENDER=org.apache.log4j.DailyRollingFileAppender
log4j.appender.TEST_API_APPENDER.File=${carbon.home}/repository/logs/${inst
ance.log}/myFirstRestAPI.log
log4j.appender.TEST_API_APPENDER.datePattern='.'yyyy-MM-dd-HH-mm
log4j.appender.TEST_API_APPENDER.layout=org.apache.log4j.PatternLayout
log4j.appender.TEST_API_APPENDER.layout.ConversionPattern=%d{ISO8601}
[%X{ip}-%X{host}] [%t] %5p %c{1} %m%n
```

This will create a file called myFirstRestAPI.log in the $EI_HOME/repository/logs folder where our debug information will be written when using a log mediator with DEBUG level.

You need to restart for these changes to take effect.

The way to proceed to enable per proxy service logging is quite similar. We will suppose that we have a proxy service called my1stProxyService. Then, we will follow these steps:

1. Open $EI_HOME/conf/log4j.properties.
2. Add the following section for the DEBUG level in the SERVICE_LOGGER category:

```
log4j.category.SERVICE_LOGGER.my1stProxyService=DEBUG, SQ_PROXY_APPENDER
log4j.additivity.SERVICE_LOGGER. my1stProxyService =false
log4j.appender.SQ_PROXY_APPENDER=org.apache.log4j.DailyRollingFileAppender
log4j.appender.SQ_PROXY_APPENDER.File=logs/my1stProxyService-proxy-
service.log
log4j.appender.SQ_PROXY_APPENDER.datePattern='.'yyyy-MM-dd-HH-mm
log4j.appender.SQ_PROXY_APPENDER.layout=org.apache.log4j.PatternLayout
log4j.appender.SQ_PROXY_APPENDER.layout.ConversionPattern=%d{ISO8601}
\[%X{ip}-%X{host}\] \[%t\] %5p %c{1} %m%n
```

This will create a file called $EI_HOME/repository/logs/my1stProxyService-proxy-service.log, where the debug information logged with the log mediator in our my1stProxyService proxy will be written.

Summary

In this chapter, we learned how to log any information about the message received or the properties we set during our service orchestration. We also learned how to log when we are developing a piece of JavaScript code in our service.

Now that we have learned the main topics to build our services, we will learn how to test our services in the next chapter.

10

WSO2 Enterprise Integration Testing

In the previous chapters, we learned how to log the logic we implemented in our service orchestration, to help us during the development as well as being a useful tool to find error causes. At this point, we have learned many instruments to build our services but we still need to learn how to test them. That is the aim of this chapter, where we will learn the following things:

- Testing the services using the TryIt built-in feature
- Testing the services using SOAPUI
- Other ways of testing: CURL and TCPMon

Testing with a built-in tester

WSO2 EI provides a built-in feature to try SOAP services. This feature can be used to test SOAP services, including proxy services and data services. It is a basic feature that does not allow us to test REST services, so data services that are exposed as resources will not be able to test their resources from this feature. For this purpose, we will use SOAPUI, as we will describe in the next section.

We can access this testing window from the list of services:

Alternatively, we can access it from the service dashboard:

The testing window, as you might have seen earlier in the book, looks like this:

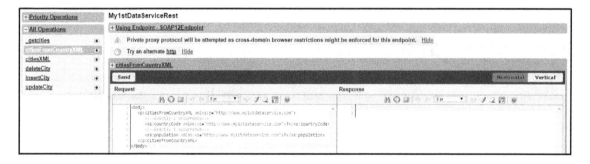

There are three main sections in this window. On the left-hand side of the window, we have the list of SOAP operations available in the service:

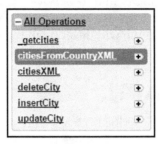

We just need to click on any of them to generate a template request. In the top section, we can choose the endpoint to send the request. The typical options available are SOAP 1.1 and SOAP 1.2, as well as the HTTP and HTTPS endpoints:

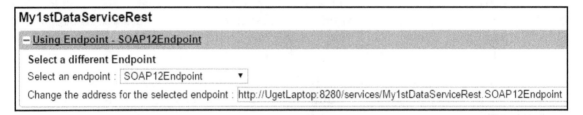

Once you choose the endpoint, you will be able to change the URL of the final endpoint to be called if you need it. Under this section, we find the work area where we can type the request we are sending, and next to it, we will see the response received:

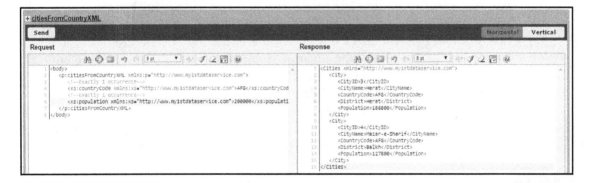

After typing the request, we just need to click on **Send**, and we will see the response in the right-hand side window.

As you can imagine, there are many modifications you can perform on a request that you are not able to perform in this basic tester; for instance, the **Accept:application/ json** header needed to receive the response in JSON in data services. In spite of the fact that this basic tester may be enough in some scenarios, we recommend you test the service with more advanced tools such as SOAPUI, as we will describe in the next section.

Testing with SOAPUI

As you may remember, when we describe how to create data services and expose them as REST services, we use SOAPUI to test them since we need to add a property to the request header. You cannot perform this customization using the built-in tester, so we use the SOAPUI tool, which allows you to do this kind of modification and any others you may need.

SOAPUI is an open source testing tool for SOAP and REST services that enables you to build any kind of request. As they say on their website, it is *The Most Advanced REST and SOAP Testing Tool in the World,* and there is a free open source version and a professional one. We will work with the free SOAPUI open source version.

This tool allows you to not only create fully customized requests to test a service, but also gives you many other features that are quite useful on a daily basis in a professional environment:

- **Mock services of your web services**: Most of the time, when you have to build an orchestration in your service where several web services are involved, you will have to start the development using mock services generated from their contracts Web Services Description Language (**WSDL**). Then, in the further stages, you will be able to perform test cases using the real service. SOAPUI allows you to create this mock service with just a few clicks.
- **Test case**: Another quite useful feature that you cannot perform with the built-in tester, but that you can do with SOAPUI, are test cases. It is a best practice to develop a set of test cases to validate that the service is working as expected. It is also quite easy to create this test case.
- **Performance test**: It is quite easy to build a performance test with SOAPUI so that you can check whether your logic is complying with your SLA, for instance.

For all these reasons, we recommend that you test your services with SOAPUI, or another advanced tool that offers similar features.

According to the scope of this book, we will learn the basic concepts to use SOAPUI for testing, and how they are related, so that the reader can easily go ahead with them on their own.

You can download and install SOAPUI open source from `https://www.soapui.org/downloads/soapui.html`. We are working with SOAPUI 5.3 in this book, but because we are dealing with basic concepts, you will learn how to work with it generally rather than how to work with a specific version.

Creating a web service client

Here, we learn how to create a web service client in SOAPUI to test our services. We use the data service from `Chapter 4`, *Building Data Services*, that publishes the information as a SOAP service and REST service.

Remember that due to an issue in this WSO2 EI version, we have to upload the data service manually or create it from the management console so that the SOAP and REST versions work properly.

For a SOAP service, we just need its contract; this is its WSDL. We can set it from a URL or from a file in the filesystem. So, to create the client, we just need to go to **File** | **New SOAP Project** in SOAPUI and set the WSDL:

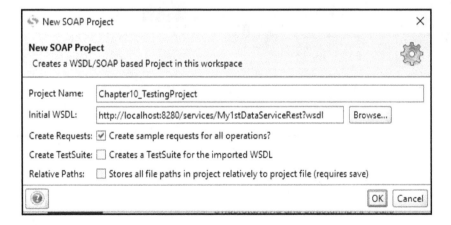

Then, a new project will be created and will have the list of operations available in the service. WSO2 EI publishes, by default, the operations in SOAP 1.1 and SOAP 1.2 versions. Thus, the project in SOAPUI looks like this:

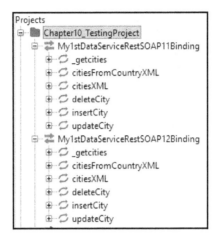

You can expand each operation to access the request where we can consume the service:

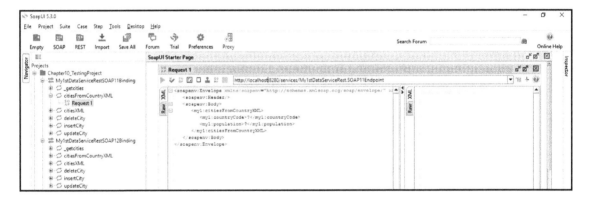

Double-clicking on the **Request 1** will open a new window with a default request created based on the schema defined in the WSDL for that operation, so we just need to set the proper values and click on the Play button to send the request:

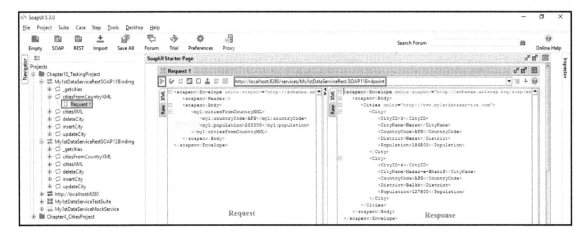

The response received will be shown in the right-hand section of the request window. The endpoint of the service is obtained from the WSDL, so when we are not using the contract from just the service we are consuming, the autogenerated endpoint might not be right one. In this case, we just need to edit it to set the proper one.

Now we will add a client for the REST operation we created in the data service, which will give us a list of the cities. We select the project and right-click on it, and then we choose **New REST Service from URI**:

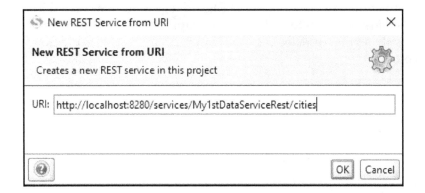

We set the URI where the REST service is published and click on **OK**. Then, the REST client will be added to the project, and a request template will be generated:

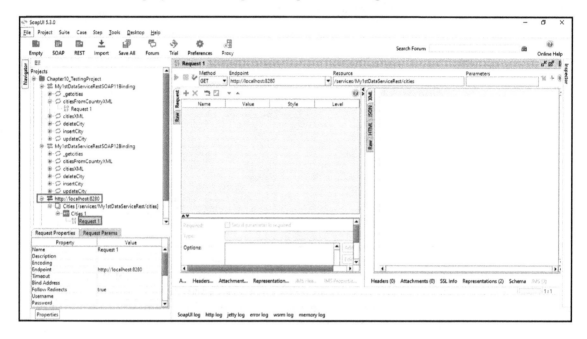

In the request window, we can change all parameters related to the API, such as the method, the endpoint, the resource, and the parameters. We can also modify the request properties, add security headers, and modify the headers.

You may remember that for consuming the REST data service we created in `Chapter 4`, *Building Data Services*, we need to add the **Accept:application/json** property to the header. Well, we can easily do that by selecting the **Header** tab in the request window and clicking on the add icon (+):

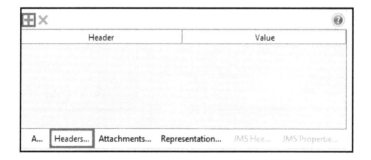

Then, we add the `Accept` property to the window:

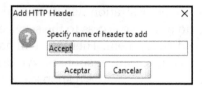

Also, we set its value in the list of properties:

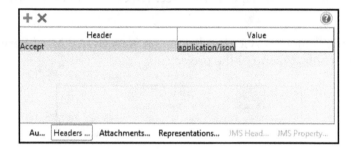

Then, we can call the REST service by clicking on the Play button, and we will get the response of the service:

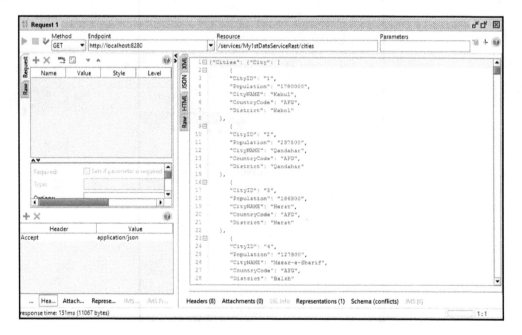

Creating a mock service

When we are developing a service orchestration where several services are implied, it will be a common scenario that we do not have access to the service in a developer environment, at least for the first stages of the development. Then, we will have to work the contract of the service and, if we are lucky, same sample responses. We can solve this situation, creating a mock service where we set the sample responses as the response of the service.

Thus, we can start developing our service by invoking a mock service of the real service until we are able to integrate with the real service. We can do that for both REST and SOAP services.

We can easily create the mock service by clicking on **New SOAP MockService** / **New REST MockService** in the context menu of the project:

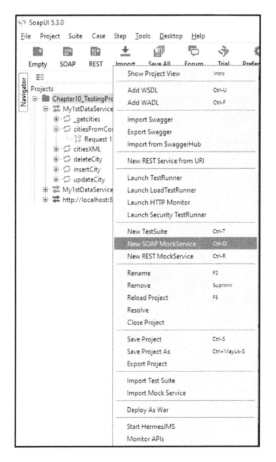

In this case, we choose a **New SOAP MockService**:

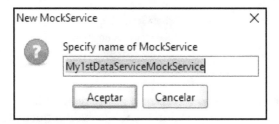

We just set a name, and it will be added to the project. Now, we just need to add the mock operation for each operation we need. To do that, the fastest way is to right-click on the request of the desired operation, and click on **Add to MockService**:

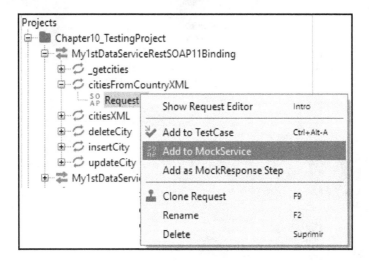

Then, we select the MockService:

Finally, the mock operation is added to the service:

If it is the case that we have received a response in the request from where we start, the value set as response in the mock operation is the received request. Otherwise, SOAPUI will autogenerate a response template from the WSDL:

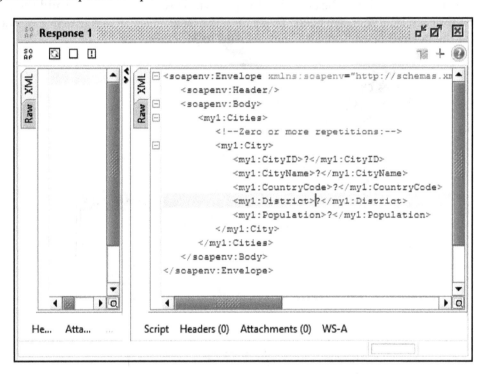

As you can imagine, the response window is quite similar to the request window. In this window, the editable section is the right-hand part of the window, while in the request window, the editable section is the left-hand side.

We can repeat this process to add as many mock operations as we need. Then, we just need to start the MockService by right-clicking on the MockService and click onMockService**Start Minimized**:

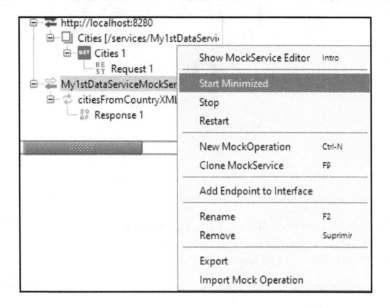

Now the service is running, and we can call it; for instance, from the request client just adding the endpoint where the MockService is listening. The fastest way to do this is by right-clicking on the **Response 1** in the MockService and clicking on **Open Request**:

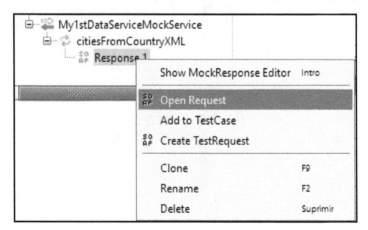

This will open a request with the proper endpoint of the MockService set, just ready to introduce the request parameters:

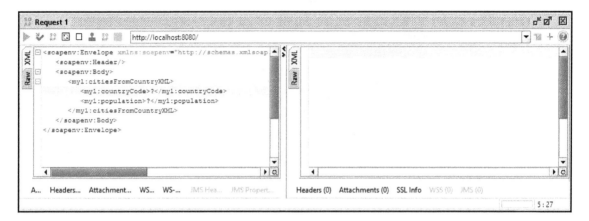

To test this MockService, we type any dummy values on the request and call the endpoint of the MockService. If we open the mock response, we will be able to verify that the request has been received, and that it is the request we just typed:

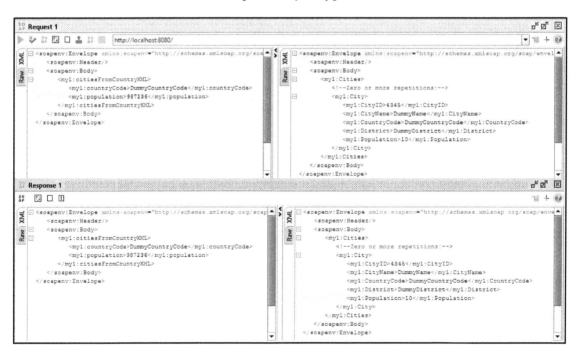

You can proceed to create a REST MockService in the same way as we created this SOAP MockService, starting from the REST request in this case.

Creating a test case

Another useful tool that SOAPUI gives us is the test case. Test cases allow us to create a set of tests over a service to validate whether the service is working properly, for instance. Test cases are wrapped in a test suite. So, we can create a Test Suite in the same way we created a MockService, just by right-clicking on the project and clicking on New TestSuite:

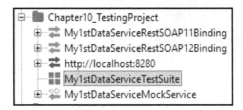

In this test suite, we will create a test case to contain all of our test steps. We can do that by right-clicking on the TestSuite and New TestCase:

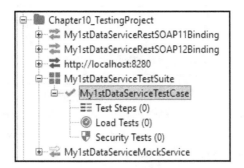

Finally, here we can add Test Steps to validate some scenarios, **Load Tests** to test the performance of the service, and **Security Tests**. Here, we will also learn how to create a **Test Step** to illustrate this powerful tool. You can check the SOAPUI documentation to find out more about how to tap the full potential of this tool.

We can add as many **Test Steps** as we need by just right-clicking on the request we want to test, and clicking on **Add to TestCase**:

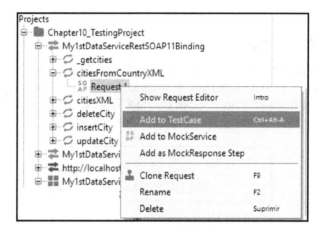

Then, we choose the TestCase we just created and in the next step, we can set some useful default validations, such as **Add Schema Assertion**, **Add Not SOAP Fault Assertion**, and **Add SOAP Response Assertion**:

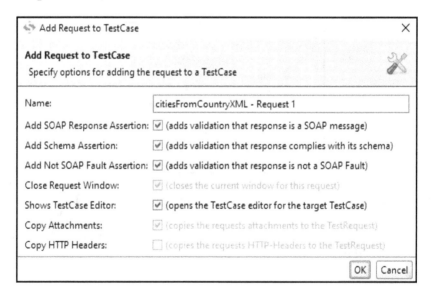

The request has been added to the TestCase now, and we can modify it like any other request to try different scenarios. Repeating these steps, we can add as many tests as we need:

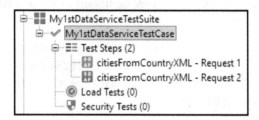

Finally, we can run all of them by double-clicking on the TestCase, and clicking on the Play button. If everything is okay, the progress bar will turn green, otherwise it will turn red:

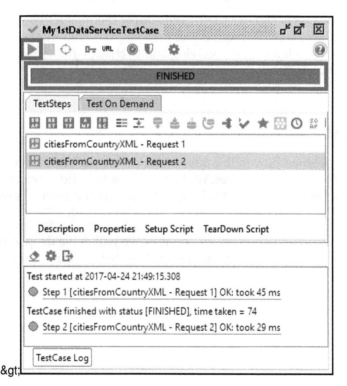

>

Other ways of testing

SOAPUI may cover all needs required for a professional delivery in an integration project. However, there are a couple of tools that may be useful in some situations. These tools are as listed:

- CURL: This is a command-line tool to make requests using URL syntax. This will be useful, for instance, to perform a quick test over a REST API. For example, we can call a REST API called `my1stAPI` with the search operation from the command line using this command:

  ```
  curl -v http://localhost:8280/my1stAPI/search
  ```

  Many of the samples provided by WSO2 use curl to test them.

- TCPMon: This is another useful and simple tool that allows you to inspect and modify the raw HTTP request and response received in a port. This is quite useful to see what we are receiving and to check whether we are sending the information to the endpoint properly.

Summary

In this chapter, we learned how to test our services using the basic built-in feature and a more powerful tool--SOAPUI. Besides, we learned how to build mock services and test suites to create a set of test cases that help us validate that the service is working as we expect.

Once we know how to build and test our services, we will delve deeper into enterprise integrations, and we also learn how to build services that integrate with a **Virtual File System** (**VFS**).

11
Integrating with VFS

The main topic in the previous chapter was the testing of the services that we deployed in Enterprise Integrator, with internal tools from WSO2, and also, external programs for creating requests and consuming those services. The subsequent chapters will go through different protocols of integration from EI, such as **Virtual File System** (**VFS**), **Java Message Service** (**JMS**), and connectors that will bring us the opportunity to expand the default functionality of the server and create more complete services that can interact with other servers.

This chapter focuses on the integration of Enterprise Integrator with files, local or remote, handled using the VFS protocol from Apache Commons. We will learn how to do the following in this chapter:

- Configuring the server for VFS protocol
- Global properties used by VFS implementation
- Reading files from the local, samba, FTP, FTPS, and SFTP repositories
- Polling a directory waiting for a file
- Transferring large files without processing
- Installing and using the file connector
- Writing files

Configuring the server

The VFS implementation that uses the Enterprise Integrator server is based on the Apache Commons VFS implementation deployed in the `commons-vfs2_2.0.0.wso2v15.jar` library that contains the required resources to work with files.

The use of the VFS transport is disabled in the server by default, so we need to enable it in the `<EI_HOME>/conf/axis2/axis2.xml` file and restart the server in order to apply the changes. We have two different implementations that we can enable: one for reading the files and the other for writing the files:

- `<transportReceiver name="vfs" class="org.apache.synapse.transport.vfs.VFSTransportListener"/>`
- `<transportSender name="vfs" class="org.apache.synapse.transport.vfs.VFSTransportSender"/>`

Large files

Sometimes when we work with large files with the VFS transport, we can get out of memory errors. To avoid these errors, we need to configure the EI server with the following properties.

The first file that we need to set up is `<EI_HOME>/conf/axis2/axis2.xml`, adding the `messageBuilder` and the `messageFormatter` for the `application/binary` content type. In the `messageBuilders` section, we will add this:

```
<messageBuilder contentType="application/binary"
class="org.apache.axis2.format.BinaryBuilder"/>
```

Also, in the `messageFormatters` section, we will add the following:

```
<messageFormatter contentType="application/binary"
class="org.apache.axis2.format.BinaryFormatter"/>
```

We must restart the Enterprise Integrator after modifying this file in order to apply the changes.

Now that the server is configured to handle big files, the second step is to configure the proxy services as well. In the VFS proxy, we need to add a parameter called `transport.vfs.Streaming` with a `true` value, as follows:

```
<parameter name="transport.vfs.Streaming">true</parameter>
```

When we have a proxy that performs the operation VFS origin to VFS destination, we need to add this property before the send mediator:

```
<property name="ClientApiNonBlocking" value="true"
scope="axis2" action="remove"/>
```

Reading files

The process for reading files is usually in integration projects in which we have different servers that need to communicate with others that produce a text file. It is very important in legacy applications that don't have a web service or another way to handle big data input information, so generating and reading the files is a good approach to integrate with them.

VFS properties

When we are reading a file, we can choose between different scenarios; for example, we can read a file for a directory on demand when we make a request to a service, or we can create a service that automatically polls the directory waiting until the file exists to process the information contained in it.

There is a list of properties that we can configure in the VFS proxy or file inbound endpoint for setting up the behavior of the service. Here's the list of properties.

transport.vfs.FileURI

This is a required parameter for VFS services in the URI where the files that we want to process are located; these can be local, FTP, SFTP, FTPS, SMB, and so on. We can specify the `sftpPathFromRoot` to access the absolute path of the URI.

Here is the syntax:

```
<parameter name="transport.vfs.FileURI">
protocol://[ username[: password]@] hostname[: port][ absolute-
path]?sftpPathFromRoot=true</parameter>
```

Consider the following example:

```
<parameter name="transport.vfs.FileURI">
    file:///home/user/vfs/in
</parameter>
```

transport.vfs.ContentType

Content type of the files is processed, while encoding split with a semi-colon character is optional.

Consider this example:

```
<parameter name="transport.vfs.ContentType">
    text/xml;charset=UTF-8
</parameter>
```

If we want to change the content type of the file after processing it, we can use the following property in our service:

```
<property name="CHARACTER_SET_ENCODING"
value="UTF-8" scope="axis2" type="STRING"/>
```

transport.vfs.FileNamePattern

This property contains a regular expression for processing only the files in the directory configuration in the `transport.vfs.FileURI` property that matches this expression. For example, we have a directory that contains a list of files in which we only want to process the XML files, so we must configure this property as follows:

```
<parameter name="transport.vfs.FileNamePattern">
    .*\.xml
</parameter>
```

transport.PollInterval

This defines the time in seconds that the service must to poll the directory for new files. Also we can add the ms suffix for milliseconds.

For example, to poll every 5 seconds, we can use the following:

```
<parameter name="transport.PollInterval">5</parameter>
<parameter name="transport.PollInterval">5000ms</parameter>
```

transport.vfs.ActionAfterProcess

Once the transport has processed the file, we can choose between moving the file to another directory, deleting it, or taking no action with the MOVE, DELETE (default), or NONE values.

We must be careful if we take no action with the file, because it will remain in the same directory and will be processed again in future pollings.

---

transport.vfs.ActionAfterFailure

Following with the preceding configuration, we can choose from MOVE, DELETE (default), or NONE if the processing of the file fails.

transport.vfs.MoveAfterProcess

Only if we configure the `transport.vfs.ActionAfterProcess` to MOVE, do we need to specify this property with the destination URI to move the processed files.

transport.vfs.MoveAfterFailure

Only if we configure the `transport.vfs.ActionAfterFailure` to MOVE, do we need to specify this property with the destination URI to move the processed files.

transport.vfs.ReplyFileURI

In this parameter, we need to specify a valid URI where reply files should be written by the transport.

transport.vfs.ReplyFileName

This is the full name, extension included, for the reply files.

transport.vfs.MoveTimestampFormat

This is a valid format for the timestamps that are prefixed to the filenames when are moving from origin path to destination target. More information about valid formats can be found in the official Java documentation at `http://docs.oracle.com/javase/7/docs/api/java/text/SimpleDateFormat.html`.

transport.vfs.Streaming

This is a boolean parameter that enables or disables the streaming transfer mode that is useful for large files.

transport.vfs.ReconnectTimeout

This is the time in seconds to wait until we try to connect again after an error in transferring files; it is 30 seconds by default.

transport.vfs.MaxRetryCount

This is the maximum number of retries when we get an error; this property will work along with the previous one in case of an error. The number of retries is three by default.

transport.vfs.Append

This is a boolean property that lets us add content to an existing file instead of replacing it (Replace the file is the default behavior when a file with the same name exists in the destination location). This property is not a parameter of the service, and must to be defined in the out or reply file URI.

Consider the following example:

```
<parameter name="transport.vfs.ReplyFileURI">
    file:///home/user/vfs/out?transport.vfs.Append=true
</parameter>
```

transport.vfs.MoveAfterFailedMove

This is a valid URI where we move the failed processed files.

transport.vfs.FailedRecordsFileName

This is a name for the file that contains the list of files that get an error during processing. The default name is vfs-move-failed-records.properties.

transport.vfs.FailedRecordsFileDestination

This is a URI to store the preceding file containing the error files.

transport.vfs.MoveFailedRecordTimestampFormat

This is the file that contains the error processing files that store the name of the file and the timestamp of the failure. With this property, we can configure the timestamp format; by default, we have the dd-MM-yyyy HH:mm:ss pattern.

transport.vfs.FailedRecordNextRetryDuration

This is the time in milliseconds between retries after a failure, which is 3 seconds by default.

transport.vfs.Locking

This lets us configure the locking behaviour of the files that are processed. The possible values are enable (default) or disable.

transport.vfs.FileProcessCount

With this parameter, we can enable the batch process for files and configure the number of files that should be processed in each batch.

transport.vfs.FileProcessInterval

This is the time in milliseconds between two files processed.

transport.vfs.ClusterAware

This is the boolean parameter that enables or disables the VFS coordination support in a clustered deployment.

transport.vfs.FileSizeLimit

This is the limit for the files to be processed, expressed in bytes. Only the files that have the same or lower size will be processed by the server. Also, we can set up this parameter to -1 for an unlimited file size.

transport.vfs.AutoLockReleaseInterval

This is the time in milliseconds to ignore the file locks and process the file. The default value is 20000, and we can configure -1 to never ignore the locked files.

Local filesystem

We can configure an inboundEndpoint with the parameters outlined in the previous section in order to use the VFS transport and process a file for a local or samba repository. In the transport.vfs.FileURI parameter, we can configure a local file with the file:// prefix, and a samba file with the smb:// prefix:

```
<inboundEndpoint name="FileInbound"
            onError="fault"
            protocol="file"
            sequence="main"
            statistics="enable"
            suspend="false"
            trace="enable">
    <parameters>
        <parameter name="interval">5</parameter>
        <parameter name="sequential">true</parameter>
        <parameter name="coordination">true</parameter>
        <parameter name="transport.vfs.FileURI">
        file:///home/user/vfs/in
    </parameter>
        <parameter name="transport.vfs.ContentType">
            text/xml
        </parameter>
        <parameter name="transport.vfs.FileNamePattern">
            .*\.xml
        </parameter>
        <parameter name="transport.vfs.Locking">
            enable
        </parameter>
        <parameter name="transport.vfs.ActionAfterProcess">
            DELETE
        </parameter>
        <parameter name="transport.vfs.ActionAfterFailure">
            DELETE
        </parameter>
        <parameter name="transport.vfs.AutoLockRelease">
            false
        </parameter>
        <parameter name="transport.vfs.LockReleaseSameNode">
```

```
                        false
                    </parameter>
                    <parameter name="transport.vfs.DistributedLock">
                        false
                    </parameter>
                </parameters>
        </inboundEndpoint>
```

FTP and FTPS

Similar to the preceding example, we can create an inbound endpoint that polls an FTP/FTPS remote directory. In this case, the `transport.vfs.FileURI` parameter must have the following structure:

```
vfs:ftps://[user[:password]@]hostname[:port][path][?URL parameters]
```

In addition to the mentioned VFS parameters, we can use other URL parameters inside some other parameters, which make a connection with the remote server, such as `transport.vfs.FileURI` and `transport.vfs.MoveAfterProcess`. This is the list of the URL parameters:

- `vfs.passive`: Boolean parameter to enable the passive mode required when the client and server are in different networks. It's configured to `false` by default.
- `transport.vfs.Append`: This is a boolean parameter to add the content to an existing file instead of overwriting it; it's disabled by default.
- `vfs.protection`: Configures the data protection level with the FTP PROT command. The possible values are C (Clear, is the default value), S (Safe, for SSL protocol only), E (Confidential, for SSL protocol only) and P (Private).
- `vfs.ssl.keystore`: Path of the keystore that will be used for mutual SSL; it must be signed by a certificate authority.
- `vfs.ssl.kspassword`: Password of the key store.
- `vfs.ssl.keypassword`: Password of the key.
- `vfs.ssl.truststore`: Trust store to use for FTPS.
- `vfs.ssl.tspassword`: Password for the trust store.
- `transport.vfs.CreateFolder`: Boolean parameter to create the folder if it does not exist; it is `false` by default.
- `transport. vfs.SendFileSynchronously`: Boolean parameter to send the files synchronously, which is disabled by default.

Here's an example of the `transport.vfs.FileURI` parameter with the preceding URL parameters inside, for a connection with an FTPS server:

```
<parameter name="transport.vfs.FileURI">
 vfs:ftps://username:password@ftpsServerHost:ftpsServerPort/full/path?
 vfs.passive=true&
 transport.vfs.Append=true&
 vfs.protection=S&
 vfs.ssl.keystore=/home/user/jks/keystore.jks&
 vfs.ssl.kspassword=wso2carbon&
 vfs.ssl.keypassword=wso2carbon&
 vfs.ssl.truststore=/home/user/jks/truststore.jks&
 vfs.ssl.tspassword=wso2carbon&
 transport.vfs.CreateFolder=true&
 transport.vfs.SendFileSynchronously=true
 </parameter>
```

SFTP

When we work with SFTP servers, we need to configure the following parameters:

- `transport.vfs.SFTPIdentities`: Full path for the private key
- `transport.vfs.SFTPIdentityPassPhrase`: Password for the private key
- `transport.vfs.SFTPUserDirIsRoot`: Boolean parameter for treating the user directory as root

Writing files

Now that we know how to read files, we will learn how to use the VFS transport for writing content to files, no matter what the source of the data is: another file, API, Proxy service, inbound endpoint, task, or any other.

For writing the file, we need to create an endpoint with the path where the file will be created:

- Local
- FTP
- Samba

This endpoint will be used inside a send or call mediator, as follows:

```
<call>
    <endpoint>
        <address uri="vfs:file:///home/user/vfs/out"/>
    </endpoint>
</call>
```

When we want to create a file, we need to use the `OUT_ONLY` property, because this is a single-way operation and the server does not need to wait for a response. Another property that we use in the write file process is `ReplyFileName`, which will specify the name and extension of the file that will be created. We can use the `MessageID` property to get a unique filename for every file that is created (for example, we can use it to store all the incoming requests and look for the `MessageID` when an error occurs):

```
<api xmlns="http://ws.apache.org/ns/synapse" name="vfs" context="/vfs">
    <resource methods="POST" url-mapping="/writeSimple">
        <inSequence>
            <property name="OUT_ONLY" value="true"
            scope="default" type="STRING"/>
            <property name="transport.vfs.ReplyFileName"
expression="fn:concat(fn:substring-after(get-
            property(' MessageID'), 'urn:uuid:'), '.xml')" scope="transport"/>
            <call>
                <endpoint>
                    <address uri="vfs:file:///home/user/vfs/out"/>
                </endpoint>
            </call>
            <payloadFactory media-type="json">
                <format>{"status":"File created"}</format>
                <args/>
            </payloadFactory>
            <respond/>
        </inSequence>
    </resource>
</api>
```

The problem in this solution is that we need to know the target destination path to store the files, because this will be set up in the endpoint and hence all the files will be created in the same directory. In the next example, we will dynamically create a file with the information received in the request to the API. In order to do that, we need to configure the `To` header with the full path and the name of the file.

For the content of the file, we will use the `PayloadFactory` mediator, replacing the content of the payload with the value of the property content of the incoming request. This is the request to the API:

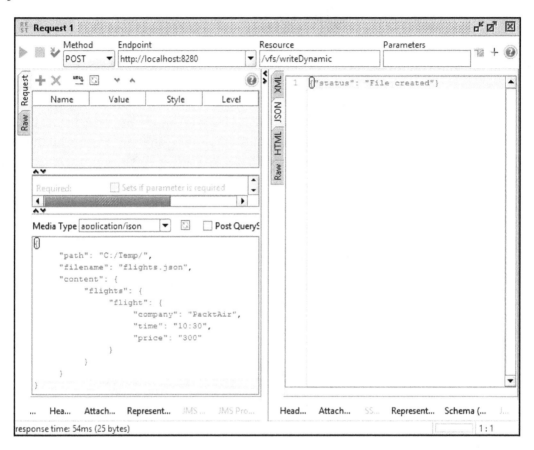

As we can see in the preceding SoapUI request, the service is waiting for the path where the file will be created, the name of the file, and the content for the file. The API will return a JSON format message, explaining that the file has been created:

```
<api xmlns="http://ws.apache.org/ns/synapse" name="vfs" context="/vfs">
    <resource methods="POST" uri-template="/writeDynamic">
        <inSequence>
            <log level="custom">
                <property name="LOG" value="Get Parameters"/>
            </log>
            <property name="PATH"
                            expression="json-eval($.path)"/>
            <property name="FILENAME"
```

```
                             expression="json-eval($.filename)"/>
        <property name="CONTENT"
                             expression="json-eval($.content)"/>
        <header name="To" expression="fn:concat(
               'vfs:file:///',
               $ctx:PATH,
               $ctx:FILENAME)"/>
        <property name="OUT_ONLY" value="true"
        scope="default" type="STRING"/>
        <log level="custom">
            <property name="LOG" value="Creating file"/>
        </log>
        <payloadFactory media-type="json">
            <format>$1</format>
            <args>
                <arg evaluator="xml"
                expression="$ctx:CONTENT"/>
            </args>
        </payloadFactory>
        <call/>
        <log level="custom">
            <property name="LOG" value="Creating response"/>
        </log>
        <payloadFactory media-type="json">
            <format>{"status":"File created"}</format>
            <args/>
        </payloadFactory>
        <respond/>
      </inSequence>
    </resource>
  </api>
```

Transferring files

Transferring files is usually required in big integrations where we need to move some files
without processing them. For example, we can be polling for a file in a local directory and
once the file appears, we move it to another folder, such as a remote FTP server. In that
scenario, we must take care of big files in order to not use too much memory resources
(refer to the *Large files* configuration section at the beginning of the chapter).

In the next example, we will use an `inboundEndpoint` to poll a directory for a file, and then we will send that file to a FTP server. In order to do that, we need to create two resources: the `inboundEndpoint` that is waiting for the file, and a sequence that will send the file to the remote FTP server:

```
<inboundEndpoint name="TransferFile" onError="fault" protocol="file"
sequence="TransferFileSequence" suspend="false">
    <parameters>
        <parameter name="interval">1000</parameter>
        <parameter name="sequential">true</parameter>
        <parameter name="coordination">true</parameter>
        <parameter name="transport.vfs.FileURI">
            file:///home/user/vfs/in
        </parameter>
        <parameter name="transport.vfs.ContentType">
            text/plain
        </parameter>
        <parameter name="transport.vfs.Locking">
            enable
        </parameter>
        <parameter name="transport.vfs.ActionAfterProcess">
            DELETE
        </parameter>
        <parameter name="transport.vfs.ActionAfterFailure">
            DELETE
        </parameter>
        <parameter name="transport.vfs.AutoLockRelease">
            false
        </parameter>
        <parameter name="transport.vfs.LockReleaseSameNode">
            false
        </parameter>
        <parameter name="transport.vfs.DistributedLock">
            false
        </parameter>
        <parameter name="transport.vfs.FileSortAttribute">
            NONE
        </parameter>
        <parameter name="transport.vfs.FileSortAscending">
            true
        </parameter>
        <parameter name="transport.vfs.CreateFolder">
            true
        </parameter>
        <parameter name="transport.vfs.Streaming">
            false
        </parameter>
```

```
      <parameter name="transport.vfs.Build">
         false
      </parameter>
   </parameters>
</inboundEndpoint>

<sequence name="TransferFileSequence">
   <property expression="get-
   property('transport','FILE_NAME')"
   name="transport.vfs.ReplyFileName" scope="transport"
   xmlns:ns="http://org.apache.synapse/xsd"/>
   <property name="OUT_ONLY" scope="default" type="STRING"
   value="true"/>
      <send>
         <endpoint>
            <address uri="vfs:file:///home/user/vfs/out"/>
         </endpoint>
      </send>
</sequence>
```

In the preceding sequence, we get the name of the original file with the FILE_NAME property and set up the same as the name of the destiny file.

File connector

Connectors are the way that we have in the WSO2 servers for adding functionalities that are not supported by default. WSO2 has a virtual *store* where we can look for and download the required connector and install it in our servers; all of these connectors are open source and free to use. The URL of the store where we can find the connectors for all the servers is https://store.wso2.com/store; also, the WSO2 official documentation confluence has a dedicated project at https://docs.wso2.com/display/ESBCONNECTORS.

A file connector allows us to perform various operations with the filesystems from the Enterprise Integrator server. The link to the store where we can find the connector to download and install it in the server is: https://store.wso2.com/store/assets/esbconnector/details/48bab332-c6a6-4f5a-9b7 9-17e29c7ad4c6, and the official documentation confluence page is https://docs.wso2.com/display/ESBCONNECTORS/File+Connector+Version+2. Here, we have a list of all the operations that we can perform with the file connector:

- append
- archive

- copy
- create
- delete
- isFileExist
- listFileZip
- move
- read Reads
- search
- unzip
- ftpOverProxy
- send

Configuring

In order to install the file connector, we need to download the `.zip` folder of the WSO2 *store* and upload it to the Enterprise Integrator server from the form located at **Home** | **Manage** | **Connectors** | **Add**:

After that, the connector must be in the list of connectors deployed in the Enterprise Integrator server without restarting the server:

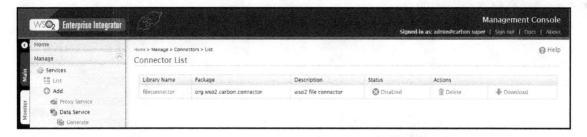

The connector is uploaded as disabled by default, as we can see in the preceding screenshot, so we need to enable it before use by clicking on the **Disabled** link of the status column.

Working

In the next example, we will create an API that receives a JSON payload request with flights information and the file to store it. The service will check whether a file exists. If the file exists, the information data will be added; if not, a file will be created with the following content:

```
<api xmlns="http://ws.apache.org/ns/synapse" name="flights"
context="/flights">
    <resource methods="POST" url-mapping="/fileConnector">
        <inSequence>
            <property name="PATH"
                            expression="json-eval($.path)"/>
            <property name="FILENAME"
                            expression="json-eval($.filename)"/>
            <property name="CONTENT"
                            expression="json-eval($.content)"/>
            <property name="source"
            expression="fn:concat('file://',$ctx:PATH,$ctx:FILENAME)"/>
            <fileconnector.isFileExist>
                <source>{$ctx:source}</source>
            </fileconnector.isFileExist>
            <property name="exists"
             expression="json-eval($.fileExist)" type="BOOLEAN"/>
            <filter xpath="$ctx:exists">
                <then>
                    <fileconnector.append>
                        <destination>{$ctx:source}</destination>
                        <inputContent>{$ctx:CONTENT}</inputContent>
```

```xml
                    </fileconnector.append>
                    <payloadFactory media-type="json">
                        <format>{"status":"File updated"}</format>
                        <args/>
                    </payloadFactory>
                </then>
                <else>
                    <fileconnector.create>
                        <source>{$ctx:source}</source>
                        <inputContent>{$ctx:CONTENT}</inputContent>
                    </fileconnector.create>
                    <payloadFactory media-type="json">
                        <format>{"status":"File created"}</format>
                        <args/>
                    </payloadFactory>
                </else>
            </filter>
            <respond/>
        </inSequence>
    </resource>
</api>
```

We can test the API with the SoapUI program, as follows:

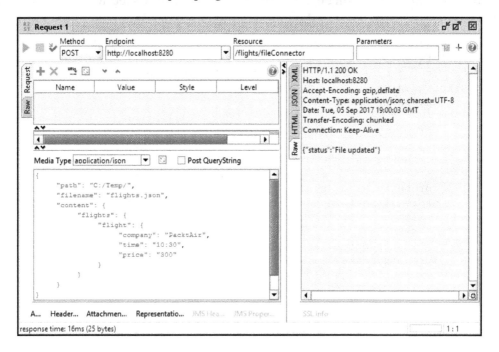

Summary

In this chapter, we worked with the VFS protocol in order to interact with files from the Enterprise Integrator server. The use of files is really common in big integration projects where we have different servers (some of them can be legacy), and the action of reading and writing files is a normal input/output for servers. In the chapter, we covered a variety of file scenarios such as read, write, and transfer without processing files over different locations, such as the local, samba, FTP, FTPS, and SFTP repositories.

In the next chapter, we will continue with another protocol very important to integration scenarios, that is, JMS. This protocol will allow us to use business queues where we can store the messages temporarily to process later; this is used for reliable messaging and for minimizing the errors in the logic of our services.

12
Integrating with JMS - WSO2 EI Message Brokering

In the previous chapters, we learned how to integrate with the **Virtual File System** (**VFS**) that allows us to access FTP, read and write messages from/to the filesystem, monitor a folder, and much more, which is quite a common task on a daily basis. In this chapter, we shall learn how to integrate with a Message Broker, which is a must in scenarios such as the following:

- High-performance integrations
- Integrations with reliable messaging and guaranteed delivery
- Asynchronous integrations
- Message throttling

You can find out more about this pattern and many others at: http://www. enterpriseintegrationpatterns.com.

In the Message Broker, what we will use is WSO2 Message Broker, which is integrated in WSO2 EI and supports **Java Message Service** (**JMS**) 2.0. The JMS API is a standard API to create, send, receive, and read messages that can be implemented by any providers.

We have already learned how to install and start up WSO2 EI, and now we will learn to do the following:

- Create message queues for our services
- Publish messages to a queue from our service
- Consume messages from a queue in our service

Creating message queues

WSO2 Message Broker allows us to easily create as many queues as we need for our services. As you may remember from the first chapter, you can start up all components automatically, or you can just start the required components, which are WSO2 EI and WSO2 Message Broker in this case. As shown in `chapter 1`, *Getting Started with SOA and WSO2*, we follow these steps to start WSO2 Message Broker:

1. From command prompt (Windows) or shell (Linux/Mac), go to the `<EI_HOME>/wso2/ broker/bin` directory.
2. Type the following command:
    - On Linux or Mac OS: `sh wso2server.sh`
    - On Windows: `wso2server.bat`

By default, we will find WSO2 MB Management Console in port 9446.

We can create two different message queues in WSO2 Message Broker depending on the messaging pattern we are using. For the point-to-point channel messaging pattern (`http://www.enterpriseintegrationpatterns.com/patterns/messaging/PointToPointChannel.html`), we will create **Queues**, and for the publish-subscribe pattern, we will create **Topics**:

We just need to click on the **Add** button to add a queue or a topic. Both **Queues** and **Topics** have similar add forms:

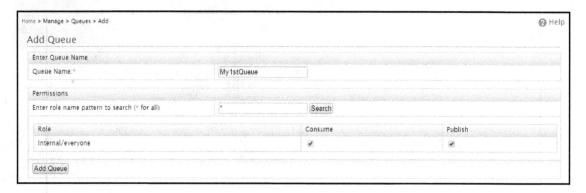

We will create our first queue with the following data:

- **Queue Name**: My1stQueue
- **Permissions**: We will allow everyone to consume messages from our queue as well as publish messages to it, so we will check both **Consume** and **Publish**

Now, we just need to click on **Queue List** section to see a list of the existing queues, including the one we have just created:

The administration of the queue is quite a simple task in WSO2 Message Broker:

- **Editing the queue**: By clicking on the queue name, we will go to the creation/edit window

- **Publishing messages to the queue**: If we click on the **Publish Messages** link of a row, a window for sending a message to the queue will show up:

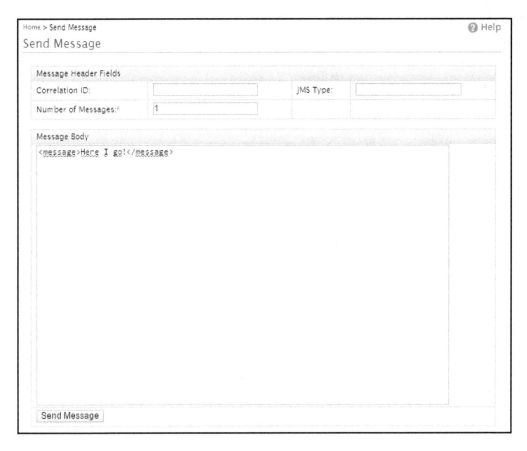

This is a useful feature that allows us to easily send new messages to the queue when developing a service. We only have to set the **Message Body** and the number of messages we want to publish.

- **Browse the queue messages**: We click on the **Browse** column of a queue to browse all messages in the queue:

- **Empty the queue**: If we click on **Purge Messages**, all messages will be removed
- **Remove the queue**: We will click on **Delete** to remove the queue

The way topics and queues are handled is quite similar, so what we learned here about queues is that it will also help us to work with queues in WSO2 Message Broker.

Publishing messages to a queue

At this point, we have our queue ready to receive new messages. Here, we will learn how to send a message from **WSO2 EI** to a **JMS Queue**, which in this case will be the queue we created in the previous section:

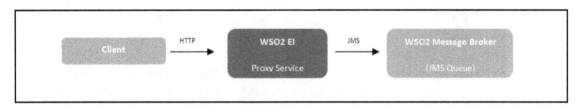

First of all, we have to enable the JMS transport sender in WSO2 EI so that we can send messages to a JMS endpoint; in this case, the `My1stQueue` queue. You may remember what we learned in the first chapter about how to configure different transports in WSO2 EI. Assuming this background, we will follow these steps to enable the JMS transport for WSO2 Message Broker:

1. Open the `axis2.xml` file.
2. Look for the following string in this file:

    ```
    transportSender name="jms"
    class="org.apache.axis2.transport.jms.JMSSender"
    ```

    You must find an XML tag that is commented by default when you download a fresh WSO2 EI:

```
<!-- uncomment this and configure to use connection pools for sending messages>
  <transportSender name="jms" class="org.apache.axis2.transport.jms.JMSSender"/-->
```

3. As you can imagine from the comment preceding the XML tag, we just need to uncomment the transportSender tag:

```
<!-- uncomment this and configure to use connection pools for
sending messages-->
<transportSender name="jms"
class="org.apache.axis2.transport.jms.JMSSender"/>
```

Check the XML syntax as any error will result in WSO2 EI failing to start up.

4. Save the file.

5. Copy the following files from the <EI_HOME>/wso2/broker/clent-lib/ directory to the <EI_HOME>/lib/directory:

   - andes-client-3.2.4.jar
   - geronimo-jms_1.1_spec-1.1.0.wso2v1.jar
   - org.wso2.securevault-1.0.0-wso2v2.jar

6. Edit the <EI_HOME>/conf/jndi.properties file to set the connection factories required for sending the messages to the JMS queue. We will set topic connection factory as well to avoid errors during WSO2 EI startup. We will also set these values:

```
connectionfactory.QueueConnectionFactory =
amqp://admin:admin@clientID/carbon?brokerlist='tcp://localhost:5675
'
connectionfactory.TopicConnectionFactory =
amqp://admin:admin@clientID/carbon?brokerlist='tcp://localhost:5675
'
```

These values are for the default installation of WSO2 EI. You must also set the proper host and port (bold values) depending on the case. You can verify that the port is connected by taking a look at the WSO2 Message Broker startup log:

```
[EI-Broker] INFO
{org.wso2.carbon.andes.internal.QpidServiceComponent} -
Successfully connected to AMQP server on port 5675
```

7. Save the file.

8. Ensure that WSO2 EI Broker is up, and then restart WSO2 EI.

Now we are ready to send messages to a JMS queue in our services. To achieve this, we have to do the following:

1. Add these properties before the `send` mediator in our sequence:

```
<property name="OUT_ONLY" value="true"/>
<property name="FORCE_SC_ACCEPTED" scope="axis2" value="true"/>
```

This service will not have any response since the message is sent to the queue to be processed later, which is called one-way. The only response sent to the consumer of the service will be an HTTP accepted code, the 202 code. This reason is why we have to add these properties to the service.

2. Use the send mediator, using an endpoint in which the URL is defined as follows:

```
jms:/My1stQueue?transport.jms.ConnectionFactoryJNDIName=QueueConnec
tionFactory&java.naming.factory.initial=org.wso2.andes.jndi.Propert
iesFileInitialContextFactory&java.naming.provider.url=conf/jndi.pro
perties&transport.jms.DestinationType=queue
```

Here, the bold string is the name of the queue in the JMS server. If you set this URL in using Management Console, you will have to replace the `&` character with `&amp;`.

For instance, our sequence can look like this:

```
<sequence name="InQueueSequence" trace="enable"
xmlns="http://ws.apache.org/ns/synapse">
<log level="full"/>
<property name="OUT_ONLY" value="true"/>
<property name="FORCE_SC_ACCEPTED" scope="axis2" value="true"/>
<send>
<endpoint>
<address
uri="jms:/My1stQueue?transport.jms.ConnectionFactoryJNDIName=QueueConnectio
nFactory&amp;java.naming.factory.initial=org.wso2.andes.jndi.PropertiesFile
InitialContextFactory&amp;java.naming.provider.url=conf/jndi.properties&amp
;transport.jms.DestinationType=queue"/>
</endpoint>
</send>
</sequence>
```

We just need to create a proxy, called `My1stProxyPublisher` for instance, which will call this sequence, and we can check how the message is sent to the queue. This proxy will look like this:

```
<proxy name="My1stProxyPublisher" startOnLoad="true" transports="http
https" xmlns="http://ws.apache.org/ns/synapse">
<target>
<inSequence>
    <sequence key="InQueueSequence"/>
</inSequence>
<outSequence/>
<faultSequence/>
</target>
<publishWSDL>
<wsdl:definitions >
<!-- your wsdl here --> .....
</wsdl:definitions>
</publishWSDL>
</proxy>
```

You can find this proxy in this chapter's resources. So, consider that we consume the service, as shown in this SoapUI request:

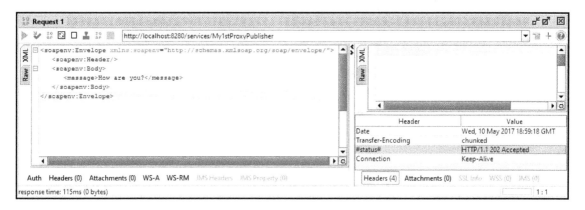

We will see that there is nothing in the XML tab of the response, but in the header, we have received the **HTTP/1.1 202 Accepted** property.

In WSO2 EI, we will see the logged request received due to the log mediator being added to the sequence:

```
[2017-05-10 20:59:18,579] []  INFO - LogMediator To: /services/My1stProxyPublisher
, WSAction: urn:mediate, SOAPAction: urn:mediate, MessageID: urn:uuid:8fb98897-583
2-4ee3-8993-2da79505822a, Direction: request, Envelope: <?xml version='1.0' encodi
ng='utf-8'?><soapenv:Envelope xmlns:soapenv="http://schemas.xmlsoap.org/soap/envel
ope/"><soapenv:Body>
    <message>How are you?</message>
  </soapenv:Body></soapenv:Envelope>
```

Finally, we can see that the message is stored in the queue we created:

Queue Content My1stQueue

Content Type	Message ID	Redelivered	Timestamp	Properties	Message Summary
[T] Text	ID:a77a0370-9fd8-3289-aa15-f2082379f6b7	false	1494442746437	JMS_QPID_DESTTYPE = 1,	<message>Here I more..
[T] Text	ID:901b3e21-5262-33f4-9912-35bc064684b4	false	1494442758662	SOAPAction = "urn:mediate", Accept-Encoding = gzip,deflate, Connection = Keep-Alive, Content-Length = 192, Content-Type = text/xml;charset=UTF-8, Host = localhost:8280, User-Agent = Apache-HttpClient/4.1.1 (java 1.5), JMS_QPID_DESTTYPE = 1,	<?xml version=' more..

We can check the content by clicking on **more..** in the second row:

Home > Message Content

Message Content

```
<?xml version='1.0' encoding='UTF-8'?><soapenv:Envelope xmlns:soapenv="http://schemas.xmlsoap.org/soap/envelope/"><soapenv:Body>
    <message>How are you?</message>
  </soapenv:Body></soapenv:Envelope>
```

Consuming messages from a queue

Now, we will learn how to consume messages from a queue. A common way to consume these queues is using a proxy that is attached to the queue. This proxy monitors the queue, consuming every message that is received in the queue:

In order to achieve this, we have to enable the transport receiver so that the proxy will be able to connect to the **JMS Queue**, where messages await to be consumed. We will proceed in the same way as we did for the transport sender in the previous section, but in this case, we have to enable the transport receiver:

1. Open the `axis2.xml` file.
2. Look for the following string in this file:

   ```
   transportReceiver name="jms"
   class="org.apache.axis2.transport.jms.JMSListener"
   ```

   You must find an XML tag that is commented by default when you download a fresh WSO2 EI:

```
<!--Uncomment this and configure as appropriate for JMS transport support with WSO2 MB 2.x.x -->
<!--transportReceiver name="jms" class="org.apache.axis2.transport.jms.JMSListener">
```

   In our case, we will `uncomment` the WSO2 Message Broker configuration, but other sample configurations for most common JMS Servers, such as ActiveMQ and Apache Qpid, are provided.

3. As you may imagine from the comment preceding the XML tag, we just need to uncomment the `transportReciver` tag. We do not need to configure any values here since the WSO2 MB configuration is delegated in the `EI_HOME>/conf/jndi.properties` file:

```
<!--Uncomment this and configure as appropriate for JMS
transport support with WSO2 MB 2.x.x -->
<transportReceiver name="jms"
class="org.apache.axis2.transport.jms.JMSListener">
<parameter name="myTopicConnectionFactory" locked="false">
<parameter name="java.naming.factory.initial"
locked="false">org.wso2.andes.jndi.PropertiesFileInitialContext
Factory</parameter>
<parameter name="java.naming.provider.url"
locked="false">conf/jndi.properties</parameter>
<parameter name="transport.jms.ConnectionFactoryJNDIName"
locked="false">TopicConnectionFactory</parameter>
<parameter name="transport.jms.ConnectionFactoryType"
locked="false">topic</parameter>
</parameter>
<parameter name="myQueueConnectionFactory" locked="false">
<parameter name="java.naming.factory.initial"
locked="false">org.wso2.andes.jndi.PropertiesFileInitialContext
Factory</parameter>
<parameter name="java.naming.provider.url"
locked="false">conf/jndi.properties</parameter>
<parameter name="transport.jms.ConnectionFactoryJNDIName"
locked="false">QueueConnectionFactory</parameter>
<parameter name="transport.jms.ConnectionFactoryType"
locked="false">queue</parameter>
</parameter>
<parameter name="default" locked="false">
<parameter name="java.naming.factory.initial"
locked="false">org.wso2.andes.jndi.PropertiesFileInitialContext
Factory</parameter>
<parameter name="java.naming.provider.url"
locked="false">conf/jndi.properties</parameter>
<parameter name="transport.jms.ConnectionFactoryJNDIName"
locked="false">QueueConnectionFactory</parameter>
<parameter name="transport.jms.ConnectionFactoryType"
locked="false">queue</parameter>
</parameter>
</transportReceiver>
```

Check the XML syntax as any error will result in WSO2 EI failing to start up.

4. Save the file.

5. Copy the following files from the `<EI_HOME>`/wso2/broker/clent-lib/ directory to the `<EI_HOME>`/lib/ directory:

   - `andes-client-3.2.4.jar`
   - `geronimo-jms_1.1_spec-1.1.0.wso2v1.jar`
   - `org.wso2.securevault-1.0.0-wso2v2.jar`

6. Edit the `<EI_HOME>`/conf/jndi.properties file to set the connection factories required for sending the messages to the JMS queue. We will set the topic connection factory as well, to avoid errors during WSO2 EI startup. We will set these values:

```
connectionfactory.QueueConnectionFactory =
amqp://admin:admin@clientID/carbon?brokerlist='tcp://localhost:5675
'
connectionfactory.TopicConnectionFactory =
amqp://admin:admin@clientID/carbon?brokerlist='tcp://localhost:5675
'
```

These values are for the default installation of WSO2 EI. You must set the proper host and port (bold values) depending on the case. You can verify that the port is correct by taking a look at the WSO2 Message Broker startup log:

```
[EI-Broker] INFO
{org.wso2.carbon.andes.internal.QpidServiceComponent} -
Successfully connected to AMQP server on port 5675
```

7. Save the file.

8. Ensure that WSO2 EI Broker is up, and then restart WSO2 EI.

Now, we are ready to consume messages from a JMS queue in our services. To achieve this, we have to perform the following steps:

1. Create a proxy where the transport is set to JMS:

This will set the transport attribute to **jms** in the proxy definition:

```
<proxy xmlns="http://ws.apache.org/ns/synapse" name="My1stProxyConsumer"
startOnLoad="true"statistics="disable"trace="disable"transports="jms">
```

2. Set the name of the queue we are consuming. We can do it in two ways:
   - Set the name using a parameter in the proxy:

     ```
     <parameter
     name="transport.jms.Destination">QueueName</parameter>
     ```

   - Omit the `transport.jms.Destination` parameter, which will result in the proxy consuming a queue with the same name as the proxy

3. Set the `contentType` of the message you will receive. For soap messages, we will set `application/soap+xml`. We do this by adding a new parameter to the proxy:

   ```
   <parameter name="transport.jms.ContentType">
   <rules xmlns="">
   <jmsProperty>contentType</jmsProperty>
   <default>application/soap+xml</default>
   </rules>
   </parameter>
   ```

4. Add this property to the sequence before the send mediator:

   ```
   <property name="OUT_ONLY" value="true"/>
   ```

After all this configuration in our proxy definition, we will be ready to consume messages from a JMS queue. Putting everything together, the proxy that consumes the queue and processes the message in a defined sequence will look like this:

```
<proxy xmlns="http://ws.apache.org/ns/synapse"
name="My1stProxyConsumer"startOnLoad="true"statistics="enable"
trace="enable"transports="jms">
<target inSequence="InJMSSequence"/>
<parameter name="transport.jms.Destination">My1stQueue</parameter>
<parameter name="transport.jms.ContentType">
<rules xmlns="">
<jmsProperty>contentType</jmsProperty>
<default>application/soap+xml</default>
</rules>
</parameter>
<description/>
</proxy>
```

Once the message is consumed, you can work with it as usual and send it to a sequence where you shall implement your logic; just remember to set the `OUT_ONLY` property.

In order to illustrate a complete cycle, we will build this scenario using the services we created earlier:

1. The `My1stProxyPublisher` proxy will receive a message to insert a new city in the database. It has been modified to publish the same WSDL as the `My1stDataService`. This proxy will then insert the message in the `My1stQueue` queue.

2. The `My1stProxyConsumer` proxy will consume the message from the queue and send it to the `My1stDataService` service, which we created earlier when we learned to build data services. This proxy uses a sequence called `InJMSSequence`, where we just set the `OUT_ONLY` property and send the message to the `My1stDataService` endpoint.

You can find these resources in the `My1stCompositeApplication_1.0.6.car` carbon file. After deploying it, you will also be able to send a message using the SoapUI project called `Chapter12_JMS_Publisher&Consumer-soapui-project.xml`.

Now we will take a look at the evidence:

1. Here, we see the result of the invocation of the `My1stProxyPublisher` service that will send the message to the `My1stQueue` queue. Note the **202 Accepted** response:

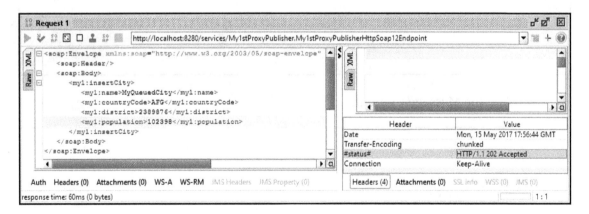

2. Here, check the log message generated by `My1stProxyPublisher` before sending the message to the queue, where we can see the message we have just sent:

```
[2017-05-15 19:56:44,260] []  INFO - LogMediator To: /services/My1stProxyPublisher.My1stProxyPublisherHttpSoap12Endpoi
nt, WSAction: urn:insertCity, SOAPAction: urn:insertCity, MessageID: urn:uuid:ece942ec-f932-474c-9eeb-8e2bea1c1cd6, Di
rection: request, Status = Sending message to My1stQueue, Envelope: <?xml version='1.0' encoding='utf-8'?><soap:Envelo
pe xmlns:soap="http://www.w3.org/2003/05/soap-envelope" xmlns:my1="http://www.my1stdataservice.com"><soap:Body>
    <my1:insertCity>
        <my1:name>MyQueuedCity</my1:name>
        <my1:countryCode>AFG</my1:countryCode>
        <my1:district>2389876</my1:district>
        <my1:population>102398</my1:population>
    </my1:insertCity>
</soap:Body></soap:Envelope>
```

3. Here, we see the queue content with the message we have just sent. As the `My1stProxyConsumer` proxy is running, you will probably not be able to find the message if you try to look for it in the queue. This is because the message is consumed immediately after being inserted, so you may not be fast enough to catch it there. Nevertheless, you can deactivate `My1stProxyConsumer` in its dashboard. Once you have checked how messages are being queued, you can activate it again, and the messages will be consumed in a few seconds:

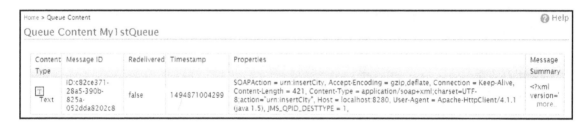

Home > Queue Content

Queue Content My1stQueue

Content Type	Message ID	Redelivered	Timestamp	Properties	Message Summary
Text	ID:c82ce371-28a5-390b-825a-052dda8202c8	false	1494871004299	SOAPAction = urn:insertCity, Accept-Encoding = gzip,deflate, Connection = Keep-Alive, Content-Length = 421, Content-Type = application/soap+xml;charset=UTF-8;action="urn:insertCity", Host = localhost:8280, User-Agent = Apache-HttpClient/4.1.1 (java 1.5), JMS_QPID_DESTTYPE = 1,	<?xml version=' more.

And the **Message Content**:

Home > Message Content

Message Content

```
<?xml version='1.0' encoding='UTF-8'?><soap:Envelope xmlns:soap="http://www.w3.org/2003/05/soap-envelope" xmlns:my1="http://www.my1stdataservice.com"><soap:Body>
    <my1:insertCity>
        <my1:name>MyQueuedCity</my1:name>
        <my1:countryCode>AFG</my1:countryCode>
        <my1:district>2389876</my1:district>
        <my1:population>102398</my1:population>
    </my1:insertCity>
</soap:Body></soap:Envelope>
```

4. Now, the message is consumed when we activate the proxy again, so the queue will get empty:

5. If we take a look at the WSO2 EI log, we will see the log generated by the `My1stProxyConsumer` proxy when processing the message from the queue:

```
[2017-05-15 20:16:38,356] []  INFO - ServiceTaskManager Task manager for service : My1stPr
oxyConsumer [re-]initialized
[2017-05-15 20:16:38,834] []  INFO - LogMediator To: , WSAction: urn:insertCity, SOAPActio
n: urn:insertCity, MessageID: ID:c82ce371-28a5-390b-825a-052dda8202c8, Direction: request,
Status = Consuming message from My1stQueue and sending to My1stDataService  Envelope: <?x
ml version='1.0' encoding='utf-8'?><soap:Envelope xmlns:soap="http://www.w3.org/2003/05/so
ap-envelope" xmlns:my1="http://www.my1stdataservice.com"><soap:Body>
    <my1:insertCity>
        <my1:name>MyQueuedCity</my1:name>
        <my1:countryCode>AFG</my1:countryCode>
        <my1:district>2389876</my1:district>
        <my1:population>102398</my1:population>
    </my1:insertCity>
  </soap:Body></soap:Envelope>
```

6. Finally, the message will be sent to the data service, and the new city will be added to the city, as we see here:

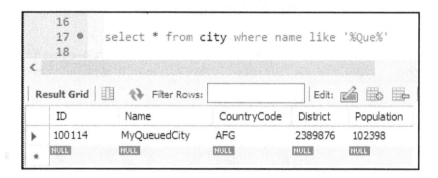

You can find in this chapter's resources all the services needed to perform this example, as well as the SoapUI project called `Chapter12_JMS_Publisher&Consumer-soapui-project.xml`. The carbon file with this scenario is `My1stCompositeApplication_1.0.7.car`.

Dead Letter Channel

Dead Letter Channel pattern is a must when working with queues and integration, and when you need to guarantee a message's delivery. In this pattern, when a message delivery fails, normally after several retries, it is moved from its queue to a special queue for an ad hoc treatment later.

You can find out more about this pattern by visiting: `http://www.enterpriseintegrationpatterns.com/patterns/messaging/DeadLetterChannel.html`, where we can see the following explanation diagram:

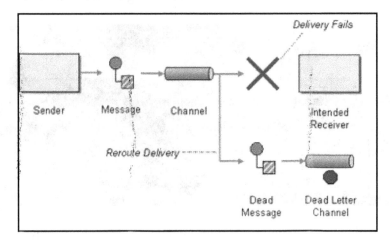

The Dead Letter Channel where the message finally ends is typically another queue that receives special treatment from administrators because all messages in this queue mean an error in the system.

WSO2 EI Message Broker implements this pattern out of the box, so we just need to set a number of retries, which, by default, is set to 10. We can modify it by following these steps:

1. Edit the `$EI_HOME/wso2/broker/conf/broker.xml` file.
2. Locate the `maximumRedeliveryAttempts` XML tag and set the desired attempts.
3. Save and restart.

Taking advantage of this pattern requires that your project uses transactions. This means that the information processing in your system is split into individual and indivisible operations, called transactions. This way, you work with a temporal state of your system that is persisted if all operations succeed (commit) or discarded if any of them fail (rollback).

So, if you need to use the Dead Letter Channel pattern, you have to keep in mind the following considerations:

- Use transactions in the client that consume the queue. This way, the message is removed from the queue when all operations in your client succeed (perform a commit). If anything fails (rollback), the message is kept in the queue until the next retry. When the number of retries expires, the message will be moved to the Dead Letter Channel.
- Configure WSO2 Message Broker properly for the number of retries.
- Configure your client (Java, WSO2 EI, and so on) properly to use transactions. This may imply using special drivers for accessing database and additional libraries.

Transactions can be local or distributed. A local transaction represents an atomic work on a single connection to a data source. Distributed transactions represent an atomic work on several distributed resources; for instance, a JMS queue and a database. Unfortunately, WSO2 Message Broker does not support JMS-distributed transactions.

You can find more information about transactions at: `https://docs.wso2.com/display/EI600/JMS+Transactions`.

Connectors

In previous chapters, we have learned how to integrate the WSO2 EI server with the on-premise environment but nowadays is frequently that we need to integrate also with cloud-based Software as a Service (SaaS) applications. Most of these SaaS applications exposes standard interfaces to consume their core functionalities by SOAP or REST APIs that could be consumed externally by third-party servers like WSO2 EI.

WSO2 provides us *connectors* that allow us to interact with the functionality of a third-party product from the WSO2 message flow in a fast and easy way for developers.

Types of Connectors

Depends on the technology exposed for the backend application that we want to integrate, WSO2 provides us 3 different types of connectors:

SOAP-based connectors

When we want to integrate with SOAP APIs we can write the entire connector with Synapse configurations. The next example shows a SOAP-based connector for Salesforce to execute the query method of the API:

```
<template name="query" xmlns="http://ws.apache.org/ns/synapse">
 <parameter name="sessionId"/>
 <parameter name="url"/>
 <parameter name="queryString"/>
 <sequence>
   <payloadFactory>
     <format>
       <soapenv:Envelope
         xmlns:soapenv="http://schemas.xmlsoap.org/soap/envelope/"
         xmlns:urn="urn:partner.soap.sforce.com">
         <soapenv:Header>
           <urn:SessionHeader>
           <urn:sessionId>$1</urn:sessionId>
           </urn:SessionHeader>
         </soapenv:Header>
         <soapenv:Body>
           <urn:query>
             <urn:queryString>$2</urn:queryString>
           </urn:query>
         </soapenv:Body>
       </soapenv:Envelope>
     </format>
     <args>
       <arg expression="$func:sessionId"/>
       <arg expression="$func:queryString"/>
     </args>
   </payloadFactory>
   <property name="messageType" scope="axis2" value="text/xml"/>
   <header name="Action"
 value="urn:partner.soap.sforce.com/Soap/queryRequest"/>
   <property value="true" name="FORCE_ERROR_ON_SOAP_FAULT"/>
   <property name="HTTP_METHOD" scope="axis2" value="POST"/>
   <header name="To" expression="$func:url"/>
   <call>
     <endpoint>
```

```
      <default format="soap11">
      <timeout>
        <duration>60000</duration>
        <responseAction>fault</responseAction>
      </timeout>
      <suspendOnFailure>
        <initialDuration>2000</initialDuration>
        <progressionFactor>1.0</progressionFactor>
        <maximumDuration>3000</maximumDuration>
      </suspendOnFailure>
    </default>
  </endpoint>
  </call>
 </sequence>
</template>
```

REST-based connectors

The REST-based connectors are similar to the previous one with the difference in the underlying communication mechanism. For example, to integrate with the Twitter rest API we can use the following source code:

```
<template xmlns="http://ws.apache.org/ns/synapse" name="search">
 <parameter name="search"/>
 <parameter name="accessToken"/>
 <sequence>
   <property name="uri.var.twitter.search" expression="$func:search"/>
   <property name="Authorization" expression="$func:accessToken"
scope="transport"/>
   <property name="messageType" value="application/x-www-form-urlencoded"
scope="axis2"/>
   <payloadFactory media-type="xml">
     <format>
       <soapenv:Envelope
xmlns:soapenv="http://schemas.xmlsoap.org/soap/envelope/">
         <soapenv:Header/>
         <soapenv:Body/>
       </soapenv:Envelope>
     </format>
   <args/>
   </payloadFactory>
   <call>
     <endpoint>
       <http method="GET" uri-
template="https://api.twitter.com/1.1/search/tweets.json?q={uri.var.twitter
.search}"/>
     </endpoint>
```

```
    </call>
  </sequence>
</template>
```

Java API-based connectors

For integrating with JAVA APIs through connectors, we need to use the class mediator for implement the logical inside a Java class that extends the AbstractConnector class and implement the actions in the connect method. Once implemented the Java program we can use it from the synapse configuration. In the next example we use a JAVA API-based connector for integrate with Twilio and send an SMS:

```
import java.util.HashMap;
import java.util.Map;
import org.apache.axiom.om.OMElement;
import org.apache.synapse.MessageContext;
import org.apache.synapse.SynapseException;
import org.apache.synapse.SynapseLog;
import org.wso2.carbon.connector.core.AbstractConnector;
import org.wso2.carbon.connector.core.util.ConnectorUtils;
import org.wso2.carbon.connector.twilio.util.TwilioUtil;
import com.twilio.sdk.TwilioRestClient;
import com.twilio.sdk.resource.factory.SmsFactory;
import com.twilio.sdk.resource.instance.Sms;

public class SendSms extends AbstractConnector {
    public void connect(MessageContext messageContext) {
        SynapseLog log = getLog(messageContext);
        log.auditLog("Start: send SMS");
        String to = (String)
ConnectorUtils.lookupTemplateParamater(messageContext,
TwilioUtil.PARAM_TO);
        String from = (String)
ConnectorUtils.lookupTemplateParamater(messageContext,
TwilioUtil.PARAM_FROM);
        String body = (String)
ConnectorUtils.lookupTemplateParamater(messageContext,
TwilioUtil.PARAM_BODY);
        String statusCallBackUrl = (String)
ConnectorUtils.lookupTemplateParamater(messageContext,
 TwilioUtil.PARAM_STATUS_CALLBACK_URL);
        String applicationSid = (String)
ConnectorUtils.lookupTemplateParamater(messageContext,
 TwilioUtil.PARAM_APPLICATION_SID);
        Map<string, string> params = new HashMap<string, string>();
```

```
        params.put(TwilioUtil.TWILIO_TO, to);
        params.put(TwilioUtil.TWILIO_FROM, from);
        params.put(TwilioUtil.TWILIO_BODY, body);

        if (applicationSid != null) {
            params.put(TwilioUtil.TWILIO_APPLICATION_SID, applicationSid);
        }
        if (statusCallBackUrl != null) {
            params.put(TwilioUtil.TWILIO_STATUS_CALLBACK,
statusCallBackUrl);
        }

        try {
            TwilioRestClient twilioRestClient =
TwilioUtil.getTwilioRestClient(messageContext);
            SmsFactory messageFactory =
twilioRestClient.getAccount().getSmsFactory();
            Sms message = messageFactory.create(params);
            OMElement omResponse =
TwilioUtil.parseResponse("sms.create.success");

            TwilioUtil.addElement(omResponse,
TwilioUtil.PARAM_MESSAGE_SID, message.getSid());
            TwilioUtil.addElement(omResponse, TwilioUtil.PARAM_STATUS,
message.getStatus());
            TwilioUtil.preparePayload(messageContext, omResponse);
        } catch (Exception e) {
            log.error(e.getMessage());
            messageContext.setProperty(SynapseConstants.ERROR_EXCEPTION,
e);
            messageContext.setProperty(SynapseConstants.ERROR_MESSAGE,
e.getMessage());
            messageContext.setProperty(SynapseConstants.ERROR_CODE,
"0007");
            throw new SynapseException(e);
        }
        log.auditLog("End: send SMS");
    }
}
```

The synapse configuration that uses this Java implementation using the class mediator is as follows:

```
<template name="sendSms" xmlns="http://ws.apache.org/ns/synapse">
 <parameter name="body"/>
 <parameter name="to"/>
 <parameter name="from"/>
 <parameter name="statusCallBackUrl"/>
 <parameter name="applicationSid"/>
 <sequence>
     <class name="org.wso2.carbon.connector.twilio.sms.SendSms"/>
 </sequence>
</template>
```

Have a look at `chapter 11`, *Integrating with VFS*, in which we install and use the WSO2 File Connector

Summary

In this chapter, we learned how to send messages to a JMS queue as well as consume them. We also learned to build a typical high-performance scenario where a message is stored in a queue to be processed further by another service, which allows the service to handle a high figure of messages per second. At the end of the chapter, we get in deep about the WSO2 connector to integrate with third-party APIs in a fast-easy way.

Now, we will move on to the next chapter, where we will learn about the newest integration programming language called Ballerina.

>

13
Introduction to Ballerina

In the last chapter, we learned how to integrate with Message Broker using JMS protocol and so on. Now we are facing the last chapter of the book where we will learn about the newest thing in the WSO2 company-the Ballerina programming language.

This chapter is an introduction to this new language that is born to be a reference in the integration languages; in this chapter, we will cover the following:

- The Ballerina language history
- Main concepts about Ballerina
- Ballerina tools
- Working with Ballerina
- Summary

The Ballerina language history

In the WSO2 conference USA 2017 celebrated in San Francisco, WSO2 announced a new integration programming language, called Ballerina. The main target of this programming language is to focus on system integration with easy understanding for everyone, not only programmers. For this reason, we can develop our Ballerina programs in two different ways--writing the code or dragging and dropping the functionality to the design view, which is easy to understand for more people. In the design view, we can draw sequence diagrams that will be automatically translated into code syntax so that we can change from one view to the other and are synchronized in real time.

For example, the echo service that returns the message that we send is as follows in Ballerina code:

```
import ballerina.net.http;
@BasePath("/echo")
service echo {
    @POST
    resource echo(message m) {
        http:convertToResponse(m);
        reply m;
    }
}
```

The ballerina language is easy to read and understand because it uses frequent standard nomenclature like any other programming languages, such as Java or C. In this simple example, we can see how we need to import the core libraries before using them (not auto-import them) or how to define the path and HTTP method of the REST service using annotations syntax. The following is a graphical representation of the preceding code in the sequence diagram:

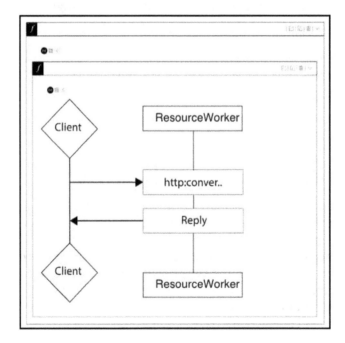

Apart from the visual sequence diagramming tool, Ballerina has a graphical data mapper, a visual Swagger editor, mockup tool, and plugins for different IDEs such as IntelliJ IDEA, Vim, Atom, Sublime Text, or VSCode.

The main concepts of Ballerina

Ballerina has been built for integration purposes, having the native ability for working with JSON and XML messages, and easy build for APIs using HTTP, REST, and Swagger to define and implement it.

We can make two different types of applications in this programming language--network services and main functions. On the one hand, we have the network services that keep waiting once launched for incoming requests, until the process is stopped. On the other hand, the main function does a specific action when it is launched and then finished until the next execution.

Connectors

Apart from the Ballerina core syntax, we can use different connectors for integrating with a list of commonly used servers in an easy and fast way. These connectors are constantly improving, offering us the newest integration for the latest APIs. We can find authentication connectors, such as BasicAuth, OAuth, or AmazonAuth, and also web APIs for social networks or frequently used cloud servers such as Twitter, Gmail, Facebook, LinkedIn, Jira, Google Spreadsheet, or Salesforce.

The users can also create and use their custom connector, so it's an important extension point to use in Ballerina. We have a set of methods to use with connectors:

- `setKeyValue`: Set the key/value pair

- `getValue`: Get the value of a given key

- `updateValue`: Update the value of a key

- `deleteKey`: Delete a key

- `createDir`: Create a directory

- `listDir`: List the directories

- `deleteDir`: Delete a directory

Type system

The Ballerina language comes with four types of attributes--`boolean`, `int`, `float`, and `string`. Apart from these types, the users can create their custom types using struct types, as we do in the C programming language. The next diagram contains all the type systems of Ballerina:

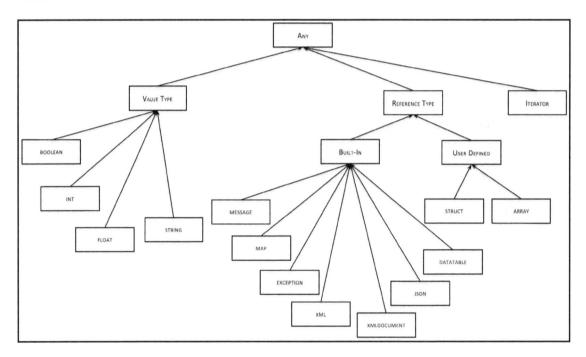

The language statements that we can use are as listed:

- `assignment`
- `if`
- `while`
- `break`
- `try/catch/throw`
- `return`
- `action invocation`
- `fork/join`
- `worker initiation/invocation/join/reply`

Community

The Ballerina has a strong community of supporters that help improve the language from version to version; here is a list to join it and get up to date:

- Users: ballerina-user@googlegroups.com
- Slack: #ballerinalang
- Twitter: @ballerinalang
- StackOverflow: #ballerinalang
- Developers: ballerina-dev@googlegroups.com

Ballerina tools

Ballerina is not only the programming language, but a list of components that provide us with a set of tools that we need since it starts the analysis and requirement phase of our projects, until the programming, documentation, or testing in all the states of the project.

Composer

The Ballerina composer is a browser-based tool for developing the Ballerina projects using three different views. It is possible to go switching between all views because they are real-time synchronized:

- Design view: Is a visual sequence diagram in which we can drag and drop the different components into a canvas place:

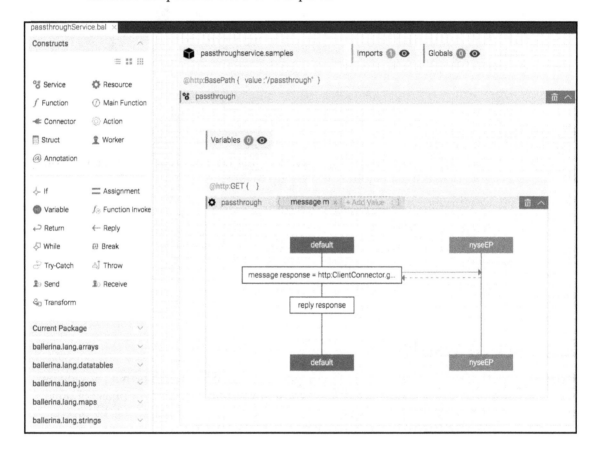

- Source view: To write the code that we need directly:

```
passthroughService.bal ×

1  package passthroughservice.samples;
2
3  import ballerina.net.http;
4
5  @http:BasePath {value:"/passthrough"}
6  service passthrough {
7
8      @http:GET{}
9      resource passthrough (message m) {
10         http:ClientConnector nyseEP = create http:ClientConnector("http://localhost:9090");
11         message response = http:ClientConnector.get(nyseEP, "/nyseStock", m);
12         reply response;
13
14     }
15
16 }
```

- Swagger view: Needed to define services:

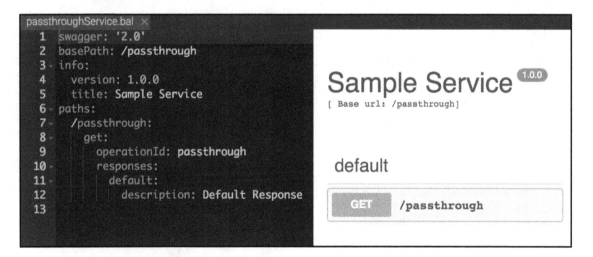

Docerina

Docerina is a tool for generating documentation for the Ballerina language in HTML format, although it can be extended to support other formats as well. All the Ballerina code is documented using Docerina.

The annotations available are as follows:

- @doc:Description: Used to provide a general description of resources, structs, functions, and so on
- @doc:Param: Explain the incoming parameters
- @doc:Return: Explain the outgoing parameters
- @doc:Field: Detail fields inside structs

In the following example, we have a simple Ballerina program that will help us understand the use of the docerina documentation in functions and structs types:

```
import ballerina.lang.system;

@doc:Description{value:"Contains information related to a specific flight"}
@doc:Field{value:"company: Name of the company"}
@doc:Field{value:"time: Time for takeoff"}
@doc:Field{value:"price: General price"}
struct Flight {
    string company;
    string time;
    float price;
}

@doc:Description{value:"Given a flight get the general price"}
@doc:Param{value:"flight: flight to get the price"}
@doc:Return{value:"price: Current price of the flight"}
function getPrice (Flight flight) (float price) {
    return flight.price;
}

function main (string[] args) {
    Flight f1={company:"PacktAir",time:"10:30",price:300.0};
    float price = getPrice(f1);
    system:print(price);
}
```

Testerina

Testerina is the test and mocking framework for the Ballerina programs that we can run with the `ballerina test <package_name>` command. All the test files should contain the `_test.bal` suffix, and the test functions should contain the`test` prefix and must contain at least one assert. Here's the list of all the available test functions:

- `startService (string servicename)`
- `assertTrue(boolean condition)`
- `assertTrue(boolean condition, string message)`
- `assertFalse(boolean condition)`
- `assertFalse(boolean condition, string message)`
- `assertEquals(string actual, string expected)`
- `assertEquals(string actual, string expected, string message)`
- `assertEquals(int actual, int expected)`
- `assertEquals(int actual, int expected, string message)`
- `assertEquals(float actual, float expected)`
- `assertEquals(float actual, float expected, string message)`
- `assertEquals(boolean actual, boolean expected)`
- `assertEquals(boolean actual, boolean expected, string message)`
- `assertEquals(string[] actual, string[] expected)`
- `assertEquals(string[] actual, string[] expected, string message)`
- `assertEquals(float[] actual, float[] expected)`
- `assertEquals(float[] actual, float[] expected, string message)`
- `assertEquals(int[] actual, int[] expected)`
- `assertEquals(int[] actual, int[] expected, string message)`
- `setValue(string pathExpressionToMockableConnector)`

In the next example, we have the following Ballerina program:

```
package samples.foo.bar;

import ballerina.lang.system;
function main (string[] args) {
    int i = intAdd(1, 2);
    system:println("Result: " + i);
}
function intAdd(int a, int b) (int) {
```

```
        return a + b;
    }
```

The text file for the preceding program to check whether the `intAdd` function works as expected will be like this:

```
package samples.foo.bar;
import ballerina.test;
function testInt() {
    int answer = 0;
    answer = intAdd(1, 2);
    test:assertEquals(answer, 3, "IntAdd function failed");
}
```

Packerina

Packerina is under construction right now but will be available for a short period under this name. Packerina will be the tool to manage repositories and dependencies and build the Ballerina programs.

Working with Ballerina

It's time to put ourselves in the Ballerina programmer's shoes and start coding our first Ballerina project. After that, we need to download and install it, so we need to go to the official website and download the latest Ballerina tools distribution, which contains the runtime and the tools needed for writing our Ballerina project; for this, visit `https://ballerinalang.org/downloads/`.

After downloading it, extract the content into a directory that we call <BALLERINA_HOME>, and we need to set the PATH environment variable to the <BALLERINA_HOME>/bin directory:

```
export PATH = $PATH:/User/user/ballerina-tools-0.8.3/bin
```

Now, we are ready to start with the classic first example to understand a new programming language, the Hello World project!

To execute the `helloWorld` project, we must use the following command in a terminal from the <BALLERINA_HOME>/samples directory:

```
ballerina run main helloWorld/helloWorld.bal
```

This will return the following message:

Hello, World!

The program is really simple; here's the content inside it:

```
import ballerina.lang.system;
function main(string[] args) {
    system:println("Hello, World!");
}
```

The preceding example is a *main function* type of Ballerina program; the next example will be a *network service* type with the same "Hello, World!" message. The main difference is that while the preceding example is executed once and then it's finished, the next one will be a REST HTTP service that will be waiting for an incoming request to return the message response. To start the helloWorld service, we need to use the following command in a terminal from the <BALLERINA_HOME>/samples directory:

ballerina run service helloWorldService/helloWorldService.bal

We will see the following output in the terminal:

**ballerina: deploying service(s) in
'helloWorldService/helloWorldService.bal'
ballerina: started server connector http-9090**

As we can see in the output, the service is listening on the 9090 port, and we don't have any response yet like the previous example execution. To test the service, we can make a request to that port and the /hello path:

```
$ curl -v http://localhost:9090/hello
> GET /hello HTTP/1.1
> Host: localhost:9090
> User-Agent: curl/7.51.0
> Accept: */*
>
< HTTP/1.1 200 OK
< Content-Type: text/plain
< Content-Length: 13
<
* Curl_http_done: called premature == 0
* Connection #0 to host localhost left intact
Hello, World!
```

In the last line, we can see that the server responds with the same "Hello, World!" as in the last example. Now, let's take a look at the code and compare the differences between both code programs:

```
import ballerina.lang.messages;
@http:BasePath ("/hello")
service helloWorld {
    @http:GET
    resource sayHello (message m) {
        message response = {};
        messages:setStringPayload(response, "Hello, World!");
        reply response;
    }
}
```

As we can see in the code, Ballerina use annotations for defining the path (/hello) and the HTTP method (GET) for the service.

The next example is a little more complex; it uses a .bsz archive file that contains all the artifacts required to run the service. This service contains a simple integration connecting with another service that returns to us as a message. To run the service, we need to use the following command in a terminal from the <BALLERINA_HOME>/samples directory:

ballerina run service passthroughService/passthroughService.bsz

Then, we will see the following output in the terminal:

**ballerina: deploying service(s) in
'passthroughService/passthroughService.bsz'
ballerina: started server connector http-9090**

Now we have started the server, and it's waiting for a request to begin the logical process. To consume the service, we use the following curl command:

```
curl -v http://localhost:9090/passthrough
> GET /passthrough HTTP/1.1
> Host: localhost:9090
> User-Agent: curl/7.51.0
> Accept: */*
>
< HTTP/1.1 200 OK
< Content-Type: application/json
< Content-Length: 49
<
* Curl_http_done: called premature == 0
* Connection #0 to host localhost left intact
{"exchange":"nyse","name":"IBM","value":"127.50"}
```

The main service that we make the request in is the `passthroughservice.bal` file and it contains the following:

```
package passthroughservice.samples;
import ballerina.net.http;
@http :BasePath ("/passthrough")
service passthrough {
   @http :GET
   resource passthrough (message m) {
      http:ClientConnector nyseEP = create
      http:ClientConnector("http://localhost:9090");
      message response =
          http:ClientConnector.get(nyseEP, "/nyseStock", m);
      reply response;
   }
}
```

This service is making a request to another service in the `9090` port of localhost with the `/nyseStock` path and returns the same message that we get as a response. These types of services are called `passthrough`. This service is located in the `nyseStockService.bal.` file with the following content:

```
package passthroughservice.samples;
import ballerina.lang.messages;
@http :BasePath ("/nyseStock")
service nyseStockQuote {
   @http :GET
   resource stocks (message m) {
      json payload = `{"exchange":"nyse","name":"IBM",
"value":"127.50"}`;
      message response = {};
      messages:setJsonPayload(response, payload);
      reply response;
   }
}
```

This service is waiting for a request and just formats a JSON payload to respond to the client.

Summary

In the course of the book, we went in depth into different sections from simple and generic to more complex and powerful WSO2 capabilities. At first, we made an introduction to the service-oriented architecture in general and focused on the WSO2 world in order to put in context the principles and the target area where we can apply the knowledge and the techniques of the book. This was a very important chapter, because it contained the core basics for all the other chapters, and let the reader understand the SOA architecture even without any previous knowledge about it, making the book readable for all the people interested in learning to develop with WSO2 servers, with or without prior experience.

The second section of the book joins all the chapters with the main focus of how to build services, from Chapter 3, *Building Web Services*, to Chapter 8, *Tasks Scheduling*, both included. In this section, we learned how to use *mediators* for creating APIs and Proxy services, in which we can perform different actions such as transforming the payload or making a conditional route inside to create smarter web services. Also, we learned how to handle the *quality of service configuration* to apply security, throttling, and caching to the services.

In the third section, we don't speak about giving more functionality to our services, but abot logging and testing them. When we develop a service, it is important that it does the actions that it's designed for, and always gives the same response for the same request. For this reason, it's important that we test our services and debug all that we need.

The last section has the main focus of integrating the WSO2 EI with other servers using different protocols. We learned how to use the VFS protocol to work with files: read, write, move, and so on. Using the JMS protocol, we know how to integrate with the WSO2 Message Broker that is inside the WSO2 Enterprise Integrator, although this configuration is valid for other queue messaging systems such as ActiveMQ or RabbitMQ. In this section, we also used the *connectors* to integrate with other commonly used servers, such as social networks, email, calendar, and so on, in an easy way. Finally, we got an introduction to the new programming language called Ballerina, which will be the future of the company.

Index